D1087626

Democracy in Crisis

POINTS OF VIEW

Series editor: Alex Holzman

So much of what passes for debate on contemporary social, political, and economic issues focuses more on "winning" than on making sense. The books in the Points of View series are designed to elevate the discussion—with reasoned arguments and lively writing bent on encouraging real problem solving.

DEMOCRACY
IN CRISIS

Why, Where,
How to Respond

Roland Rich

LYNNE
RIENNER
PUBLISHERS

BOULDER
LONDON

Published in the United States of America in 2017 by
Lynne Rienner Publishers, Inc.
1800 30th Street, Boulder, Colorado 80301
www.rienner.com

and in the United Kingdom by
Lynne Rienner Publishers, Inc.
3 Henrietta Street, Covent Garden, London WC2E 8LU

© 2017 by Lynne Rienner Publishers, Inc. All rights reserved

Library of Congress Cataloging-in-Publication Data
A Cataloging-in-Publication record for this book
is available from the Library of Congress.

ISBN 978-1-62637-671-7 (hardcover : alk. paper)

British Cataloguing in Publication Data
A Cataloguing in Publication record for this book
is available from the British Library.

Printed and bound in the United States of America

 The paper used in this publication meets the requirements
of the American National Standard for Permanence of
Paper for Printed Library Materials Z39.48-1992.

5   4   3   2   1

For my children—
Elliat, Zak, and Julia

Contents

1

Democracy Is in Crisis

I am embarrassed to admit that I was disappointed the first time I met Leonard. He was too tall, almost five foot two! I had imagined pygmies to be shorter. Leonard was at the United Nations in New York for the Permanent Forum of the world's indigenous peoples. They had fought for many years to be granted this annual meeting and also succeeded in having the UN adopt a Declaration on the Rights of Indigenous Peoples. Who are the world's indigenous people? The best answer is that they are original inhabitants of territories that were later settled by outsiders. Obviously this includes America's First Nations, Australian Aborigines, and New Zealand Maori, but it also includes the remnants of other now marginalized ancient communities around the world, including the pygmies of the Congo basin.

Leonard had done his homework, and he played me expertly. As head of the UN Democracy Fund (UNDEF) I was constantly listening to entreaties from different civil society groups seeking cash grants from our fund. I listened to homilies about how improved health or higher-quality education or committed peacebuilding would contribute to democracy, all true to an extent; but my answer was invariably that the UN had created this as a democracy fund, not a health fund or an education fund or a peacebuilding fund. Leonard's pitch was more sophisticated—fund his NGO to go into the forest and register his people to vote so that the politicians of Gabon would take an interest in their plight. Perfect! Of course, Leonard and I both knew that this story, though it had considerable truth, was not the primary reason for registration. Without an identity card in Gabon, one cannot send kids to school or seek care from a hospital. And Leonard's back story was also compelling. Taken in by French expats who saw to his schooling, allowing him to be the first of his people to graduate with a university degree, Leonard could not ignore his origins. He had no option in his own mind but to dedicate his life to the pygmy people.

Leonard's NGO applied and was given a significant grant after a rigorous competitive process. A couple of years later we concluded that the project had been, on balance, a minor success. The paperwork was a mess and the Excel sheets did not add up just right, but our monitors on the ground reported that some two thousand people had been registered to vote and because many of these were heads of households, perhaps up to ten thousand people now had access to health and education services in Gabon. A pretty good return for an investment of $180,000.

Now multiply Leonard's project by 600 and you get a pretty good idea of the very fulfilling work of UNDEF. While the General Assembly resolution that created UNDEF included the term *civil society* as something of an afterthought, this is the area on which the fund came to be focused. This was the way we could fund people to help themselves rather than to be helped by paternalistic governments or well-meaning international organizations. And so the money flowed to women's groups, tribal communities, slum dwellers, election observer groups and many other types of advocacy associations in more than 130 countries around the world. The common thread was that all these groups wanted to have a voice in the politics of their country or region and UNDEF was offering not only a cash grant but was also lending them a little bit of the UN brand to help their cause.

Having headed the Australian democracy institute assisting countries in Asia and the Pacific and then heading the UN Democracy Fund with a stint as a researcher at the National Endowment for Democracy (NED) in Washington in the middle, I had been in the business of promoting democracy for fifteen years. Fifteen years of professional optimism. Fifteen years of encouraging, supporting, and defending champions of democracy in so many countries. Fifteen years of cajoling, placating, and inspiring government donor agencies to continue their support. All of a sudden, with my retirement from the UN, it was no longer my job to be a professional optimist. I could look at the world without my professional lenses. And what I saw was not pretty.

People lucky enough to live in consolidated democracies think of their system of government as constant as the Northern Star. Votes are cast and counted, politicians come and go, policies succeed or fail, but the system goes on regardless. It is this very expectation of constancy that acts as a bulwark against unconstitutional changes in governance. Locked into what may seem an unending virtuous cycle, it is understandable that an element of complacency may creep in, that the level of participation may decline, and that democracy itself may be taken for granted.

Yet, were one to take an historical perspective of this supposed constancy of the virtuous cycle of democracy and compress the world's written history into a 24-hour clock, democracy as the default best practice form of government has only been around for the last several minutes before midnight. Even more bracing is the realization that democracy made several previous appearances in world history, in ancient Athens, ancient India, and perhaps ancient Mesopotamia, without consolidating itself as the governance norm.

The majority of the world's population is too young to remember, but for that older segment of the world's population that was politically conscious during the Cold War, there will surely be a memory of the fragility of democracy in the face of an opposing Soviet system that seemed at a certain stage to be so powerful that its supporters thought of its eventual dominance in terms of teleological inevitability. The communists were ultimately shown to be deeply mistaken. But those Cold War doubts we occasionally felt and quickly banished remain an important and useful reference point.

The purpose of this book is to sound a warning of a crisis in democracy all over the world. Modern democracy is a fragile system of government that has not yet been consolidated on a global scale and may yet prove to be as historically fleeting as its predecessors. Modern democracy is a vulnerable system open to manipulation from inside and intimidation from outside. There is nothing certain about the maintenance of our democratic systems in a world history that has seen the rise and fall of previous systems. There can be no confidence in the impregnability of democracy simply because it has existed for those short few minutes in human history. Democracies have traversed crises in the past and have demonstrated an admirable ability to self-correct and renew, but having done so in the past is no guarantee that they can continue to do so in the future. To be forewarned is to be forearmed.

The internal and external challenges must be confronted with resolution and competence, qualities that are at times in short supply. Deep problems exist in both the established and the transition democracies. The first-wave democracies are witnessing some ugly politics associated with the rise of demagoguery. The disregard of what the demagogues like to call *political correctness* is in reality a rejection of political civility, which is the software that allows democracy to work in complex mass societies. In the third-wave democracies we are seeing very few successes and too many cases where the next election is faced with the dread of looming chaos. Democracy faces some daunting challengers on the world stage. The authoritarianism we know well from the Cold War era is resurgent. There is a new challenger, messianic jihadism, which we are grappling to understand. But perhaps the most significant challenge is China's Leninist capitalism. Will democracy settle for a kind of moral equivalence with these systems as it did fleetingly with the Soviet system? This would lead to a loss of moral authority, which, to date, has been democracy's greatest asset.

The diagnosis is concerning, but despair is not a useful response. The book will conclude with some policy ideas on how to strengthen democracy and support democratization around the world. Criticism needs to be constructive. I do not pretend to have all the answers, but I do posit some thoughts on key questions. One of the most prominent ways that rich countries relate to poor countries is through official development assistance (ODA). I propose that ODA be radically changed and itself democratized. I cast doubt on the dominant theory of democratization, modernization theory, and call for a women-led process before tackling the issue of how established democracies can renew and invigorate their struggling democratic systems. The writing was concluded at the time of the 2016 US election campaign, and so a further question is posed in the postscript—has democracy been trumped?

Democracy's Soft Power in Decline

When we are not taking democracy for granted, we often mock it because of the frustration and despair we experience with it. Established democracies are not performing well. Gridlock among elected representatives, vetocracy engineered by cashed-up interest groups, and apathy among voters—in particular toward their political parties—are all symptoms of a deep malaise. Chapter 2 deals with democracy's declining soft power, which can be tracked through the work and effectiveness of the various democracy support bodies established to hasten along the third wave of democratization.

Francis Fukuyama's 1992 book, *The End of History and the Last Man*, began life as a philosophical treatise on Platonic, Kantian, and Hegelian thought but quickly morphed into a bumper sticker. Its argument that liberal democracy has been accepted as the best way to satisfy human needs became the intellectual ballast for the triumphalism that many in the West expressed. The title of the book came to be complacently interpreted as obviating the need to work toward the best form of governance—it had already been found.

The high point of democracy's soft power began in the Cold War years with the Carter administration's emphasis on human rights; it strengthened with the Reagan administration's self-confidence to challenge the Soviet Union in treasure rather than blood; it intensified with Gorbachev's failure to reform the Soviet system and also his reluctance to impose Soviet orthodoxy on its fractious empire by force of arms; it solidified with the collapse of the United States' sole global strategic competitor; and it was ratified with glib interpretations of academic theories about the end of history and the Washington consensus. The sense of democracy's superiority as a political system increased to the point of expectation of the near inevitability of its triumph over other forms of governance.

Promoting transitions to and consolidation of democracy by a handful of modest institutions from the established democracies became a measure of the strength of democracy's soft power. The entire enterprise was always plagued by a seed of doubt at its core. Wasn't democracy something that had to emerge from and be fought for by the citizens of the country in question? So what role could foreigners play in that process? And what role had they played in the past? Let's be honest and admit that during the Cold War the West was not so interested in supporting transitions to democracy, a remote theoretical concept at the time; rather, it was determined to undermine the authoritarian Soviet government. Vladimir Putin, incidentally, still thinks this is what the West is trying to do. The key protagonists for this activity at that time were the West's intelligence agencies, and the work was in part to support dissidents and their samizdat publications and, regrettably, at other times to get rid of inconvenient new governments regardless of whether they had come to power through election results.

Democracy promotion came about through a little piece of serendipity. When the Iberian dictators died, first Salazar and then Franco, and their personalistic fascist regimes collapsed, political parties reemerged to contest power. Having been outlawed in the long Portuguese and Spanish fascist period, these parties were unskilled, to say the least. They needed help. In Weimar Germany, a Socialist politician, Friedrich Ebert, left a modest legacy to establish a (subsequently eponymous) foundation to deepen support for his party through civic education. The political party foundation was born and then given fresh life in the post–World War II era when the German conservatives followed suit and established the Konrad Adenauer Foundation. Not only were these foundations given the role of delivering civic education domestically, they also were financed to deliver official development assistance abroad. So when the upstart Social Democrat and Christian Democrat political parties of Portugal and Spain called for help, there happened to be sister party foundations in Germany with the staff and the skills to respond. The success of the transition to democracy in Spain and Portugal was facilitated by this German assistance.

It is one of the notable achievements of the Reagan administration that it took notice of these developments. Homage to democracy is in the American DNA. American democracy was going to be the shining light that would persuade other countries of its merit, and there were certainly times under Presidents Wilson and Roosevelt when the United States took a more hands-on role. An ongoing mission to promote democracy fitted neatly with America's self-perception, and the German foundations' example provided the precedent. The National Endowment for Democracy and the two American political party foundations were born in 1983. Others around the world followed; their work is described in Chapter 2.

While giving credit to one Republican administration for putting the United States in the position to take full advantage of democracy's post–Cold War soft power, it was another Republican administration that squandered it. One can hardly blame George W. Bush for the *Bush v. Gore* legal fiasco in 2000, because he was simply trying to win. But the fact that the world's leading democracy could not competently run an election and then was seen to inject partisanship into the adjudication process dealt a nasty blow to the reputation of democracy. Why would others wish to emulate that fiasco? Blame, however, can squarely be laid at the feet of W's administration in its third attempt at an excuse for the ill-conceived Iraq invasion after the first two were found to be contrived. To impose democracy on a foreign country by force of arms represented the antithesis of everything the institutions of democracy promotion stood for. It suggested, to many in the global South in particular, that democracy was simply being used as a stalking horse for American power; it showed others, Putin included, that the old ways of "might is right" still represented the rules of the game; and it hollowed out democracy's rhetoric, which previously had been among its most powerful weapons but which Bush greatly devalued.

Democracy support work around the world did not end. Committed people everywhere continued its important work. I certainly did not let up, and neither did my colleagues in New York, Washington, Brussels, Berlin, Stockholm, London, and elsewhere. But Bush put a blemish on our product and gave our opponents powerful ammunition. We continue to debate whether that blemish is indelible.

Global Frustrations of Democratic Transitions

The Iraq war grabbed the world's attention and dominated discussion, but a parallel phenomenon is further sapping democracy's soft power. It is not as dramatic as shock-and-awe, but in many ways it is more telling and insidious. Democracy is not living up to its promise in so many of the third-wave countries. It is not embedding itself into the national culture; it is not producing competent leadership; it is simply not delivering.

The scholarly community has already identified the issue. It presents itself as one of terminology. The word in question is *transition*. That word gave rise to vast expectations that could not possibly be met. It suggested that regardless of the path by which a country came to its "transition," once having accomplished that magic word, the path to democracy was as well-established as a yellow brick road. Indeed, a country could virtually be certain of progressing down this road once it had passed the very first milestone, the transition election. The word *transition* thus gave a sense of inevitability to a process that in the established democracies took a great deal of time and effort with many setbacks.

Having attended a conference at Ditchley House, Oxford, in 2015 celebrating the 800th anniversary of the Magna Carta, it came home to me how long the process took in England. It took centuries after those first tentative steps limiting absolutism before its system of government could be described as a democracy. It took over a century or so in the United States before the wisdom of the Declaration of Independence and the Constitution could find concrete expression in the reality of the political system, a process that was ongoing when the Voting Rights Act was finally passed in 1965. It has taken some fifty years in Costa Rica for a culture of democracy and peace to become the norm among its people.

Yet by passing through the magic door of transition, the public in democratic nations and beyond anticipates democracy's advance to occur within a few short years. First, the various "square people," to adopt Thomas Friedman's felicitous expression describing those demonstrators camped in their town squares demanding change, put a start to the process of ridding the nation of its dictator. That is quickly followed by the international community bankrolling an election fiesta, usually putting in power the leader of the nation's largest ethnic group. Presto, democracy has arrived.

Chapter 3 will conduct a bracing tour of Africa, Asia, and Latin America to point out the many examples where a decade or two after that presto moment, countries remain on the same complicated path on which they were traveling before democracy supposedly arrived. Even sadder, the tour will drop in on Europe, to Hungary, which has every chance of making democracy a reality in very quick time but which is reverting to strongman leadership.

If transition has any meaning, it must be interpreted as a transition *from* rather than a transition *to*. The *from* is well known. It is the military dictatorship that sees the world in black and white, friend or foe, us or them. It is the personalistic dictatorship ruled by the whim of the dictator and, invariably, his scheming wife and avaricious children. It is the Leninist single-party system that talks about equality but is dedicated to welfare of the elite, the *nomenklatura*. Transition *to* also has a clear meaning in theory but remains shrouded in a fog of reality. Freedom House may call it democracy, but in most third-wave transition countries it hardly lives up to that grand term.

Chapter 3 will also attempt to categorize various outcomes. We have seen some of the rhetoric change, but we are still left with many of the old autocrats. We also have some new forms of governance in the form of Islamist obscurantists dressing up old forms of domination in the form of patriarchy and sectarianism. But perhaps most distressing are the many feckless illiberal democracies going nowhere. Democracies are in crisis, and this has led to a crisis in democracy itself.

Democracy's Three Challengers

Oh how meek were the autocrats when the Berlin Wall was pulled down. In the binary world of the Cold War, the competition between the United States and the Soviet Union had provided the world's autocrats with a game at which they could excel. By simply siding with one or the other, any criticism could be deflected as Cold War rhetoric. The more subtle actors played one side against the other and thus sidetracked criticism from the outset as each side tried to woo the recalcitrant leader. One side or the other not only provided some form of military umbrella for its acolytes but also enveloped them in a coherent-sounding ideological framework. Even the field of human rights was divided, with the Soviet camp claiming ownership over economic and social rights while the Western camp privileged civil and political rights. Some valued the stability this world provided; others despaired at its stasis. The end of the

Cold War put an end to this binary world. For a brief moment there was a unipolar world dominated by the United States, but it quickly turned to a world of uncertainty. In this more chaotic world, the autocrats are resurgent. The resurgence of authoritarianism is detailed in Chapter 4.

Russian president Vladimir Putin has single-handedly rehabilitated authoritarianism. He has not invented anything new or original but has dusted off the old tactics. Deploying his oil wealth, he has given autocracy a patina of respectability and become the tactical leader of the authoritarian camp. Among the old tactics are appeals to nationalism and Russian exceptionalism taking the form of paranoia ("they wish to deny Russia its destiny!"). Many of the old Soviet tactics remain useful—show trials, exemplary assassinations or punishments, nomenklatura patronage for those close to the leader, control of media, and "big lie" propaganda. Putin has added a powerful new tactic unavailable to the Soviet Union because of the Marxist disquiet with religion—he can appeal to traditionalism and religious authority. He has had to move with the times and allow elections, but these proved to be negligible inconveniences once his power was consolidated. Opposition parties can rather easily be intimidated and their leaders merrily imprisoned or banished. Control of the popular electronic media through pliant oligarchs provides an insurmountable electoral advantage.

Putin has had to tolerate certain trappings of a liberal state, among them the existence of civil society. Civil society has never been a feature of Russian life, but a few buds emerged in the Yeltsin years. As in other globalized urban settings, civil society will develop if permitted to operate. It is on this issue that Putin has demonstrated his global leadership of the authoritarian world. He attacked civil society at its weakest point—its links with the international community. In a world where people, goods, money, and ideas travel quite freely, it is only to be expected that civil society will have links to like-minded groups in other parts of this globalized world. Putin attacked those links and portrayed them as unpatriotic and even seditious. He attacked the flow of money to Russian civil society and required groups receiving foreign funds to register as "foreign agents," which retains its 007 meaning in Russian.

One group funded by the UN Democracy Fund in a provincial capital was required to so register but refused. It was prosecuted. I prefer not to name this group because it would increase its vulnerability. To our pleasant surprise the presiding judge decided in favor of our grantee, noting that the group was simply undertaking activities specifically allowed by Russian law. The outraged prosecutor appealed, but to our further surprise, the regional appeal court upheld the original judgment. The fact that the money was coming from the UN rather than George Soros may have had some influence on these courts. Should the prosecutor appeal to the Moscow-based federal court, I have little doubt that proximity to Putin would lead to a different outcome.

But even in Russia there can be cyclical downswings affecting the government's patronage and popularity, and in these circumstances Putin resorted to a dangerous ploy available to the autocrat; fighting foreign enemies, near and far. Keeping neighbors destabilized through festering Russian-supported insurgencies in its border areas is a well-known play. Annexing foreign territory—though, admittedly, Crimea has strong links to Russia—is a far more dangerous play. Putin cannot resurrect the Cold War because he has no ideology, a single resource based economy, and limited global military reach, but he can certainly become a regional trouble maker. In any case, enemies near and far simply serve to bolster his nationalist and exceptionalist credentials.

Not content with all these powerful controls on Russian society, Putin has pioneered another. Racism and anti-Semitism are well-known tools, but they are quite difficult to deploy in a world awash with human rights doctrines and rhetoric. So Putin has had to identify a new fifth column within Russia to attract the attention of bigots whose support he covets. Thus he has privileged the fight against homosexuality as an excellent domestic diversion and a battle in which Russia can again be a world leader. Gays are the new Jews.

Putin is significant not simply because of the way he has returned Russia to its introspective petulant traditionalism but because he has emboldened other authoritarian regimes to adopt his tactics. From the former Soviet republics of Central Asia, to various parts of Africa, Asia, and the Middle East, autocrats are being tempted to follow the Putin course and rid themselves of troublesome opposition figures and pesky NGOs. The return of old-style authoritarianism is Putin's gift to the world, and it represents a return of the old challenge to democracy.

The new challenge, coming from China, is outlined in Chapter 5. It is both a traditional rising power challenge and a brand new systems challenge. The genius of the Chinese challenge is to appropriate the economic half of the democratic system and allow its people a certain economic freedom while developing the art of soft authoritarianism and granting its people very limited political freedom. It is a far more potent threat than the old-fashioned Russian authoritarian challenge because of its impressive achievements. Lifting six hundred million people out of poverty in a single generation is a feat never before achieved. We need to be respectful of this unprecedented accomplishment.

But is the Chinese system simply another example of run-of-the-mill authoritarianism? Yes and no. The Communist Party continues to use the normal authoritarian instruments of repression: disallowing free speech, punishing dissent, deploying propaganda. But this is not the full story. It is a form of soft authoritarianism pioneered by Malaysia and Singapore that allows significant room for dissent but punishes the most threatening or at times simply capriciously punishes at random. In either case, the message gets through. But the soft nature of the repression leaves open an important safety valve allowing some of the steam of fury to escape . . . and mostly evaporate. There are one hundred thousand protests in China every year. Occasionally they may even have an impact if they do not threaten the fundamentals of single-party rule. And there is significant economic freedom and even Confucian meritocracy for those with the right education.

Perhaps the most important distinction is the Chinese leadership's ability, thus far at least, to deal with the Achilles' heel of authoritarianism: leadership succession. Next door in North Korea the solution has been dynastic, however inappropriate may be the next in line. There are clearly elements of this in China with Maoist and Dengist nomenklatura continuing to insist on its privileges. But one can only admire the apparent ease and regularity of recent leadership transitions in China. Of course, the ugly bits happen behind locked doors and the eligible cohort is tiny. One reason for this orderly procession of leaders is that it is good for the business of government and the entire political camp benefits. But there is an important, unstated, underlying premise behind the process; it is no longer a winner-takes-all game. The outgoing leader retains status and privilege and even influence, and his family members retain the massive wealth they have accumulated.

This is an important advance on the usual method of bloody coup. It is true that Zhao Ziyang was purged because he showed sympathy toward the Tiananmen demonstrators, but with that political exception, succession has been peaceful and orderly. Until now. President Xi Jinping's current anticorruption purge is bringing down some very big fish and undermining the unstated underlying premise. The purge is without a doubt political and not simply following the course of blind justice. If all corruption were targeted, then the regime would fall. One of the theses advanced in this book is that Leninist capitalism *necessarily* leads to corruption.

Another important advance made by China is its ability to use the carrot even more than the stick. China's growth and relative wealth has allowed it the resources to solve many problems. The purge under guise of an anticorruption campaign has been used quite sparingly. There has been no need to descend to Stalinist or Maoist levels because the government has the resources and often the competence to fix many problems. Indeed, it is this aspect that provides its greatest claim to legitimacy. China's soft authoritarianism rests on performance legitimacy, and as long as it is able to maintain this level of performance, it will remain a challenge to liberal democracy.

The third challenge to democracy comes from an ancient source. Chapter 6 opens with a discussion of the relationship between democracy and religion. They are incompatible if one adopts a fundamentalist perspective on religion. If laws are god-given, then humans had better stay out of the game of debating, negotiating, and passing laws. If laws are god-given, then there is no room for a parliamentary or even an executive branch of government because the priests can perform this role, though I guess there may be room for priestly judges to try to unravel the inevitable inconsistencies and lacunae of any legal system and for priestly police to implement it. Societies around the world grappled with the religion problem and found varying solutions. A very sophisticated solution is that god gave humans the gift of freewill, thus allowing humans to govern themselves individually and collectively. A complementary though accidental solution to the problem emerged in the New World, the destination for the sects and religions fleeing persecution in the Old World. These settlers believed deeply in religion but feared the wrath they had experienced under a dominant or state religion. They pragmatically agreed that no single religion should be allowed to become a state religion in the United States. Thus was born modern secularism.

Employing the concept of free will and deploying the practice of secularism, religion found a way to coexist with democracy, and though various tensions may at times occur, this dynamic can and does apply to all religions. But if a group rejects these concepts of coexistence and insists that its religion contains all the certainties and provides all the answers any society needs, then democracy is clearly being challenged. Islam has demonstrated over the course of many centuries and in many different parts of the world that it can coexist with temporal government. Accordingly, Islam can also happily coexist with democracy, and several such examples are emerging. But one small group within the Islamic world, feeding on grievances and intoxicated with the prospect of power, rejects temporal power and democracy in favor of an Islamic caliphate where the Koran is the constitution. For want of a better term, the consensus is to call these people jihadis and their ideology jihadism. Admittedly, this has denatured a common meaning of *jihad* as a personal struggle for righteousness. But usage changes language, and, regrettably, jihad now has a nasty political meaning.

This book argues that religion becomes incompatible with democracy when it mutates from a belief system to a political ideology. Jihadism has thus mutated. Jihadism has certain attractions. Doctrinally, it is simple to understand. The world it describes is one of black and white, right and wrong, allowed and forbidden, *halal* and *haram*. There are no difficult gray areas. Tactically, jihad is particularly convenient. After all, when god has established heaven on earth and shown the path toward it (through jihad), nothing can stand in the way. Everything done in service to progress along that path is justified. Concepts such as human rights or humanitarian law are simply seen as imperfect and inferior positive law at best and the tricks of the enemies of god at worst. Emotionally, jihad is exciting. The concept of a soldier of god has been a recruiting tool for millennia. Why spend years studying, then competing with many others, while often being discriminated against, simply to achieve a boring middle-class existence, when the prospect of adventure in the service of god beckons? Simple, convenient, exciting; no wonder thousands of Muslims from all over the world including Western countries are flocking to the Levant in the service of jihad.

Which leads to another important distinction between jihadism and democracy—the former is utopian while the latter is resigned to pragmatism and least-worst outcomes. Demagogues seeking a path to power have been deploying visions of utopia for millennia, and even in a sophisticated Internet-enabled world, utopia still sells. Jihadism is selling a vague mirage-like version of utopia based on Islam's creation myths and in doing so has rejected modernity and its institutions though not its weaponry. Democracy is correctly seen as an institution of modernity and therefore has no place in the jihadi vision.

Who Are the Allies of Democratization?

The dominant theory of democratization is modernization. It has much to commend it. It links democracy tightly to economic development and wealth accumulation, processes that have near universal approval. It sees democracy as the almost inevitable result of the end of large-scale poverty. Modernization theory does not depend on an individual leader or thinker. Like Marxism, it depends on the demands of an entire economic class—in this case the middle class rather than the working class. According to modernization theory, it is only upon becoming a significant class in society that the middle class will exert its influence. By that point it will be sufficiently powerful economically and politically that national leaders will find it difficult to ignore its demands. Having achieved material security, modernization theory posits that middle-class people will shift the goal posts. The new goals will broaden beyond the economy and turn to more political issues concerning government services, quality of life, and individual freedom. Before too long, the middle class will see democracy as the instrument to achieve its goals and will insist on democracy's adoption.

Modernization theory attempts to supplant Marxism as the better explanation of the march of history. It has some powerful empirical evidence in support. After all, most of the wealthy countries of the world are democratic. And some of the more phoenix-like transitions from poverty and authoritarianism to wealth and democracy, as in South Korea and Taiwan, tend to fit the thesis of middle-class leadership. Supporters of modernization theory explain exceptions to the rule, such as autocratic Gulf monarchies, as the odd results of rentier economies buoyed by petro dollars. It is also true, with the towering exceptions of India and perhaps Indonesia, that poor countries struggle to build democratic systems.

The middle class is a comforting group to take on the mantle of the transformational actor in society. Middle-class people have achieved a lot. They live relatively comfortably and send their children to school and, often, university. They plan ahead and husband their resources to meet their future needs. In other words, middle-class people have much to lose. The middle-class concept of transition is based on dialogue and peaceful protest, on building coalitions of supporters, and on changing leaders through elections. The middle class prefers pacted transitions over violent overthrow, truth commissions over street justice, and order over chaos so as to maintain its business interests and comfortable lifestyles. Contrast the middle-class scenario with the Marxist precedent: working-class rage directed at society at large, leading inevitably to violence and destruction and without a single precedent of establishing a functioning democracy in its wake.

Chapter 7 examines modernization theory and compares it with other ideas on the process of democratization. As is so often the case in the social sciences, it is difficult to come to a definitive answer that responds to every situation, but clearly, modernization theory retains a powerful explanatory capacity. It seems to work best, however, where the middle class is not only politically strong but also constitutes a majority. What happens when the middle class is powerful and succeeds in having a democratic system adopted but the majority remains poor and aggrieved? One effect of democratization in this case is that poor people, underprivileged people, and rural people will be significant beneficiaries of the middle class's agitation. They will gain the right to vote and to participate in the politics of their nations. When those underprivileged classes in society seize the possibilities opened by the middle class and proceed to elect their own champions, and those champions begin the process of opening greater opportunity for their political base, where will the middle class stand?

I have probably landed in Bangkok more than in any other city in the world, having served much of my diplomatic career in Southeast Asia, for which Bangkok is the key hub. As a student of democracy, I found Thailand in the late 1990s and early 2000s to be worth watching as it embarked on one of the great deliberative democracy experiments of our time. I spoke to many people in Bangkok involved in drafting a new constitution that would cement Thai democracy once and for all. The middle class at its best. The result, elaborated at greater length in Chapter 7, was such a success that people other than the urban middle class and the elite it supported became interested in democracy. It would not take long before a politician would add up the numbers and start targeting the votes of the non-middle-class majority. Through cynicism, electoral calculation, and attractive policies Thaksin Shinawatra, Thailand's richest person, accidentally became their hero. An outsider to the established Bangkok elite, he began the process of reshaping the established elite to his commercial needs. They fought back.

I am shocked and embarrassed that nearly all my friends and colleagues in Bangkok who worked so hard to bring democracy to their country now side with the antidemocratic forces that adopted the (late) king as their mascot. They disparage the majority of their fellow citizens as country bumpkins and buffoons. They create the strawman argument that Thaksin wished to overthrow the monarchy, when all he wanted was to ingratiate himself with the royal family using the vast means at his disposal. And, most distressing of all, they argue that one aspect of democracy—elections—are, after all, not really appropriate to their country (because the Thaksin forces peskily keep winning them).

Thailand is an unusual country, proud never to have been colonized, and perhaps we can simply call it an outlier of modernization theory or idiosyncratic in various ways. The middle class according to modernization theory builds democracy, it doesn't undermine it. Or perhaps it does both, depending on where its interests lie. Thailand, it turns out, is not that unusual. On three other continents in three other countries we can trace a not dissimilar phenomenon of the middle class turning against electoral democracy. The middle class in each country is distinctive, each has traveled by a different path, and each may have valid reasons for some of its actions, but the point remains that in Egypt, Turkey, and Venezuela, the middle class rejects the electoral will of the majority and now harbors doubts about the validity of democracy in its country.

Perhaps the middle class is democracy's champion only when it is a majority. That may be the case in Western countries, but it is never the case in the global South. So is there another candidate? According to Alexis de Tocqueville, civil society fits the bill. Tocqueville noted that associational life in the New World was spontaneous and self-generating. It provided a context in which the community holds a conversation and prepares the foundations for the marketplace of ideas so central to a living democracy. This organized realm of public life is not generated by the profit motive, thus taking it outside the parallel realm of rational economic choice. Clearly, civil society cannot be part of the state, thus creating the contestability so necessary for sound policy formulation. And from the perspective of the global South, perhaps the most critical aspect of civil society is that it is outside the family and thus has the opportunity to be outside all the ascriptive allegiances of religion, ethnicity, and patriarchy that so bedevil its politics. Civil society builds the social capital on which democracies thrive.

In the course of my time as head of the UN Democracy Fund, we received more than twenty thousand applications for funding from all over the global South and we made grants to some six hundred civil society organizations. These are sufficiently large numbers to allow me to draw some tentative conclusions about civil society, especially in the global South. The first and most obvious conclusion is that people are clamoring to take part in the public conversations of their nations. UNDEF projects are voice projects, and we funded dozens of ways for civil society to have voice: dissemination of views; advocacy for policy positions; commentary on constitutional or legislative amendment; networking among the like-minded; production of tools such as websites and repositories to aid in the public conversation; production of media products for newspaper, television, and radio; and, of course, the ubiquitous training processes for all sorts of people from civil society leaders to youth leaders to newly elected legislators, local and national. UNDEF funded the demand side of democratization.

Another conclusion is that the quality of civil society varies greatly. At one end were well-meaning groups that had little idea how to achieve an impact while at the other were highly experienced organizations that knew how to deliver projects. What we have seen over the past couple of decades is both an exhilarating growth of civil society organizations in nearly every country and a flinty professionalism among the top tier born from Darwinian competition for scarce resources. Which gets us to the nub of the problem. While civil society is essential for democracy, its cost needs to be met by private discretionary funding and perhaps competitive grants from disinterested public funds. Wealthy countries have the tax base, philanthropists, discretionary income, discretionary time, active retired folk, rich parents, and dedicated self-funded people to staff the needs of civil society. Poor countries have far less of each of these pools of funding. A solution to this dilemma flows from global solidarity. Part of the mission of civil society in the global North is to contribute to the funding of civil society in the global South. But this solution is also an Achilles' heel—if autocrats can choke off the flow of funding from North to South by internal regulations, then they can financially asphyxiate their own civil societies. As noted, Vladimir Putin has anointed himself as leader of the world's autocrats and pioneered the means of suffocating infant civil societies. That autocrats consider it necessary to attack civil society in their countries is perhaps the best piece of evidence of its efficacy in democratization. Autocrats fear civil society.

There are various ways one can analyze societies. The discussion on civil society depicts society as a three-circle Venn diagram of government sector, commercial sector, and civil society sector overlapping each other to a greater or lesser extent nation by nation. But an even more basic way of looking at society is as a Venn diagram of two gendered circles with the overlap representing those who do not fit neatly into one circle or the other for reasons of physiology or predilection. Different-sized circles can be used for different issues. Because women generally live longer than men, the female circle will be the larger when considering population size. If, however, one were to consider ownership of land, the male circle would be vast compared to the tiny size of the women's circle. And though it is a difficult phenomenon to measure, a gendered Venn diagram of political power in the world would be not dissimilar to the circles of land ownership. We cannot discuss democracy without also discussing gender, and this is the subject of Chapter 8.

I am somewhat reluctant to launch into this area because of my gender. Some feminists may believe that only women can fully understand the relevant issues. They may be correct, but to abandon a subject to only those who identify with the subject matter is to adopt a deeply unscholarly approach. Should only Christians comment on Christianity? Should only Americans debate American politics? The issue of the role of women in society is one for everybody to engage with. I am a lawyer who focuses on politics, a diplomat who concentrates on nonstate actors, and a man prepared to write about women's empowerment.

The starting point of any discussion of women and politics is an acknowledgment that all our forbearer agricultural societies began as patriarchies. Troglodyte societies provide us with the iconic meme of a club-wielding caveman dragging a woman back to his cave. This image seems to have two deep truths. The first is that the man is normally the stronger and can overpower the woman. The second is that the man is treating the woman as a chattel to be used for various purposes such as food gathering and preparation, child bearing and rearing, and of course sex. It has been ten thousand years since humankind left the caves for built environments, but we are still negotiating a path away from that caveman trope. Many issues continue to flow from the power/chattel dynamic. Gender violence is almost uniformly unidirectional and manifests itself in everyday life in the home. Violence in wartime strikes the mainly male warriors, but when it engulfs the civilian population it is again women who suffer disproportionately, including through that thus far historically inescapable act of war known as rape. The impact of being considered as a chattel also continues with women usually working land they do not own, unable to escape relationships of dependency and legally blocked from inheriting wealth-producing assets. That cave does not seem so far away. But the great irony that will be elaborated in Chapter 8 is that we are the cavemen and our hunter-gatherer forebears were the metrosexuals.

The insidious aspect of the situation of most women on the planet is that although they continue to live under the shadow of violence and continue to be treated as little more than chattels, the package in which this system is wrapped is called *tradition*, which women are taught to respect and defend. I had a terrible experience of this in Sierra Leone when I visited an admirable group of women who were delivering a project to help give voice to victims of sexual violence—in other words, other women and girls. They worked so hard to comfort the victims and help them to bear witness. They stood as advocates between the victims and the system of police and courts. They even found the money to pay for bus fares to the hospitals and court rooms. As the subject was violence against women, I had the temerity over a delicious lunch of chicken and rice to ask them about their work in relation to female genital mutilation. I experienced immediate pushback! "We don't call it that. It is simply called cutting." It was presented as a relatively minor issue of little medical threat and no great harm. So I asked if their daughters would also be cut. Only one woman was not nodding sagely. She said she was moving to the UK and so did not have to continue this tradition.

Women are annoying chattels. They don't hold still or always do as they are told. They sometimes wish to have their own opinions. But most distressing of all, they have their own biological sex drives to satisfy a Darwinian urge to reproduce. This might even lead them to sneak away from the cave and allow another man to try to impregnate them. Harried men have had to confront this problem through the ages, and different societies have found their own solutions. We are familiar with the medieval chastity belt as a solid physical solution. We have read the stories of eunuchs guarding harems. But there is another physical solution that continues to allow your woman to have your children but makes sex so unpleasant as to greatly diminish the prospect that your woman will voluntarily wish to have sex with you or anybody else. Hack off the woman's clitoris and labia. Dress the practice up as an example of gender equality by calling it circumcision. And then step away from the practice altogether and inculcate it as a mother-to-daughter tradition that has nothing to do with men. Pretty damn clever!

These intelligent and committed women in Sierra Leone were now caught in the system. Their daughters cannot join the women's league in their villages unless they go through the cutting initiation ceremony. To be outside these Bondo societies is to be an outcast in one's own community. These admirable women of Sierra Leone were fighting sexual violence while inflicting it on their own daughters.

Tradition has not been kind to women. Tradition derives from patriarchy, and it retains many patriarchal practices dissimulated as genderless time-honored custom. Modernity has been kinder to women. Modernity allows women to negotiate a path away from the most noxious of the patriarchal traditions. Democracy is women's key to modernity.

Women need democracy, but democracy needs women just as much. Women are the world's largest underprivileged group. Democracy will only succeed if it offers a means for the underprivileged to have voice and a say in dealing with their own predicament. If women identify democracy as a means of their empowerment, democracy will be immeasurably strengthened. Chapter 8 will outline this process. Women need to do much of the heavy lifting, but they will not succeed without a change of attitude by men. Of course we need to continue to invest in women's rights and women's voice, but the investment will not bring the dividends we seek unless we also invest in men and boys and show that there is a path out of the cave; that they do not have to wear beards and carry guns to be men; and that the world will be in better balance when everybody can contribute to their fullest capacity.

How to Respond?

If I might be allowed to borrow from a showbiz dichotomy about death and comedy: analysis is easy, action is hard. Yes, it is best to begin action with a pretty good understanding of what one is trying to achieve or to fix. And yes, it is good to have a powerful theory to guide one's actions. But action remains so difficult because we have such limited tools at our disposal. Chapter 9 unpacks the democratization tool kit.

According to the recent Bush administration, the military is a powerful tool to bring about democratization. Fifteen years later in Afghanistan that proposition remains in great doubt, a view compounded by the tangled mess military intervention triggered in Iraq. Investment and globalization are also available tools, but they follow a market logic and are not generally undertaken at the beck and call of governments. Governments have limited means of influencing the direction of trade and investment—tax policies, trade promotion, investment treaties, and reductions of official barriers to trade and investment. These are not insignificant, but they do not fundamentally influence the rational economic decisions that direct the flow of trade and investment. Soft power is a mighty tool, but it hovers well above the world of policy prescriptions. What remains is a rather weak tool known as official development assistance (ODA).

In April 1946, Evsey Domar, a US economist, published an article that suggested there was a gap in developing countries between available financing for investment (such as through domestic savings) and the requirements for investment in productive capital, and that this gap could be filled with ODA, thus achieving the targeted growth rate. There are so many unrealistic assumptions underpinning this "financing gap" model that Domar himself quickly disavowed it, but it nevertheless became the theoretical basis for ODA and it continues to haunt the field. One of the assumptions is that capital is necessarily productive, but anyone who has tramped around the world will soon harbor doubts. I have seen abandoned rice silos in Burma built by the Australian government that crushed the rice they were supposed to store—they were apparently good wheat silos!—and an unused desiccated coconut factory in Tonga, also built from ODA, that died from lack of simple maintenance. There are highways going nowhere, stadiums with weeds growing through the cracks, and I have even dodged the dripping water in the Chinese-built parliament building in Vanuatu that leaked alarmingly, though only in the rainy season.

If ODA is the main weapon to solve the world's problems, then we are in deep trouble! I need to declare my interests at the outset of this discussion: I have had my snout in the ODA trough for many years. In all those years, I delivered my little piece of the ODA product without too much protestation. Upon retirement, I am freer to express my doubts. First of all, ODA is a bait-and-switch game. The bait is ODA as an instrument for economic development. But ODA abandoned this goal long ago in reaction to its utter inability to influence economic development in any measurable way. There is not a single case of ODA lifting any nation out of poverty. The focus of ODA switched to other goals—emergency assistance after natural and human-made catastrophe, education and health programs, expert advice on a vast range of subjects, and a switch of emphasis from economic development to human development. I am not critical of this change in focus because it is a rational response to the failure to have an appreciable impact on economic development, but of course ODA continues to be sold to the public as a key to economic development. If the world can divorce itself from its previous rhetoric (the D in ODA), then it may well be possible to use this bundle of funding for more useful purposes.

How did the rich countries develop? It was certainly not by ODA, though there is an argument that the profits from colonialism filled the financing gap in a previous age. Interestingly, the corollary to this argument is that ODA is in fact a form of reparations for the unjust profiteering from colonialism . . . but that is an issue for another time and place. Rich countries developed because their people pioneered ways of efficient production of goods, which dramatically grew the economic pie. This is often referred to as the industrial revolution. It was followed by further revolutions in literacy, health, consumption, trade, communications, and services. The fuel for these revolutions was innovation, productivity, risk-based investment, and, to a certain extent, supportive government policies. The point about this process is its self-generating basis, with the people playing the major part and the government cast in a critical supporting role.

ODA adopts the exact opposite approach. The government is cast as the main player, and the people have a lesser, often passive role. It is as if all the lessons learned from the economic success of the donor countries have been conveniently forgotten to allow a system of cozy government-to-government relations in which ODA is used as a means to obtain an array of donor government objectives, originally as part of the alliance-building process of the Cold War, then supporting globalization in the fields of trade and investment, and now in the various policies we have chosen to call wars—against drugs and terrorism. Then let's stop calling it ODA and call it "official bribery assistance" instead. As I said, I have been a part of the ODA game for quite a while and can attest to the fact that many others involved in ODA share this disquiet.

In Chapter 9 I will outline a better philosophy and direction for ODA. Let's get the proportions right. The people have the major role to play in civic, economic, social, and cultural development, and governments have an important but discreet supportive role. So let's have the major flow of ODA directed at the people and a modest flow going to governments. This sounds like such a simple prescription, but it would in fact represent a radical turnaround. How can ODA support the people? Thankfully, there is nothing new to invent here. For many years ODA has recognized the limitations of directing its flow solely through governments, which lack the capacity (another term for *incompetence*) and commitment (a euphemism for *corruption*) to best use these funds. Many different processes have been developed to directly fund people: competitive scholarships, competitive grants to civil society, blind investment trusts where decisionmaking is outside the hands of donor and receiving governments. In a strange way, Evsey Domar's discredited theory had a kernel of truth. There is a financing gap, and ODA can help fill this financing gap—but not if the means of doing so is to funnel the financing through the receiving government. By directly funding individuals, civil society organizations, and businesses, ODA can help fill the financing gap to help society grow in an organic way. Let's help empower people, and then those people can empower their own governments through taxes and votes.

The "people first" philosophy is clearly the way forward, but it is not without problems. Of course there will be howls of protest from receiving governments, but that is what diplomacy is for. There are two more serious structural problems. While receiving governments have been assigned a more modest role in my reenvisioned ODA process, what should be the role of donor governments? As things stand, they play a dominant role, so only half the problem is solved. Donor governments have many policy objectives, and it is not much of a stretch to see ODA morphing into a weapon in the war against terrorism if they are left to their own devices. That is not ODA's purpose. Terrorism feeds off grievances, and ODA is a weapon to help deal with the causes of those grievances. The solution is to leave a modest part of ODA delivery to donor governments while developing a system to privilege the involvement of people in donor countries. There is an effective way to achieve this result—through the tax system. Chapter 9 will outline how the tax system can engineer a system of people-to-people ODA, leaving governments to deal with the more modest government-to-government slice of ODA.

There was a time when scholars and practitioners thought the solution to the democratization puzzle passed through the process of institutional design. This flowed from a sentiment that government was not an art but a science. Articulation of this sentiment came from the rescue of the ancient word *governance*. The basis of governance, the rules of governance, and the practice of governance could all be scientifically crafted to achieve societal goals and, in particular, democratization. This dovetailed with a shift in the expert advice provided by ODA from fields such as engineering and hydrology to fields such as constitutionalism and parliamentary practice. The new field was called *institutional design,* and Chapter 9 will elaborate on some of these design issues. The field encompasses a number of important areas including constitution drafting, electoral system design, executive branch efficiencies, and improvements in the systems of accountability and transparency.

I need to disclose that I was one of those "experts" in leading the Australian Centre for Democratic Institutions, which assisted parliaments and judiciaries in Southeast Asia to improve their performance. I embarked upon this venture without any particular cynicism. I shared the view that better processes and designs would inch along the curve of governance progress, passing the threshold of competence and eventually leading to a virtuous cycle of responsiveness to public needs. In retrospect, I was buoyed by undue optimism. Yes, legislators, executives, and judges can become more competent at their tasks, and many welcomed the links with their peers and access to new ideas; but increasing the skills of key actors does not change the systems in which they operate. They remain in thrall to the political economy and political culture in which they find themselves. Deep changes, as required in democratization, can only come with changes to the political economy and political culture. Democracy cannot be improved by focusing only on the supply of institutions; it has to be influenced equally by the demand for good policy and outcomes. I came to a rather dispiriting conclusion about institutional design: poor institutional design will deepen and exacerbate problems of governance, but felicitous institutional design cannot itself resolve those problems—it is only one of many aspects that will have an impact on the issues.

The final chapter will identify a few of the low-hanging fruits we can pick to kick-start the process of reforming and renewing our democracies. It focuses primarily on the United States and its dysfunctional electoral system. The electoral system is the most accessible area of institutional design and the one with the most immediate consequences. It is also an area where some useful reform work has already been accomplished and where other initiatives are in progress. It is therefore a realistic option. I am not suggesting that Americans abandon their presidential system and adopt Westminster parliamentary designs, though this may well be one way out of the current vetocracy. That would be a bridge too far. The objective needs to go beyond reforming an institution of democracy. We need to demonstrate that reform is possible, that democracy has not been caught in a time warp of originalism, and that deliberation remains a means to finding better solutions.

No society is static, and therefore all societies must continually review and address their situation. Democracy is the system that best allows this process to be conducted fairly and sustainably. Democracy needs to undertake this task and be seen to do so. Today, however, the pressure is mounting. The world is facing unprecedented challenges. Climate change is the most difficult to deal with. The loss of prestige of globalization threatens to undermine the global economic system. The large and growing reality of inequality in nearly every country in the world cannot long continue without causing inevitable explosions. And conflicts stubbornly continue to erupt. There has never been a time when we are in greater need of functioning democratic systems to help us deal with and adjust to these challenges. Are those systems in place?

Democracy is in crisis all over the world, and the time for action has come.

2

Democracy Is Squandering
Its Soft Power

Academics judge success in terms of publications and cita-tions, carefully crafted syllabi, and contented students as well as that rare phenomenon, admiring colleagues, but perhaps the ultimate indicator of success is to have coined an intelligent oxymoron that becomes universally acknowledged and employed even by people who have never read the primary text. Isaiah Berlin's *negative liberty* is initially jarring and discordant but becomes expressive and meaningful when one understands it to be about freedom from external restraints. Marshall McLuhan's *global village* was a breakthrough concept as well as a self-fulfilling prophecy coined prior to the digital revolution. Robert Putnam's *social capital* employed Marxist terminology but turned it on its head by referring to people instead of machinery. And Joseph Nye's *soft power* sounds deeply contradictory but has an insidiously captivating quality pointing to the true nature of everyday influence in the world. It is Nye's intelligent oxymoron that is of most utility to this discussion.

Soft power has been primarily applied as an attribute of states, with the focus being largely on the world's most powerful state, the United States. It refers to the degree to which the American ethos is admired globally; the way admiration morphs into emulation; and the consequential power accumulated in the hands of the admiree. Yet the concept of soft power transcends national and even geographic boundaries and also attaches itself to movements and concepts. It is not difficult to see this elision in the case of religions such as Christianity and Islam, which over the centuries employed both hard and soft power. History demonstrates that the soft-power influences were more enduring than those seized by hard power. For much of the twentieth century Marxism enjoyed considerable soft power given its critique of economic exploitation and its championing of workers. It was the hard-power misapplication of Marxism that led to the demise of its soft power. The horrors of the Stalinist and Maoist periods delivered in the name of Marxism were instrumental in devaluing the theory. Today, with the exception of its faint echo in Cuba and its continued study in certain corridors of Western university campuses, Marxism is in eclipse, its soft power exhausted.

The Rise of Democracy's Soft Power

The high point of democracy's soft power came with the end of the Cold War. It is important to unpack the elements and history of democracy's soft power to situate it in today's world, a quarter of a century after the Cold War, and to compare its soft power with that of its competitors. Christianity, Islam, and Marxism all have a key facet in common that enhances their soft-power capacity: they are all utopian ideologies. They offer utopian visions of heaven on earth or heaven in heaven. These are strong selling points; utopia is by definition attractive. History has shown consistently, however, that the supposed path to utopia leads us through some pretty appalling places more akin to dystopia. This is a problem that all utopian ideologies eventually need to acknowledge. And, of course, they need to deal with the stubborn reality that outside the theory books or the religious creation myths, utopia has never been achieved on this planet.

One significant structural problem with democracy's soft power is that it makes no claims of utopian outcomes. Indeed, Churchill's dictum has it that "democracy is the worst form of government, except for all the others." Selling the least worst form of government falls well short of selling visions of utopia. And this might help explain modern democracy's gradual journey to being accepted as a viable and indeed preferable form of government. Not only does democracy make no claim to utopian outcomes but one should also beware claims of democracy as panacea. Democracy's journey toward broad popular acceptance came not through revelation or a single lightning bolt of inspiration but through decades of deliberation and debate followed by decades of trial and error. There were times in this journey when citizens may well have had cause for despair about the ability of democracy to deliver an acceptable form of governance. The world may currently be traversing one of those times. But before coming to that issue, it is best to examine democracy's soft-power journey in greater detail.

Three revolutions paved the way for modern democracy: Britain's Glorious Revolution, the American Revolution, and the French Revolution. These marked the beginnings of the modern practice of democracy in a handful of nations in what Samuel Huntington described as the first wave of democratization.[1] The accompanying deliberative processes encompassed the great debates between Hobbes and Locke on the nature of the social contract; the arguments between Burke and Mill on the extent of individual liberty; the discussion of constitutionalism between Hamilton and Madison in the Federalist Papers; and the debate as to the legacies of the French Revolution between the Jacobins and the Girondins. In the evolving practice of democratic governance, the first-wave democracies passed a number of important milestones. Various steps were taken toward universal suffrage, including eventually meeting the demands of the suffragists and minorities of color (though efforts continue to this day in some parts of the United States to deny universal suffrage through dubious arguments about averting voter fraud). The evolving system had to find the best mix of policies and practices for free and fair elections—free from Tammany Hall manipulation and fair to nonincumbents (though to this day gerrymandering remains endemic in United States lower house elections and big money has an ever greater say in electoral results). And alongside the building of democratic institutions came the mutually constitutive building of the rule of law and its corollary, the promotion and protection of human rights.

The first wave of democratization was a European phenomenon in that the countries following this path were either in Europe or were European settler societies in the Americas and Oceania. The one possible exception was Japan of the early twentieth century, whose leaders consciously borrowed from the European experience to experiment with Taishō democracy. Yet even among the first wave, democracy was neither inevitable nor irreversible, as many would turn to authoritarian rule in the between-wars period. The number of democracies in this period of fascination with fascism was reduced to less than a dozen. A contributing reason was that democracies were not performing particularly admirably in terms of economic growth and inclusive social policies. In other words, democracy's soft power was weak. The countries making the trains run on time were attracting admiration, and Benito Mussolini was plausibly able to depict democracy as a passing phase.

Huntington describes the second wave as flowing from the decolonization process. But this is to mistake an effect for a cause. The hinges of history are wars and revolutions, and the cause of the second wave of democratization was the Allied victory in World War II. It led to the defeat of both fascism and colonialism, though its effects would be spread over the several decades after the war during which many newly independent states were proclaimed and fascist governments were either defeated (as in Germany, Italy, and Japan) or eventually succumbed (as in Greece, Portugal, and Spain). Democracy's soft power increased with the Allied triumph, and it gained a distinctly American tinge. It was in this era that "the greatest generation" could aspire to build "the Great Society." And unlike most victors of most wars in history, the United States did not attempt to colonize or dominate through the usual means of military hard power but was content to extend its influence through a mix of financial (the Marshall Plan, the Bretton Woods institutions) and legal (Universal Declaration of Human Rights, the UN Charter, Japan's constitution) hard power with great dollops of soft power (Hollywood, the melting pot, scientific innovation, academia, jazz, and Elvis Presley) thrown in.

The Cold War was next to influence the extent of democracy's soft power. The Allied victory was a victory of the United States and the Soviet Union, but whereas the former was fully intact and benefiting from the industrialization imposed by the war effort, the latter lay in ruins. Wealth and success are intoxicating ingredients of soft power, and the United States had it in abundance. Democracy's status would benefit from the reflected glory. But the Soviet Union would recover lost economic ground. Those institutions that would eventually lead to its downfall—top-down centralized decisionmaking, the command economy, the Gosplan and its five-year economic prescriptions, imposed discipline through authoritarianism—were initially the means to its postwar recovery. Before too long the former allies were adversaries.

Superpower adversarialism manifested itself in every field imaginable from war to sports. The first hot war of the Cold War in Korea ended in stalemate, which could be seen as a harbinger of the result of the military contest over the next four decades. Parallel to the physical confrontations and maneuvers, virtually every intellectual theory and concept became a field of opposing interpretations. All the social sciences had Marxist interpretations, and even the field of international law—which was based on the unifying concepts of the United Nations Charter—was reinterpreted by Soviet theorists to mean a system of temporary peaceful coexistence until such time as socialist revolutions occur throughout the world, leading to the withering away of governments and the end of the necessity for international law. Imagine my surprise as a fresh-faced diplomat in Paris in the late 1970s representing Australia at an obscure UNESCO conference on library policy, a task seen as of such little significance as to be safely entrusted to a neophyte negotiator, at being confronted by a phalanx of Soviet-bloc diplomats insisting that their antibourgeois spin be the focus of the conference. The Cold War had its impact on every facet of international relations.

It follows that Cold War contestation had both spatial and intellectual dimensions. Spatially, the field of contest was what was then referred to as the Third World, where the adversaries fought out proxy wars, supported their puppet governments or national liberation movements as the case may be, and showered aid on their allies while attempting to undermine the allies of their enemy. Clearly the United States was in the stronger position to play this game given its massive economy, which dwarfed that of the Soviet Union. But the Soviet system of centralized decisionmaking had a distinct attraction to leaders of the Third World, many of whom could not see the point of tolerating a system of scheming opposition parties, carping civil society organizations, and pesky media critics. The United States would attempt to nullify this Soviet advantage by turning a blind eye to the suppression of opposition in its client states.

The spatial contest was generally limited to the Third World. With the early exceptions of the Berlin blockade and the Cuban missile crisis, there was no sustained attempt at attacking the enemy head-on. Even where opportunities arose, such as the Hungarian uprising of 1956, the West acted with great prudence. The intellectual contest extended far more broadly. It was certainly fought out among the elites of the Third World, but it was also bitterly contested in the West, and dangerously and surreptitiously in the East. The intellectual debate saw the contest for soft power at its fiercest. This is not the place for a detailed history of the intellectual contest, the key points of which are, in any case, well known. In the United States there was McCarthyism and anticommunist hyperbole that would mistakenly lead the nation to fight an ideological battle in Vietnam against an opponent fighting a nationalist war. In the Soviet Union, genocidal Stalinist social engineering would eventually give way to a more strategic attack on internal enemies that would nevertheless keep the gulags full.

From the perspective of democracy's soft power, the most damaging aspect was the creeping sense of moral, or perhaps amoral, equivalence between the two systems. They were clumped together as the two superpowers, and there was even a facile similarity in their names, as one was the US and the other the SU. This view was particularly widespread in

Europe, where in a number of countries, communist parties played active roles in domestic politics and had fraternal relations with the Soviet Communist Party. It was also held in intellectual circles in the West where the sins of colonialism, racism, and capitalist exploitation were the accepted wisdom and there was little faith in the political system that produced the governments that committed these sins. The great gap between the heroic rhetoric underpinning democracy and the distressing reality on the ground gnawed away support for the concept. Thus, at the height of the Cold War, democracy was seen by many as not much better in practice than the communism practiced by the other side.

It was at this nadir that the advantages of democracy demonstrated their worth. The 1960s and 1970s would bring the civil rights movement, a youth revolution, and a feminist awakening in a frenzy of internal contestation that only a democracy can tolerate and indeed through which democracy in the United States would be immeasurably strengthened. Violence occurred but was ultimately contained. The political system would be shaken by new ideas, new actors, and new coalitions that would wrestle with conservative forces and renew the system as a whole. The Soviet Union could have no similar sense of renewal. There was a pithy joke circulating around Moscow in this period postulating the response of each of the Soviet leaders to a situation where the train he is riding runs out of track. Lenin would call together the engineers and ask them to donate their labor; Stalin would gather the engineers and shoot every last one of them; Khrushchev would have the engineers take track from behind the train and put it in front; while Brezhnev would draw the curtains and have the engineers gently rock the carriage so he could pretend the train was still moving.

By the final decade of the Cold War, the United States had emerged from its counter-cultural churning and elected Ronald Reagan, a conservative president, who raised the stakes on cutting-edge weaponry in an attempt to price the Soviet Union out of the superpower game. The Soviet Union could no longer compete on equal terms. Clearly it could not compete financially. But even more devastatingly, it could not compete with the United States in terms of system renewal. Authoritarian systems have well-known problems of leadership succession, but these pale compared to the problem of system and social succession. Mikhail Gorbachev tried a top-down method of changing Soviet society through his introduction of the concept of perestroika, but however well-meaning his attempt, it only advanced the collapse of the entire system.

With its competitor's political collapse, the United States began its unipolar moment on the world stage. The conduct of the executive branch in this period was reasoned and relatively modest. George Bush the elder introduced the concept of a new world order in terms of high-level international agreement for direction and existing multilateral machinery for delivery. The Kuwait war was fought within this context. And the Clinton administration was also relatively modest in its management of the unipolar moment by rebranding the United States as the indispensable nation without which progress on the world's difficult issues would be impossible.

The same modesty was absent, however, in the ideological space where a sense of triumphalism dominated, and the search began for an ideological equivalent to the unipolar moment. Francis Fukuyama's 1992 book, *The End of History and the Last Man*, argued that liberal democracy has been shown to be best able to satisfy human needs. It became the intellectual ballast for the triumphalism that many in the West expressed. The title of the book (another oxymoron) came to be a bumper sticker meaning that the hard work of crafting the best form of government was done and that we need look no further.

The triumphalists needed to add a pleasing economic component to the Fukuyama bumper sticker, and they found it by appropriating another academic publication to their needs. John Williamson coined the term *Washington Consensus* to refer to a set of ten economic policy prescriptions that experts from the Washington-based international financial institutions as well as the US Treasury were advising Latin American governments to follow.[2] The ten policies deal with quite basic and indeed unremarkable prescriptions such as avoiding deficits and subsidies, achieving market-determined interest rates, liberalizing trade and investment, privatizing inefficient state enterprises, avoiding unnecessary regulation, and securing property rights. The term was, however, appropriated to be the standard bearer for a neoliberal agenda of supply-side economics, monetarism, low tax regimes, and minimal state machinery. And it was under this appropriated guise that it would be attacked by the antiglobalization movement. The Washington Consensus would quietly pass with the advent of the 2008 global financial crisis.

The high point of democracy's soft power thus began with the Reagan administration's self-confidence to challenge the Soviet Union in treasure rather than blood; intensified with Gorbachev's failure to reform the Soviet system but also his reluctance to impose Soviet orthodoxy by force of arms on its fractious empire; solidified with the collapse of the United States' only competitor; and was ratified with glib interpretations of academic theories about the end of history and the Washington Consensus. The sense of democracy's superiority as a political system increased to the point of expectation of the near inevitability of its triumph over other forms of governance.

The concept and even the word *democracy* inspired individuals and terrified autocrats in this brief period. In many parts of Asia, Africa, Central and South America, and Eastern Europe the demand for democracy took hold. People all over the world who had often been described as apathetic, passive, or uninterested in politics suddenly found a passion for that subject and articulated it in demands for democratization. The word *democracy* acted as a heading for all their frustrations of the past and their hopes for the future. For the autocrats of the day, democracy was an enemy difficult to overcome or subvert. Ferdinand Marcos was left stranded in Malacañang Palace with an American helicopter ride and exile in Hawaii his only means of evacuation; Nicolae Ceauşescu saw his stage-managed support rally in Bucharest turn into an ugly mob baying for his blood; and even the Soviet Politburo members who attempted to overthrow Gorbachev could not defy the Moscow mob led by Boris Yeltsin standing on a tank.

The high point of democracy's soft power also translated into the high point of global democratic transitions. Huntington describes the third wave as beginning with the Iberian revolutions of the 1970s, but those events clearly belong to the second-wave era of defeating fascism and colonialism. The third wave is tied to the end of the Cold War, and peak activity coincides pretty closely with the Gorbachev years. Beginning the third wave in the Gorbachev period has the advantage of tying a major global development to a major global event between which there is strong evidence of causality. The evidence in favor of this periodicity comes from a study of democratic transitions that uses the Gastil Index, on which the Freedom House measures are based, to plot the transitions to the greater practice of democracy in the period from 1972 to 2003, thus encompassing both Huntington's suggested 1974 start of the third wave and the Gorbachev incumbency. As Figure 2.1 demonstrates, while the global practice of democracy rises and falls in the post-Iberian revolutions period, the Gorbachev years see the greatest increase in democratic transition.

Some have criticized Huntington's adoption of the wave simile as insufficiently accurate and descriptive of events.[3] It certainly breaks down when the odd concept of reverse waves is introduced. But my problem is less with the imagery and more with the periodicity. Three waves or periods or generations make sense, but they need to be tied to major historical shifts. The first wave saw the slow and contested end of royal absolutism. The second wave was caused by the violent defeat

Figure 2.1　The Average Path of Democracy in 171 Countries, 1972–2003

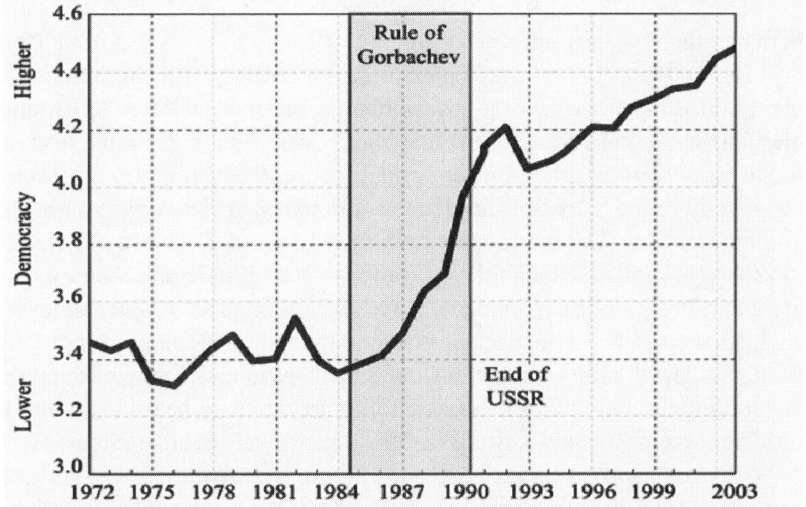

Source: Vani Borooah and Martin Paldam, "Why Is the World Short of Democracy? A Cross-Country Analysis of Barriers to Representative Government," paper presented at the European Public Choice Society Annual Conference, University of Durham, March 31–April 3, 2005.

of fascism. And the third wave flows from the overnight evaporation of communism.

Living through the period of democratic soft power's high-water mark was exhilarating. The possibilities and opportunities seemed limitless, and the tax-payer-funded democracy promotion bodies were seen as influential. Even an individual philanthropist such as George Soros was able to exert extraordinary influence on the direction of the public debate in the countries of Central Europe and, to a lesser extent, in Russia itself.

Democracy Support Machinery

The nations of the world are interdependent. The world has become the global village McLuhan so presciently foresaw. In many ways, the world forms one investment market, one trading space, and one, highly fractured and controlled, labor market. The Westphalian notion of sovereignty continues to exist, but its meaning is becoming ever more hollow. North Korea continues to assert its sovereign right to starve, torture, and deceive its own people, but it is, fortunately, a distant outlier to the norm of behaving in concert and cooperation with one's fellow global villagers. In other words, it is not an option to ignore what is happening elsewhere simply because there is an international border between the observer and the action.

The other way in which Westphalian sovereignty is losing its bite is the diminishing capacity of a government to be the only voice of its people. This was part of the Soviet "vanguard" theory that many other leaders found quite convenient, but it never made sense in a democracy where the cacophony of the marketplace of ideas dominates. Technology has played an important role in giving voice to nongovernment actors. In the Soviet days it was samizdat technology, sometimes as simple as carbon paper and hand-held pen to reproduce the forbidden texts and at other times as sophisticated as the mimeograph machine to crank out copies. Today it is more digital, with micro blogs, tweets, and anonymizers. But whatever the technology, it is simply a means to allow voices to be heard beyond the official perspective, and beyond the borders of one's own country.

So what happens when voices all around the world are demanding democracy and governments are resisting? What is the role and duty of a democratic state in these circumstances? The realist school of international relations would simply ask what is in the state's national interest whereas the ideational school would argue that democracy is a goal worth pursuing. In this instance it is not necessary to take a position in this difficult debate, as both perspectives pointed to the same action— support democratic forces especially but not exclusively in the Soviet sphere of influence. And perhaps the most forceful argument for taking action was one borrowed from the anarchist and leftist side of politics, the notion of solidarity or *fraternité*. In his 1982 speech to Westminster, Ronald Reagan said:

> No, democracy is not a fragile flower. Still it needs cultivating. If the rest of this century is to witness the gradual growth of freedom and democratic ideals, we must take actions to assist the campaign for democracy. ... Leaders of the national Republican and Democratic Party organizations are initiating a study with the bipartisan American political foundation to determine how the United States can best contribute as a nation to the global campaign for democracy now gathering force.[4]

This was the context for the establishment in 1983 of the National Endowment for Democracy, the International Republican Institute, and the National Democratic Institute for International Affairs, three bodies that had as their primary goal the support of democratization around the world. One could be forgiven for understanding this development as an American invention given the money and rhetoric that was eventually put at its disposal. But the reality is that democracy promotion was a serendipitous innovation, the origins of which emerged on the Iberian Peninsula with its principle actors being the major German party foundations.

Friedrich Ebert was the Social Democrat president of Weimar Germany from 1919 until his death in 1925. His will requested that a *stiftung*, or foundation, be established to fund scholarships, and the Friedrich Ebert Foundation (FES) was duly established and then duly banned in the Nazi era. When it was resuscitated after the war its goal was sharpened to advancing "democratic education." The Christian Democrats followed suit a few years later and established the Konrad Adenauer Foundation (KAS) with a similar goal. At the time of the fall of Caetano, Salazar's successor in Portugal, and the death of Franco in Spain in the mid-1970s, the two major German parties each had well-functioning foundations whose work was focused on civic education in Germany and modest development assistance in the Third World. With the end of fascism on the Iberian Peninsula, political parties sprang up mirroring the owner/worker cleavage that had taken hold in the rest of democratic Europe—basically Social Democrat (progressives) versus Christian Democrat (conservatives). They sought help, and the only European parties with supporting foundations complete with staff and resources were FES and KAS. Each foundation assisted its sister parties in Spain and Portugal with advice on party organization, platform development, membership drives, candidate selection, and election campaigning. The assistance proved to be invaluable and was seen as a key contributor to the consolidation of democratic systems in both Iberian countries.

Washington took keen note of this development, and when the various political and international stars aligned, the United States embarked on its journey to promote democracy around the world. Having followed the serendipitous German example, the US effort would, in the ways of soft power, generate many collegial institutions around the world.

The democracy support institutions in Figure 2.2 meet four key conditions:

1. They are primarily taxpayer funded though ostensibly independent.
2. They primarily work internationally, though a few work also in their home country.
3. Democracy support is their primary work.
4. They are not primarily research institutes.

Figure 2.2 International Democracy Support Foundations

Name and Nation	Established	Continuing?
Friedrich-Ebert-Stiftung (Germany)	1925	Yes
Konrad-Adenauer-Stiftung (Germany)	1955	Yes
Friedrich Naumann Foundation (Germany)	1958	Yes
Hanns Seidel Foundation (Germany)	1966	Yes
National Endowment for Democracy (USA)	1983	Yes
National Democratic Institute (USA)	1983	Yes
International Republican Institute (USA)	1983	Yes
Center Party's International Foundation (Sweden)	1983	Yes
IDASA, African Democracy Institute (South Africa)	1986	No
International Foundation for Electoral Systems (USA)	1987	Yes
Heinrich Böll Foundation (Germany)	1987	Yes
Rights & Democracy (Canada)	1988	No
Rosa Luxemburg Foundation (Germany)	1990	Yes
Jarl Hjalmarson Foundation (Sweden)	1990	Yes
Westminster Foundation for Democracy (UK)	1992	Yes
Fondation Jean-Jaurès (France)	1992	Yes
Olof Palme International Center (Sweden)	1992	Yes
King Prajadhipok's Institute (Thailand)	1994	Yes[a]
The Christian Democratic International Center (Sweden)	1994	Yes
International Institute for Democracy and Electoral Assistance	1995	Yes
Swedish International Liberal Center	1997	Yes
Centre for Democratic Institutions (Australia)	1998	No
Netherlands Institute for Multiparty Democracy	2000	Yes
The Korea Democracy Foundation	2001	Yes
Taiwan Foundation for Democracy	2002	Yes
Demo Finland	2004	Yes
United Nations Democracy Fund	2005	Yes
European Instrument for Democracy and Human Rights	2006	Yes
Arab Democracy Foundation (Qatar)	2007	No
Danish Institute for Parties and Democracy	2010	Yes
European Endowment for Democracy	2013	Yes

Notes: a. Now working only in Thailand.

What conclusions can be drawn from this list? One obvious point is the strength of the United States' soft power. Yes, Germany invented party foundations, but once the United States adopted the practice, many others followed the example. In Australia's case, the Centre for Democratic Institutions was established by the Australian government after some nudging from the United States. Also, the majority of these bodies was formed in the 1980s and 1990s, pointing to the high point of democracy's soft power. Next, the Western flavor of the list is clear, with all but five foundations from the West. An examination of the five non-Western groups is instructive. IDASA functioned largely on the basis of ODA from OECD governments, and when that dried up, it foundered. The Arab Democracy Foundation emerged from the needs of Qatari foreign policy (as did Qatar's $10 million contribution to the UN Democracy Fund around the same time as the founding of the Arab Democracy Foundation), but once Qatar's interests migrated elsewhere, so did the funding for democracy support. Thailand's King Prajadhipok's Institute (KPI) emerged from the same optimistic period as Thailand's forward-looking and far-reaching 1997 Constitution (since abrogated), and although its work always had a strong focus on Thailand's needs, it also attempted to promote democracy in neighboring countries. But democratic optimism has now faded in Thailand, and KPI can only afford to try to prop up the crumbling democracy in its own country.

The Korea Democracy Foundation also began with a strong domestic focus, largely to document and memorialize the struggle for democracy in South Korea. But the fact of Korea's growing strength and influence militated against that exclusive focus, and it became drawn into democracy promotion in other Asian countries through research and capacity building. Interestingly, Korea is also today bankrolling a new international institution, A-WEB, the Association of World Election Bodies. The Taiwan Foundation for Democracy (TFD), in contrast, was a creation of the Taiwanese Foreign Ministry, which saw Taiwan's consolidating democracy as its strongest suit in its struggle for soft-power influence against China. From the outset, TFD was concerned with international rather than domestic democracy support, and under the tutelage of the then Millennium Democracy Party government it carved out for itself quite a reputation as a vigorous actor, giving prizes and scholarships to Asian civil society actors regardless of whether this discomfited Asian neighbors; publishing the well-regarded *Taiwan Journal of Democracy*; and holding events in Taiwan and elsewhere dealing with democracy-related issues. The change in government in Taiwan to the Kuomintang (KMT) was a crisis point for TFD, but it seems to have traversed it intact.

In relation to the Western countries on the list, it is clear that three countries dominate: Germany, Sweden, and the United States. Perhaps a word on the underlying democracy support philosophy in each country is warranted. As noted, Germany, or perhaps more accurately Friedrich Ebert, invented the political party foundation. Today, the foundations are a formal part of Germany's political structure in that they are guaranteed public funding once the associated political party reaches certain electoral thresholds. This tends to impose a certain level of uniformity on the process. When the Greens eventually met the threshold, they decided to call their foundation the *Regenboden Stiftung*, or Rainbow

Foundation, but the German establishment quickly told the Greens to find the name of a prominent German like the other foundations, hence the Heinrich Böll Foundation, named after the Nobel Prize–winning author. When the former East German communists, now rebranded as the Left Party, reached the threshold, they stole a march on their colleagues by being the first to name their foundation after a woman, Rosa Luxemburg, a communist theorist and activist. She was not only a woman but also a Jew, again scoring points in the naming stakes. It is a poignant irony, that may have been well understood when her name was selected, that the Left Party foundation is named after a person who was killed in 1919 in Berlin in the crushing of the Spartacus League by the government of none other than Friedrich Ebert.

The German foundations are a function of their history, which saw them begin their work as Germany's primary conduits for civic education and this task remains. More curiously, however, is the link of the German foundations to Germany's now considerable ODA. The political party foundations deliver a significant slice of the ODA budget, allowing them, for example, to open offices in many countries in the global South—FES has ninety offices and KAS has eighty. The impact of the ODA connection is positive as far as the viability of the foundations is concerned but questionable from the perspective of democracy work. It is true that being political party foundations, these actors have a natural affinity with the ways and means of democratic practice and are therefore in a strong position to promote democracy, but being funded by ODA clearly has a limiting effect on the breadth and depth of their activities—which, according to the OECD's ODA philosophy, need to be "owned" by the receiving country. Those democracy support providers funded by ODA must constantly navigate between their views of how to reach their goals (economic development, democracy, human rights) and those of the receiving government, inevitably leading to compromises.

The United States did not slide into the democracy promotion process by serendipity or evolution but strode in through a deliberative bipartisan process led by President Reagan as articulated in his Westminster speech and supported by large majorities of both parties in Congress. This auspicious origin has served it well ever since. One effect is that the bulk of public funding for the National Endowment for Democracy, National Democratic Institute, and International Republican Institute, the three major bodies established in 1983, comes directly from Congress and not through the State Department or the United States Agency for International Development (USAID). It is Congress that needs to be satisfied with the democracy work of these bodies, not necessarily the receiving governments. Of course, receiving governments are not irrelevant to the process. They have considerable powers through domestic law and practices to either facilitate or obstruct the work of democracy promoters, to issue visas to the staff of democracy organizations, and, sadly, to arrest those same staff members and the locals with whom they work. Nevertheless, democracy promoters funded directly by a parliament are able to take more forthright positions.

The United States also has an edge in the high-level political nature of its democracy support work. The fact that President Reagan inaugurated the process adds to its luster. President Bill Clinton then made democracy support a significant part of American foreign policy. In his 1994 State of the Union address he argued that "ultimately, the best strategy to ensure our security and stability and build a durable peace is to advance the spread of democracy because democracies don't attack each other."[5] Clinton thus based part of his foreign policy on an academic theory first advanced by Immanuel Kant in 1795 under the title of *perpetual peace* and recently supported by considerable statistical corroboration. President George W. Bush also turned to the issue of democracy in his State of the Union address of 2005, stating, "It is the policy of the United States to seek and support the growth of democratic movements and institutions in every nation and culture, with the ultimate goal of ending tyranny in our world."[6] President Barack Obama took a different tack in his 2009 speech at Cairo University, in which he said,

> I know there has been controversy about the promotion of democracy in recent years, and much of this controversy is connected to the war in Iraq. So let me be clear: No system of government can or should be imposed on one nation by any other. That does not lessen my commitment, however, to governments that reflect the will of the people. Each nation gives life to this principle in its own way, grounded in the traditions of its own people. America does not presume to know what is best for everyone, just as we would not presume to pick the outcome of a peaceful election. But I do have an unyielding belief that all people yearn for certain things: the ability to speak your mind and have a say in how you are governed; confidence in the rule of law and the equal administration of justice; government that is transparent and doesn't steal from the people; the freedom to live as you choose. These are not just American ideas; they are human rights. And that is why we will support them everywhere.[7]

This edge in high-level political rhetoric about democracy support is, however, tied to the United States' soft power at any given time. It is a two edged sword. It works wonders when the US president is popular internationally and has the opposite effect when he is not.

Coming to Sweden, it is important to note that in addition to the four party foundations listed earlier there is the intergovernmental International Institute for Democracy and Electoral Assistance (IDEA), which, though it has twenty-eight member states, is dependent on its host, Sweden, for its ongoing viability. It is invidious to summarize a nation's views on any particular issue given the multiplicity of influences in any single country, but it might be possible to hazard the opinion that Sweden's commitment to international support of democracy flows from its commitment to democracy domestically and its view that economic development cannot be separated from the political context in which it takes place. Given Sweden's position as, over time, the world's largest per capita aid donor, running consistently at around 1 percent of gross national income (about five times more than the US government ratio), it is noteworthy that it has come to the conclusion that the link between democracy and development is undeniable and support for the former is essential to accomplish the latter.

Finally, it is worth noting that apart from International IDEA, there are other multilateral actors on the list. These are important because they express the common will of a group of states. Thus, the twenty-eight states that are members of International IDEA have agreed that the work of this organization is necessary to meet an important common national goal. In the same way, the twenty-eight member states of the European Union have made democracy promotion a key goal of their organization by establishing, first, the European Instrument for Human Rights and Democracy, which makes grants to civil society organizations in the European neighborhood and the global South; and, more recently, the European Endowment for Democracy, which quickly disperses grants to civil society organizations in the European neighborhood in fast-moving situations. These two instruments thus express the commitment of an entire region to democratization. Just as practicing democracy is a membership qualification for joining the European Union, promoting democracy elsewhere is a companion goal.

The other multilateral instrument on the list is the UN Democracy Fund (UNDEF), the organization I had the great honor to lead for seven exhilarating years. The European organizations express the will of a region, and the members of IDEA, coming from five continents, express an even broader international will; but for the UN to promote democracy is to express the will of the entire international community. This considerably adds to the international legitimacy of the entire enterprise. Incidentally, the three countries I noted for having a deep involvement with democracy support—the United States, Germany, and Sweden—also happen to be three of the four major contributors to UNDEF, the fourth being India.

There are several groups not on the list that deserve a quick mention. In 1988, flush with the success of the people power revolution in Manila that allowed the election winner, Cory Aquino, to take power, the incoming foreign minister, Raul Manglapus, decided that countries like his should get together to discuss democratization. He therefore convoked the International Conference of Newly Restored Democracies.[8] Fifteen countries were invited: six from South America, five from Central America and the Caribbean, three from Europe, with the host from Asia. Participating countries were Argentina, Bolivia, Brazil, the Dominican Republic, Ecuador, El Salvador, Greece, Guatemala, Honduras, Nicaragua, Peru, the Philippines, Portugal, Spain, and Uruguay. I attended the conference as an Australian government observer and recognized that a useful reason for the meeting was to allow participants to discuss democracy without any of the venerable godfathers—the United States, United Kingdom, and France—in the room. By the 1994 second meeting in Managua, Nicaragua, this body had grown to fifty-two participating countries and slightly amended its name to the International Conference of New or Restored Democracies (ICNRD). It then met in Bucharest, Romania (1997); Cotonou, Benin (2000); and Ulaanbaatar, Mongolia (2003); with the sixth meeting in Doha, Qatar, in 2006. The Doha meeting was an extravaganza bankrolled by the Qatari government to burnish its international credentials. It was in support of this role that Qatar made its contribution to the UN Democracy Fund and established the Arab Democracy Foundation. A total of 159 countries were represented, and it was clear given the host and the range of participants that any connection with democracy was accidental at best. Having successfully discharged its role as impresario, Qatar quickly tired of the subject matter and passed the reins to Hugo Chávez of Venezuela. A decade later, having not reconvened, the only question left to answer is whether ICNRD is dead or in the deepest coma.

An organization with a not dissimilar aim was established under the aegis of the Clinton administration in 2000—the Community of Democracies (CD). Its inaugural meeting was in Warsaw in 2000 with 106 countries participating. I was also present at this gathering, and though the meeting could be considered a success guided by Polish enthusiasm and American guile, there was an underlying suspicion, fanned by

France, that the CD was being built as some sort of alternative to the UN. The CD duly met every two or three years, never resembling anything of particular significance and certainly not a challenge to the UN. Indeed, under the careless neglect of the Bush administration it looked like a similar fate as that which befell the ICNRD awaited. But Secretary of State Hillary Clinton breathed new life into the body, which was endowed with a secretariat and given greater purpose to assist governments and civil society in the transition process.

I also had the pleasure of attending the inaugural and several subsequent meetings of the third group worth mentioning, the World Movement for Democracy (WMD—the nice version). It first met in New Delhi in 1999 and, like the other bodies, continued to meet every couple of years thereafter. Unlike the intergovernmental basis of the other bodies, where civil society is an appendage, WMD puts the central emphasis on civil society, though governmental representatives attend. It has done strong work on documenting attacks on civil society by authoritarian and, sadly, democratic governments.[9]

An outside observer might see the field as oversaturated. I recall Peter Eigen, founder of Transparency International, complaining that he was in trouble with his wife. Having attended the New Delhi WMD meeting, he trooped off the following year to the Warsaw CD meeting, dutifully advising his dear spouse. She called him out, accusing him of having a girlfriend abroad on the grounds that there could not possibly be two such meetings with basically the same name! The reason none of these bodies is on the list is that they are primarily forums, though with its secretariat and sharpened purpose, the CD comes close to also being a democracy support organization.

What does it mean to be a democracy support organization? What sort of work do they do? Because democracy is such a vast and complex field with so many necessary requirements and no single sufficient cause, there is quite a range of activities in which to engage:

- Conducting and observing elections
- Strengthening legislatures
- Strengthening political parties
- Strengthening civil society
- Promoting human rights
- Promoting the rule of law
- Promoting gender equality
- Enhancing civic education
- Strengthening oversight institutions

- Contributing to a vibrant media
- Ensuring civilian control over the military

In the early days of the democracy promotion movement it was naïvely believed by a few that getting elections right would somehow ultimately lead to all the other steps. It was natural that so much attention should be lavished on elections to make them free and fair because this is the phenomenon that most overtly distinguishes democracies from autocracies. Elections remain critical, and much work continues to be undertaken to make them effective, but there is now a broad and sober realization that much more needs to be done.

The preceding list can be divided into two complementary components: actions contributing to the supply side of democratization, and actions contributing to the demand side. The supply side deals with the institutions of democracy, and these are clearly a sine qua non. One cannot have a modern democracy without elections, at least one chamber of elected representatives, effective oversight institutions to ensure accountability, a functioning court system to adjudicate disputes affecting these institutions, and effective political parties. To work on any of these issues is to work on the supply side of democratization.

As the analogy with economics makes clear, the supply side will not respond properly without a functioning demand side. It is at least equally as important to invest in civil society, human rights, gender equality, and effective media. These constitute that part of society making demands on the institutions of democracy and also act as a corrective to those institutions by engagement with and criticism of them. To invest solely in the supply side of democracy is to leave it structurally weak, because the institutions will not become responsive to society's needs unless that society has voice and the means to express it. This conclusion was the seminal finding of Amartya Sen in his work on famines—it was not lack of food that caused famines but lack of democracy!

Squandering Democracy's Soft Power

Democracy does not promise utopia, but it does promise smooth alternation of power according to the people's will. This is one of its advantages over autocracies, which have great difficulty installing the new leader and thus revert to dynastic formulae, violence, or, at best, secret back-room deal making. So when the world's leading democracy cannot achieve the smooth alternation of power according to the people's will, democracy is clearly in trouble. A decade after the end of the Cold War, *Bush v. Gore*[10] gave democracy a black eye.

The 2000 election and the subsequent Supreme Court cases cast a particularly poor light on the US electoral system. It showed incompetence in the conduct of elections, which are not conducted by a federal body but are in the hands of some nine thousand counties. There is a lot to be said for the doctrine of subsidiarity whereby government action is taken by the lowest competent level of government, but an election for the presidency is clearly an issue of national significance and should be conducted by a federal body as it is in all[11] other federations. That incompetence was symbolized by the debates over hanging chads, the punched-out bits of voting paper produced by manual voting machines. The case put the spotlight on Florida, which has a history of incompetent election conduct verging on fraudulence. The case also put the spotlight on the constitutional archaisms in the US system, whereby voters do not directly elect their president but vote for "electors" in an electoral college that then meets to elect the president. Perhaps a good rule in the eighteenth century, the electoral college certainly appears anachronistic in the twenty-first. *Bush v. Gore* also placed the Supreme Court in a poor light, with one critic charging that the court had acted in a clearly partisan manner[12] and another charging that the majority judges and their families had personal stakes in a Republican victory.[13] It is the case that the five judges forming the majority were each appointed by Republican administrations (Reagan and George H. W. Bush).

The loss in soft power brought on by this case can be seen in an observation going around at the time from an African commentator, who noted to me that the voting dispute occurred in the state in which the candidate's brother was the governor, whose administration had bent over backwards to award its electoral college votes to his candidate brother, and that all the judges who found for the candidate were appointed to the bench while the candidate's father was either president or vice president. The dismissive conclusion of this observation was that "this is the way we do things in Africa!"

President George W. Bush is also a central figure in the next painful blow to democracy's soft power, the Iraq war. The facts are by now well-known and have been raked over thoroughly, so only a few salient points need to be referred to here. The first is that the ideological arm of the Bush administration was impatient with the slow and nonlinear use of soft power to obtain its objectives. Soft power is a frustrating commodity because it does not lend itself to dramatic policy decisions—a press announcement trumpeting a 10 percent increase to the budget of the Goethe Institute is the sort of decision a government can take to enhance soft power, but it hardly leads that evening's TV news. Soft power is about getting the system of government right, strengthening institutions, bolstering economic fundamentals, and facilitating the production of highly admired cultural and scientific products. Governments are expected to manage and indeed enhance all these aspects, but praise for success tends to come in later historical accounts. This clearly was insufficient for the Bush ideologues, who were impatient to use their newfound power to shape the world to their vision. So they turned to hard power. The previous administration had pretty much exhausted the hard power tools short of war in its dealings with Iraq—embargoes and sanctions, no-fly zones, intrusive inspections by the UN, and a system of directing Iraq's oil revenues. What tools were left?

It has long been my contention that pariahs inspire bad law. In dealing with pariahs, policymakers seem to have a far freer hand and enjoy greater public acceptance in bending the rules, human rights defenders have a harder job in defending the rights of their despised clients, and adjudicatory bodies sense and too often succumb to popular pressure to impose harsh exemplary punishments. Today, simply to describe someone as a terrorist is to attempt to gain all the benefits of this pariah exceptionalism. And in Bush's day there was no greater pariah than Saddam Hussein. The great irony is that Saddam wallowed in his pariah status. It made him all the more formidable domestically and gave him a certain cachet internationally, where anti-Americanism is a river that often flows or at least trickles through the international community. So rather than convincingly deny he possessed chemical weapons, he did so furtively, intentionally suggesting the opposite. He called what he thought was the American bluff.

Here was an administration champing at the bit to use hard power. Another irony in this situation is that while the US president may well be thought of as the most powerful person in the world, when all is said and done, the amount of hard power at the presidency's disposal is quite limited. It is shared horizontally with Congress and eventually with the Supreme Court as well as vertically with the states and (though decreasingly true of the United States, where the Senate has basically stopped ratifying UN treaties) with the international community through binding treaties. The most obvious bit of hard power at the president's disposal is the military, where the United States has a vast technological advantage over every other country. To use it to attack Saddam would only require the concurrence of Congress and a simple decision to ignore the international community. The pariah card would work with Congress as long as a plausible reason was provided; this is where the administration settled on weapons of mass destruction (WMD—the nasty kind) as that plausible reason.

The rest of the story follows the fruitless months of searching for WMD and the morphing of the plausible reason to that ever useful pariah of terrorism and Saddam's associations with it. While this "axis of evil" assertion made for good sound bites, it could not withstand reasoned analysis and lacked discernible evidence. It was obvious that the nationalist, secularist, and modernist Saddam was pretty much the antithesis of the globalist (*ummah*-ist), religious, and obscurantist jihadis. Enter therefore the third and final plausible reason for the war in Iraq; to bring democracy to the Arab world. It was by definition an afterthought, but it wreaked the greatest damage to democracy's soft power.

The association of war with democracy promotion was quite poisonous to the latter.[14] Imposed democracy is not a felicitous oxymoron; it contradicts the democracy community's rhetoric of respect for local decisions and the modest role claimed by the international community. It magnified the Achilles' heel of democracy promotion, which its proponents argue is not directly tied to short-term national interests but rather serves long-term mutual interests. And it undermined the self-confidence of the democracy promotion practitioners, who subsequently had to choose whether to be part of a war effort in the service of democracy. Thus did a doyen of the movement, Larry Diamond, find himself spending a frustrating and fruitless six months in the Green Zone of Baghdad.[15]

Success might have cured imposed democracy as it did in Germany and Japan after World War II. Both countries had surrendered unconditionally after disastrous wars of aggression, embraced the system of their conqueror, and returned to previous experimentation with democratization—undertaken in the Taishō period in Japan and in the Weimar period in Germany. But, though Iraq also lived through a pre-Baathist electoral period, the analogy ends there because *success* is the last word one could use for the American invasion. Instead, the costs have been staggering in terms of lives lost, treasure squandered, sectarianism rekindled, jihadism strengthened, and Iranian influence bolstered. There has been no true democracy dividend, though elections continue to be held and a parliament continues to sit.

The democracy support community suffered a harsh blow from its association with the war. Clearly the congressionally funded bodies had the most to lose by this association, but the Europeans were not spared because so many of their governments became entangled with the war's tentacles; participating in the occupation, cooperating with rendition, and trying to position themselves in the post-Saddam Arab world. Even the UN Democracy Fund had to carry the burden of the Bush administration's enthusiasm for its establishment. For some critics it would take a number of years of positive contribution to the cause of democracy to expiate in their eyes the sins of association with the war. For other critics, association with the war "proved" that the democracy support community was simply part of the deeply imagined conspiracy by the United States or the West for world hegemony.

Gridlock

The major contribution to democracy's soft power is the success of its practitioners. Success comes in many forms—economic prowess and the ability to provide citizens with a comfortable material existence; security in the form of protecting democratic homelands from the scourge of war; and high quality of life by allowing an open society where individuals are free politically, economically, and socially. The underlying assumption is that this success flows from these societies' democratic form of government. While that assumption has attempted to be proven,[16] its greatest confirmation comes from the simple comparison of the life led by those living in democracies compared with the lot of those who do not. Accordingly, democracy produces better systems of government, which then benefit the citizenry.

A common criticism of this perspective is to see the global political economy as a zero-sum game in which all the advances of democracies have come at a cost to others. Thus, it is not democracy that has given its people an advantage but rather colonialism or neocolonialism or neoliberal globalization. This is not the place to debate these rather large questions, but it is necessary to refute the key supporting premise that success in the global economy is a zero-sum game. It clearly is not. Standards of living have increased dramatically on every continent; poverty stricken nations have become wealthy within a generation or two without beggaring their neighbors—indeed, whole regions have become wealthy; and resource-poor nations have found ways to use their greatest resource, the talents of their people, to become wealthy. This is not to say that all is well with the world—there is an inequality crisis both between and within nations—but there is ample evidence to conclude that the wealth of one nation has no necessary correlation to the poverty of another. Success is not a zero-sum game; it rests on factors any nation can employ.

The advantage rests on the superiority of the democratic system of government, and so it is this system that requires further comment. Democracy and its system of governance is a complex creature. In a previous publication I put forward the following analogy:

> Recurring throughout this project is the analogy of the system of democracy resembling the system of the human body. The comparison is useful because the complexity of both systems can be simplified by reference to its key parts. In this analogy, the skeleton provides the structure for the system and it resembles the institutions of democracy—parliaments, executives, elections, courts, auditors, ombudsmen and so forth. Within this structure are the organs pumping blood and oxygen into the system and they can be compared to political parties as well as politicians and perhaps other policy leaders. The flesh around the skeletal structure can be compared to the people taking the form of deliberators, civil society activists, voters as well as consumers of the impacts of policy decisions. Accordingly, the public conversation being conducted and the political culture of the populace become key themes. Living systems grow and change. Life forms, even of the same species, are individually different from each other. The analogy between the democratic system and the human body can comfortably extend to include both change and lack of uniformity. The benefit of using this analogy is that it makes clear that various parts of the system must work together to create the whole.[17]

The analogy clarifies the discussion of the health of democratic systems and, importantly, also suggests their lack of immortality. How healthy are democratic systems of government? This broad question gives rise to more specific questions. How well are the various formal and informal institutions performing? Do they produce the required outcomes? Is the public conversation in good shape? Are citizens participating actively in the public life of the polity? The answer to these questions allows a conclusion about the support of the people for the system and whether the system remains admirable in the eyes of outsiders.

Each question in relation to each democracy would require a book-length response. The following comments are therefore necessarily impressionistic. The focus is primarily on the United States as the leading democracy. The aim remains to determine the extent of democracy's soft power and whether it is waxing or waning. The good news is that the institutions continue to tick over. Elections are held, though, as noted, the 2000 presidential election left a sour taste. Elected assemblies sit and budgets are (usually) passed while civil servants continue on the whole to implement the rules and policies laid down. Homelands remain pretty secure, and individual liberties remain largely protected. So far so good. But it does not take too much drilling to find significant problems below the surface of orderly working institutions. So, what are the significant trends in democracy that are impacting on its soft power?

The third wave of democratization in the post–Cold War era brought many nations into the field of governance experimentation as they sought to design institutions that would meet their needs. Much energy went into drafting or amending constitutions. The Philippines and South Africa demonstrated the trend of constitutions broadening from narrow legal documents delineating divisions of power to broad aspirational documents setting down national goals. There has been experimentation concerning women's rights, indigenous peoples' rights, and minority rights. There has been experimentation on the functioning of institutions with leadership codes, oversight branches of government, and independent national human rights institutions. To employ the term *experimentation* is to accept failure as a possible consequence. Many experiments yielded negative unforeseen results, and many constitutions thus required early revision. Longevity of constitutions adds to their legitimacy and thus effectiveness. But at what point does this longevity turn to stasis? Can it be possible that while the international community and its constituent nations live through a globalization revolution, a digital revolution, and an environmental revolution, a national constitution setting forth the social contract of the people of that nation needs no revision or even review? That is what the United States is saying.

The US Constitution is a remarkably prescient document and became a model for all future constitutions, but it is not revealed wisdom. It was the work of intelligent deliberators prepared to listen to different views. The fact that there have been twenty-seven amendments demonstrates the principle that all constitutions require occasional renewal. But the last modern amendment was in 1971, when the voting age was lowered to 18, while the most recent amendment concerning congressional salaries finally came into force in 1992 after a journey of more than two centuries since it was first proposed. In recent years, government has amassed enormous technical means to spy on people, kill them remotely, and tax them surreptitiously, but none of this has led to a discussion of the need for constitutional renewal. It seems that the US Constitution is frozen; indeed, an influential former member of the Supreme Court (Justice Scalia) not only saw no need to change anything but wished to interpret the Constitution according to the doctrine of originalism, whereby the key question is WWTFS ("what would the founders say?"). A petrified constitution does not contribute much to democracy's soft power.

Constitutional sclerosis is simply one of many symptoms of political gridlock. Recent problems voting a federal budget, the near default by the United States, and the difficulty of filling judicial and civil service positions requiring Senate confirmation are others. The saga of health reform is an eloquent testimony to the fact that if one side of politics happens to secure a significant plank of its platform, the other side will relentlessly attempt to undermine it using every strategy available, such as serial litigation, lack of cooperation from opposition state governors, defunding its implementation, and demonizing it in the eyes of its supporters. This is a particularly eloquent example of the culture of gridlock because the underlying concept was, in fact, originally championed by the Republican side of politics but was demonized when Democrats adopted it.

Is gridlock worse today than in previous episodes? It is always invidious to compare different eras of politics, but what can be said is that the impact of government is far greater today, the access to information is far wider today, the 24-hour news cycle is more intrusive today, and therefore the impact of gridlock, particularly on soft power, is more wide-ranging today.

The Medium and the Message

An autocracy depends on controlling the flow of information, and its effectiveness is in part related to its capacity to shape the knowledge and opinions of its subjects. To understand ultimate autocratic logic one need only look at North Korea, where the propaganda has it that its subjects live in utopic conditions while the rest of the world is experiencing hell on earth. When a North Korean peasant sees starvation abound, abandoned and feral children all around, and gulag camps on the ground, it must be difficult to accept the contention that she lives in utopia. North Korea is a closed country but is not hermetically sealed. Pre-paid cell phones are smuggled in, and returning travelers whisper about life elsewhere. Because people know or at least suspect that the propaganda is a lie, the Kim dynasty must resort to repression as the means to control the population. Information control is essential but will not work without other instruments of control.

It is possible to place the Democratic People's Republic of Korea (DPRK) as an impossible outlier, but it remains only a matter of degree. The current Russian leadership is pining away for the old Soviet information policies and is heading back to state control of the key electronic media. China also understands the problem of information control and is trying to handle it with a mix of technological "Great Firewall of

China" solutions mixed in with some soft authoritarianism where selected individuals are punished as an example to others, thus encouraging self-censorship. The free flow of information from sources independent of the state remains one of the key distinctions between autocracies and democracies.

A democracy depends on freedom of expression, and its quality can be judged in part by the breadth, depth, and insightfulness of the public conversation among its citizens. The question is whether the current set-up of the media and the public conversation it carries is serving the interests of a democratic nation. The response contains a series of contradictions and contradistinctions. In terms of ownership of the major electronic and print media, Rupert Murdoch wants it all and is well on his way, but the "all" is changing dramatically. Murdoch may well end up as the undisputed emperor of twentieth-century media but merely an important player in twenty-first-century media. The digital revolution has brought such an explosion in platforms, channels, websites, and podcasts that monopolistic ownership is beyond any individual or corporation. In parallel, individual reading and viewing habits are changing in response to the breadth of options available. The change is dramatic but not instantaneous. There are still plenty of twentieth-century habits around, and Murdoch can feed on these for years to come to remain a media kingpin. The optimist may nevertheless consider that time is on the side of the democratization of production for and access to the media. The pessimist, in comparison, will decry the deformation of news in the hands of digerati—in fact, anybody with a Twitter or Facebook account can create their own news. I don't think we should blame the medium for the messages it is facilitating. Gutenberg invented printing and is remembered for his bibles, but the early beneficiaries of the new technology were scurrilous pamphleteers. Should we blame printing?

Ownership may have once been considered to be the fundamental problem of media and democracy, but the issue of partisanship has replaced it. There may have been an explosion in platforms and channels, but it has been accompanied by a striking diminution of debate. The commercial formula, once again championed by Murdoch, is to find a doggedly loyal political cleavage and cater to its particular political perspectives; to maintain that loyalty by reinforcing commitment to the original views through "news" and opinion slanted in support; and, concurrently, ridiculing the plausibility of any other view. Newtonian laws then kick in and a reaction occurs to attempt to capture the loyalty of opposing views. The effect is to either comfort or infuriate the consumer and to reinforce originally held views. What is missing is the deliberative aspect of the public conversation, the to and fro of genuine public debate and the provocation not of ire but of thought.

Changing one's view is a fundamental building block of a culture of democracy. The world is not constant, and issues continually morph and migrate, so why should views about those issues not also change? Experiments in deliberative democracy suggest that ordinary people can, if given the opportunity, debate and discuss their way to solutions to significant public policy problems, with many changing their minds in the process.[18] But the partisan approach to the public conversation is tribal—us or them. Changing one's mind is tantamount to disloyalty, even apostasy. A politician trying to find a compromise will run the risk of being ridiculed as a flip-flopper. Why should a politician run this risk, especially in the American primary nomination system that gives undue weight to small groups with deeply held extreme convictions? The effect is the rarity of compromise solutions, the lifeblood of a well-functioning democracy. Partisan-inspired gridlock in the public conversation is particularly visible and thus has a particularly deleterious impact on democracy's soft power. A great irony is that while partisanship is deepening, political parties are weakening. The guardians of partisanship are no longer party leaders but the billionaire plutocrats, the think-tank ideologues, and the media kingpins.

Finally, what about the quality of the public conversation? Does it inspire and thus contribute to soft power? In contradistinction to the previous point about partisanship, the breadth of platforms allows many views to be expressed, and many of those views are indeed inspiring. The phenomenon of citizen journalists posting on websites and video sites is a welcome development, though the quality varies wildly, as would be expected. And it is also true that there remains a place for the nonpartisan public intellectual to contribute to and perhaps guide public debate. America's great tertiary institutions of learning provide the public with this service. High-quality commentary and debate exists, but it might be in the process of being pushed to the edges of the media spectrum while the center becomes dominated by commercial, partisan, and sensationalist interests. The public conversation in a democracy may be chaotic, it may sound cacophonous, and it may at times only be of cathartic value, but it is the most visible face of democracy. The problem facing today's democracies, particularly that of the United States, is that reasoned, deliberative, and accommodating debate is being drowned out by the dogmatic, partisan, and uncompromising speech that is coming to dominate the media.

Are There Any Admirable Democracies?

Though few people have heard of it, there is a soft power index.[19] Compiled by a British public relations company with Facebook's cooperation, the Portland survey is a composite index of thirty countries that combines both objective metrics of countries' soft-power resources and subjective international polling data. The 2016 survey put the United States on top and China and Russia near the bottom. It is noteworthy, however, that in the subcategory of "government," the United States drops to mid-table. It is categories such as "enterprise" and "culture" that drag the United States to the top. While the Portland survey may not be cited as often as that of Freedom House, it is a worthy attempt at numerating an impression. I am sure we will see many more figures generated by Google searches and Facebook likes. The greatest value of the Portland survey will come over time, as we see if the order of precedence stays constant. In the meantime, we can employ the more old-fashioned informed impressions. The following impressionistic *tour d'horizon* is obviously open to the charge of subjectivity, but this extended op-ed makes no claim to being anything else. So here goes!

This chapter has already dealt with some of the ills of the United States' political system, but as I rewrite this chapter in 2016, there is clearly more to be said. So many millions of words have been written on the Trump phenomenon that I will spare readers a repetition of the most common refrains dealing with his racism, narcissism, anti-intellectualness, and plain meanness. I want to concentrate on his demagoguery because this is where his true genius lies. I was listening to his speech the first time he proposed a ban on Muslim entry into America. What shocked me was not the absurdity and undeliverability of such a policy—those words can be applied to almost all his policies—but the instant cheering that went up from the crowd. Trump knows how to play to people's worst instincts, their identity paranoias, and their delight in bullying the "other." I prefer the word *demagogue* to the rather vague word *populist*. In some parts of the world the term *populist* does not have the same pejorative connotation it has in the established democracies. The term *demagogue* is better because there is a clear implication of deceit built into its understanding. The demagogue spurns inconvenient facts and despises experts who disagree. The demagogue builds support on irrational fears and prejudices and dispenses with rational policies and arguments.

The danger to American democracy lies in the fact that so many people are prepared to be swayed by demagoguery. The Trump phenomenon has normalized demagoguery in a way that has not previously happened in recent American history. Prior to Trump, American politics had to deal with vague and unhelpful notions such as "values" and had to also deal with the rejection of science in relation to issues such as global warming and evolution. But at least some of these are based on naked and understandable self-interest. Mitch McConnell is not stupid and probably accepts the science behind climate change, but it is inconvenient for a senator from a coal-mining state to do so. If he were a true leader, he would try to prepare his constituents for the inevitable problems rather than swim in that Egyptian river, denial. But Trump's lies—crime is caused by immigrants, international trade agreements are undermining America, Muslims are disloyal citizens—are only self-interested in the narrowest narcissistic sense. His ascendency has normalized this type of campaigning, and it will be exceedingly difficult to roll it back.

Another danger to American democracy from Trump is one very well known in other parts of the world—the man on the white horse. In his convention speech, Trump fell back to the rhetoric of dictators: "Only I can save you." There is a certain consistency therefore in not announcing policy positions. It is not policies that will save America, it is Trump. It is not reasoned judgment drawing on the expertise and experience of governance practitioners that will save America, it is Trump. It is not win-win negotiations that will advance America's international interests, it is Trump's personal negotiating skills.

And the final danger to American democracy is the acceptance of foundation myth as fact. Trump did not invent this form of reactionary delirium. It has been around for a while. The Tea Party draws on it by using a revolutionary war episode. As noted previously, it has even been given legal justification by the theory of originalism pushed by the late Antonin Scalia on the Supreme Court. Harping on the word *again* is Trump's attempt to return to an imaginary time of perfection. In that sense it is no less absurd than the jihadist insistence on returning to the period of the Medina constitution in the time of the Prophet Muhammad, when the world was momentarily perfect.

Let's continue our tour with that system of democratic governance that was given its name by the mother of all parliaments, Westminster. The classic Westminster system is the two-party parliamentary system that ensures a single-party majority in the budget-proposing chamber and diminishes the conflict between the parliamentary and executive branches of government because they are necessarily fused by overlapping incumbency. The supposed admirable result is strong government. But something has gone wrong. In recent times, every major

Westminster democracy has found itself in a coalition government, thus weakening the major feature drawing admiration. The bedrock two-party systems are being fragmented by popular demands for different issue-based and ascriptive representation. The bedrock majoritarian electoral systems supporting the two-party model drawing on Duverger's famous theory[20] have had to be tinkered with or, as in New Zealand, abandoned. Policy outcomes have clearly suffered. The United Kingdom seems to have shed its two-party system, with single-issue parties (Scottish Nationalists and UK jingoists) taking significant parts of the spectrum. Australia and Canada were recently governed by climate change deniers appealing to vested energy interests trying to lull the public to adopt an ostrich posture. These are not recipes for emulation.

And sadly, we have also seen the UK subject to its own brand of demagoguery in the Brexit debate. Mining the wreckage of that debate for a silver lining, I perversely take heart from the fact that "the other" in the Brexit debate was not someone of foreign faith and dusky color, but rather the humble Polish plumber. What it demonstrates, however, is that anyone can be made into the other. Yes, you and I! The Brexit debate and vote showed that demagoguery can win out over reason and rationality. The demagogue in this case was Boris Johnson, whose support for Brexit imbued the case with a certain legitimacy. Johnson was not previously known to be anti-Europe especially as mayor of one of the world's most international cities. But, drawing on Trump-like narcissism, he fashioned himself into the movement's spokesperson in order to reap personal gain.

In 1990, European countries declared that democracy is for them the *only* form of government.[21] This is a welcome commitment to democracy, but a quarter of a century of democratic practice since that statement has not fleshed it out with inspiring democratic governance. Europe is facing a dilemma—the construction of Europe. In many ways it is the most admirable undertaking of modern times. Here is an attempt to end all wars in Europe, create a single European identity, and put an end to the harmful nationalism that so scarred the continent in the previous century. It is an attempt to build a cosmopolitan society of linguistic and cultural polyglots that goes from tolerance to celebration of regional and local differences and peculiarities. It is an attempt to build a society of rule of law, to become uncompromising defenders of human rights, and to be a community caring for the disadvantaged. The dilemma is that reality is showing the goal to be unattainable. Cosmopolitanism thrives, but, curiously, it does so alongside a stubborn nationalism or localism that will not release its grip on people's imaginations. The rule of law is generally a reality, but it is built on a vast and deeply unpopular bureaucracy that seems to grow with every expansive idea about European integration. And the identity of the component parts of Europe in the form of national governments refuses to wither away or to cede pride of place to regional or supranational government. Continued French and British membership of the UN Security Council is an obvious example. Europe's dilemma is like that of the shark that must keep moving to survive; it must keep integrating to survive. The construction process seems more important than the end product. Yet the people of Europe seem to have grown tired of this unrelenting construction phase.

My old mate Patrice de Beer stated the problem eloquently:

> Considered the most powerful and inventive idea of the 20th century, today the EU appears more to its members, and citizens alike, as limping towards an uncertain future. No longer a leading force toward progress and prosperity, it has morphed into a rudderless, bureaucratic machine obsessed with inadequate regulations, punishing unimaginative financial and fiscal policies less and less in tune with its citizens' daily lives and aspirations. And what makes it even worse is that the countries and governments who have benefited from it and who control it by nominating their own commissioners to leadership posts are the very same who, when back home, put the blame on the Commission they have crafted to implement their policies. They attempt to wash their hands of their own responsibilities by making voters believe this Brussels bogeyman is the only culprit for everything that does not work. This lack of courage has been nurturing an ever-growing anti-European feeling now widespread throughout the EU.[22]

As a society committed to human rights, Europe has another dilemma. It is finding great difficulty integrating those many people from the immediate neighborhood who have been drawn to Europe, officially and unofficially, and who now constitute a sizeable minority. Settler societies such as the United States, Canada, and Australia have a culture of acceptance and integration into the American, Canadian, or Australian dream (though the limits of that culture are currently being tested). But Europe does not. Europe gave us the Treaties of Westphalia, whereby the local prince is sovereign over the people within the designated borders and the map makers quickly started drawing the bold lines encompassing the people controlled by those princes. The culture of European cosmopolitanism is actually a culture of internal reciprocity—I will learn French if you learn German; I will open my borders if you open yours; I will value your culture if you value mine; and, more recently, I will not block German unification if you give up the Deutschmark. Those outside the relationships of reciprocity have far greater difficulty in attracting the benefits of cosmopolitanism. Rather than accommodating forms of multiculturalism, which the settler societies had little choice but to accept, European cosmopolitanism requires outsiders to become adept at European culture before society will accept them.

Finally, Europe has a dilemma in its acceptance of a deep welfare state. Putting to one side the ideological debate about the ultimate worth of the concept, it is clear that in Europe it emerged from a fuzzy social contract that tax payers were prepared to pay a little more for the social harmony that they believed the welfare state would bring. That social contract remains reflective of today's perceptions, but it is no longer clear that European societies can afford to maintain it. Nor is it clear that they wish to extend the social contract to the hundreds of thousands of asylum seekers pouring into the continent.

Perhaps Europe will work it all out, though the Brexit vote makes it that much more difficult. The German locomotive will pull the continent to robust economic growth. The doctrine of subsidiarity will work its magic on the many layers of governance to find a workable logic. The commitment to human rights will trump the continent's cultural haughtiness. Perhaps. Until such time, European society and democracy does not attract sufficient admiration to give it much soft power beyond those few candidate countries that are qualified to join it.

But there is a towering exception, Angela Merkel. Yet another irony presents itself in that a woman who grew up in East Germany and was a member of the communist party youth wing would teach the world a lesson in compassion and international fraternity when she convinced her countryfolk to accept the one million Syrian refugees pouring into Europe.

There are admirable aspects of other democracies.[23] India remains a marvel. Its commitment to democracy and its competence in holding elections are admirable. But democracy has not solved many of India's ugly problems. Grinding poverty remains widespread. Human trafficking, indentured labor, and deep caste discrimination are not hidden away, but neither are they being adequately managed. India is an admirable democracy in a host of ways, but it is not yet an admirable society. Japanese society has many admirable qualities, but robust democracy is not among them. South Korea and Taiwan have come a long way in a short period of time in developing their democracies, and this generates considerable soft power, but it is compromised by the existential security threats they each face. In time, Indonesia could be a poster child for democratization, but for the time being, there are too many continuing inequities and injustices to justify that title.

The democracies of southern Africa (Botswana, Namibia, and South Africa) are also admirable in view of the hurdles these countries have faced, but it is important not to lose sight of the reality that in almost one century combined of elections and democratic government (post-apartheid in the case of South Africa), there has never been a change in government! South America is showing some important signs of democratic consolidation in Chile, Argentina, and Uruguay, but they remain hostage to continued economic progress. Brazil has led the way in some fields, including its innovative *bolsa familia* policy, but we are now learning of how deeply corruption remains implanted in the top echelons. In Central America, Costa Rica stands out for sustaining democracy over many decades and indeed developing a culture of democracy with contestation of ideas and alternation of power. Costa Rica's soft power flows from its adherence to democracy and from the audacious and highly successful decision in 1949 to dissolve its armed forces and become a beacon for peace.

Conclusion

There are some blinking red warning lights that democracy as a word and as a concept is losing its luster. It was telling that during the Arab Spring, the D word that attracted all the attention was not *democracy* but *dignity*. It is well and good to argue as I and others have that the path to dignity is through democracy and human rights.[24] But, as will be discussed in subsequent chapters, there are other possible paths according to various views. The goal of dignity is a subtle shift that clearly resonates with people. It is, of course, unobjectionable; nobody openly advocates an undignified existence. It is also amorphous and subjective, and it lends itself to democrats and scoundrels alike. Ultimately it is an unhelpful term because of its breadth and vagueness. Unemployment is undignified, academic failure is undignified, divorce is undignified, imprisonment is undignified, even sickness is undignified. Democracy is a system. Dignity is a vague wish. Yet, its soft power seems to be trumping that of democracy.

At the end of the Cold War, it was inspiring to have Amartya Sen describe democracy as a universal value.[25] Sen defined his terms carefully, and the universality described not the practice of democracy nor its utility but rather the far narrower fact that everyone found something of value in the concept. Thus, when *juntas* and military dictatorships such as the Fijian military justified their post-coup incumbency, they drew on this play book describing democracy as a beautiful flower that, unfortunately, will not grow in Fijian (fill in the country name) soil. Variations included "we will eventually get there but the people are not ready for democracy" and "the people want food first then we can work on rights." These tactics accepted the value of democracy but rejected its applicability—for the time being. In hindsight, the time of Sen's article may well have been the halcyon days of democracy's soft power.

Notes

1. Samuel Huntington, *The Third Wave: Democratization in the Late Twentieth Century* (Norman: University of Oklahoma Press, 1991).

2. John Williamson, *The Washington Consensus as Policy Prescription for Development*, 2004, http://www.iie.com/publications/papers/williamson0204.pdf.

3. John Keane, *The Life and Death of Democracy* (New York: W. W. Norton, 2009) p. 671.

4. Ronald Reagan, Address to Members of the British Parliament, June 8, 1982, http://www.reagan.utexas.edu/archives/speeches/1982/60882a.htm.

5. William J. Clinton, State of the Union, January 25, 1994, http://www.presidency.ucsb.edu/ws/?pid=50409.

6. George W. Bush, State of the Union, February 2, 2005, http://georgewbush-whitehouse.archives.gov/stateoftheunion/2005/.

7. Barack Obama, The President's Speech in Cairo: A New Beginning, June 4, 2009, https://obamawhitehouse.archives.gov/issues/foreign-policy/presidents-speech-cairo-a-new-beginning.

8. A history of the movement can be found in Tapio Kanninen and Katerina Sehm Patomaki (eds.), *Building Democracy from Manila to Doha: The Evolution of the Movement of New and Restored Democracies*, Helsinki Process Publication Series, 2005.

9. ICNL and WMD, *Defending Civil Society Report*, 2012, http://www.movedemocracy.org/defending-civil-society-project.

10. Bush v. Gore, 531 U.S. 98 (2000).

11. With the exception of Switzerland.

12. Alan Dershowitz, *Supreme Injustice: How the High Court Hijacked Election 2000* (New York: Oxford University Press, 2001).

13. Steven Foster, *The Judiciary, Civil Liberties and Human Rights* (Edinburgh: Edinburgh University Press, 2006).

14. James Traub, *The Freedom Agenda: Why America Must Spread Democracy (Just Not the Way George Bush Did)* (New York: Farrar, Straus and Giroux, 2008).

15. Larry Diamond, *Squandered Victory: The American Occupation and the Bungled Effort to Bring Democracy to Iraq* (New York: Henry Holt, 2005).

16. See, for example, Morton Halperin, Joe Siegle, and Michael Weinstein, *The Democracy Advantage: How Democracies Promote Prosperity and Peace* (New York: Routledge, 2005).

17. Roland Rich, *Pacific Asia in Quest of Democracy* (Boulder, CO: Lynne Rienner, 2007), p. 15.

18. Mark E. Warren and Hilary Pearse (eds.), *Designing Deliberative Democracy: The British Columbia Citizens' Assembly* (Cambridge: Cambridge University Press, 2008).

19. Portland Communications, "The Soft Power 30", http://softpower30.portland -communications.com/ranking/.

20. Maurice Duverger, *Political Parties: Their Organization and Activity in the Modern State* (London: Methuen, 1954).

21. Charter of Paris for a New Europe, November 19–21, 1990, http://www .osce.org/documents/mcs/1990/11/4045_en.pdf.

22. Patrice de Beer, "Europe: Flailing or Divided?" *World Policy Journal* (Winter 2014–2015), http://www.worldpolicy.org/journal/winter2014/europe-flailing-or -divided.

23. See Ted Piccone, *Five Rising Democracies: And the Fate of the International Liberal Order* (Washington, DC: Brookings Institution, 2016).

24. Roland Rich, *Dignity Through Democracy and Human Rights* (New Delhi: Institute of Social Science, 2012).

25. Amartya Sen, "Democracy as a Universal Value," *Journal of Democracy* 10, 3 (1999): 3–17.

3

Transitions to Democracy
Are Stalled

By the turn of the millennium, democracy had many advantages.
Its soft power was strong, people in nearly every region of the world were
making demands for democratization, and the first-wave democracies
were leading a significant democracy support movement. And yet, things
were not going quite as smoothly as might have been expected.

Canaries Gasping for Air

The first realization about the transition process was its messiness and
unpredictability, not at all like the soothing analogy of switching on a
light. The world's fourth most populous country, Indonesia, went
through what seemed like a classic transition in 1998—economic crisis;
student demonstrations; diminished international legitimacy; autocrat
side-lined; and successor, promising fundamental democratic changes,
installed. In quick succession, though through constitutional means,
three inadequate leaders took charge; B. J. Habibie, Gus Dur, and
Megawati Sukarnoputri, each described in the withering local humor as
either deaf, dumb, or blind. Habibie talked incessantly but listened rarely
and was thus deaf; Gus Dur was legally blind and also blind to his own
follies; and Megawati maintained a regal air befitting a girl who grew up
in a palace but rarely said anything of consequence, thus earning the
"dumb" sobriquet. The first six years of transition were a mess, though
in hindsight one can see that some key building blocks were laid, especially by Habibie. Indonesians refer to this time of transition as the

61

"democrazy" period. National income fell, intergroup intolerance rose, terrorism reared its ugly head, and oligarchs grew their power. Indonesia has now successfully transited through its democrazy stage, but it nevertheless serves as a warning to those demanding transition that they are likely to enter into particularly difficult times where the quality of life may, initially at least, deteriorate.

Another Southeast Asian example also serves as a democracy transition warning—the Philippines' use of people power. The people power revolution that rid the Philippines of Ferdinand Marcos was lauded internationally. It has a Hollywood feel to it, thus reinforcing the one-line summary of the Philippines' colonial history as having been in a Spanish convent for 300 years and then spending 50 years in Hollywood. The bad guy was clear to see—a once-reforming president fallen victim to the enticements of incumbency as well as the wiles of his scheming wife. His most immediate crime was that he had been caught cheating in the recent elections. The good guy also seemed pretty obvious—the pious widow of the assassinated opposition leader cheated out of her electoral victory. The supporting cast was impressive, led by courageous members of civil society who were able to shine the light on electoral fraud together with conscientious members of the Catholic Church who called the people out to the streets. And the independent variable posed a great mystery—what side would the military take? People power took physical form because, whipped up by the supporting cast, people flooded onto the main road that rings Manila and gridlocked the security forces, who were unable and perhaps unwilling to support their ailing president.

That all happened in 1986, but fifteen years later another misbehaving president was in power. The problem was that "Erap" Estrada had been duly elected, though it is likely that many voters elected the character he played as a movie star rather than the actor himself. In many movies Estrada portrayed a struggling member of the poor strata of society who is pushed too far and fights back. Many Filipino voters identified with that character. It only took a few years in power for the public to realize what a dreadful error it had made. Estrada was not only corrupt but also ostentatiously incompetent. And so in 2001 people power II removed him under dubious legal means ultimately blessed by the Supreme Court and installed his (equally corrupt but perhaps less incompetent) vice president, Gloria Macapagal, the daughter of a former president. While the term *people power* may have been used to gain legitimacy by association with the 1986 version, it should be better seen as mob rule. And when mobs can be purchased (as Estrada did in an unsuccessful attempt to return to power in the people power III fracas a couple of years later), society has moved not toward democratization but one step closer to chaos. It is a sad commentary on the electorate that it has now voted in Rodrigo Duterte, the vigilante mayor of Davao, who is making vigilantism a national practice with the nodding approval of the populace.

A similar people power phenomenon played out in Pakistan recently where former sports hero turned politician Imran Khan and populist cleric Tahir al-Qadri led thousands of supporters in demonstrations in Islamabad over a number of weeks in mid-2014, claiming the 2013 elections were rigged and unsuccessfully calling for Prime Minister Sharif to step down. Imran Khan was a wonderful and charismatic cricketer, and the 2013 elections may have left much to be desired, but the ability to get a crowd out on the street cannot become the normal means of changing governments. It only leads to mob rule.

What are these gasping canaries trying to say? Transitions away from authoritarianism are ugly and difficult processes often plunging society into years or even decades of uncertainty. Theorists have already cast grave doubt on the "transition paradigm," which plays out in a linear way from overthrow of dictator to transition election to consolidation of democracy.[1] The transition paradigm may present neatly on a blank slate, but all societies have histories, cleavages, and even personalities that get in the way of this linear progression.

Ridding oneself of an autocrat is no easy process. Overthrowing authoritarianism is complicated, but at least we have moved beyond Cold War stasis. The autocrat's death may help. But often the final decision is in the hands of the military. This is a common situation all over the world. Thailand seemed to be the classic case of military intervention in politics. Since the so-called People's Party overthrow of absolute monarchy in 1932, Thailand has been a constitutional monarchy; but the use of the word *constitutional* should not give the impression that there is a basic law restraining the conduct of the military. Thailand adopted its twentieth constitution in 2016, and its history of constitionalism demonstrates that whenever the document becomes inconvenient for the military, it simply gets changed.[2] There was a recent time, however, when the military itself said it was out of the coup business and that the Thai economy was simply too complex to be ruled by soldiers. In this time of weaning the military out of politics, it was allowed to retain many of its business advantages. This seemed to be a propitious model for other militaries around the world. Alas, the 2006 coup—the first in fifteen years—put an end to this path.

Militaries in neighboring countries, especially Indonesia, the Philippines, and Myanmar, are watching the Thai precedent closely.

Having ousted the autocrat, the transition paradigm requires the next step to be the transition election, and even at the high point of democracy's soft power, problems were clearly evident. USAID produced a book in 1998 that looked at a series of transition elections held after conflict situations.[3] Of the eight case studies in that book, it is impossible to describe any, a couple of decades later, as a success in terms of leading to a consolidated democracy. El Salvador, Liberia, and perhaps Mozambique might generously be described as qualified successes. Ethiopia and Angola are clear failures in terms of pursuing the democratic path, while Cambodia, Haiti, and Nicaragua have some democratic forms but little democratic substance and hardly any democratic culture. Was it therefore worth investing so heavily in the transition election? The 1993 election in Cambodia could only take place because the international community provided 16,000 peacekeepers, 3,600 civil police, 2,500 international civil servants, and tens of thousands of locals trained and funded by donors. The 1994 election in Mozambique cost $65 million, nearly all from donor funds. The 1994 elections in El Salvador could only take place because of the presence of a UN peacekeeping force, on top of which donors contributed more than $20 million. The 1995 presidential election in Haiti came in at a relatively modest $10.5 million, but, again, this was on top of the costs of the peacekeeping force that facilitated it.

One response is that decisionmakers had no other choice at the time but to hold a national election. The postconflict and postauthoritarian period may see successful oppositionist leaders take charge, in which case they seek the legitimacy of an election to cement their incumbency. The issue of legitimacy is put on the agenda by the rhetoric of the oppositionists in part based on the sentiments of the international community and often made more pressing by accusations of the autocrat's lack of legitimacy. Democratic transitions need to be seen to be endowed with legitimacy. Where there is a gap in the legitimacy of local leadership, it is filled by the international community, usually through a UN presence based on a UN Security Council (UNSC) mandate. A study of the evolution of UNSC mandates points to their growing sophistication and ambition in terms of facilitating democratization.[4] In either situation, pressure grows for an early election to resolve the legitimacy deficit. Local leaders wish to keep the "unconstitutional" period to a minimum, and the international community wants an election as the trigger for its exit strategy.

The emphasis on the transition election may be inevitable, but it is also poor policy. The states involved are unable to replicate the transition election four or five years later or subsequently because they do not have access to the international resources lavished on the transition election. Nor has there usually been enough time, when the transition election is held, to build any sort of culture of democracy that is essential to the fairness of an election. Concepts of public debating, media fact checking, opinion leaders' analysis, and voter deliberation need time to grow. In many divided societies, the transition election is in effect a census, with voters simply supporting their ethnic or linguistic champion. A possible response would be to reverse the cascading timing of elections from national to local and start with local elections, where the policy issues are closer to the ordinary voter, the candidates should be locally better known, and the stakes are not as great.

The foregoing is based on an assumption of goodwill among the parties, a common desire to move toward democratic institutions, and the acceptance of the contestability of incumbency. Alas, this is rarely the case. In many countries of the global South and especially in Africa, the national liberation movement became the first postcolonial government and has held power ever since, even where elections regularly take place. To change from an underground armed national liberation movement to an open political party is a considerable step, with many challenges along the way: the need to set new goals; the change in tactics from radicalization to consensus-building; eschewing the use of armed force; reversing mindsets from the destroyer of the system to its defender; the need to cater to voters beyond one's immediate support base; the change from merely making promises to being held accountable for actions in government; the move from secretiveness to openness; the requirement for more open internal party debates after the habit of suppressing internal dissent; the harmonization of internal and external wings; and the need to forego Leninism and politburo control in favor of decentralization and multiparty democracy.[5]

Transition elections led to many more illiberal democracies than the human rights–respecting democracies foreseen in the transition paradigm. The term *illiberal democracy* comes from Fareed Zakaria[6] and refers to a form of government where the leader is duly elected but then rules in a centralized manner without checks and balances and with little regard for citizens' rights. It is an evocative term, but it is a description of the effect of the system of governance—illiberalism—not its cause. A more accurate term for the phenomenon is to describe the cause of this system, and for that one turns to Guillermo O'Donnell, who coined the term *delegative democracy*.[7] Once again, leaders are duly elected, but their nations have undergone such deep social trauma in the authoritarian period that no culture of democracy has yet taken hold and all power is in effect delegated by the people to the elected leader. O'Donnell postulates on the need for a second transition, from delegative democracy to representative democracy.

The canaries are gasping for air throughout the global South, demonstrating that the problem is not inherent to any particular region but is widespread. This forces us to draw some conclusions about democratic transitions and indeed about the difficulty of democracy itself as a form of government. But first, here is a brief whip around the globe, looking at particular issues plaguing various regions.

In Africa

So many people in Africa understand that the continent needs democracy for its economic and social development but the obstacles are formidable. Winner-takes-all politics means that incumbents are loathe to let go of power. To lose political power in Africa has traditionally meant far more than simply losing office or face. It means losing the power of patronage and thus the support of the large network that kept one in power. It means losing control of the security forces and thus risking life and limb of family and supporters facing the wrath of those who feel themselves to have been wronged in a traditional justice system of self-help. And it means losing one's fortune unless one has taken care to stash away the proceeds of one's corruption in a foreign bank. So who would readily relinquish power in those circumstances? Is it really a surprise that elections in an African transition democracy are treated as life-or-death events? And is it surprising that they can lead to massive violence and dislocation?

Yet even in these circumstances there are glimmers of hope. In 2010 President Gbagbo of Côte d'Ivoire lost the election but tried to manipulate the results in what he no doubt expected to be standard incumbent operating procedure. He was surprised by the level of local opposition to his maneuvers and perhaps even more surprised that the special representative of the UN Secretary-General, Choi Young-Jin, adopted the resolute position that the winner was the opposition candidate Alassane Ouattara. He did not anticipate that both the Security Council and the African Union would turn against him, and with some French military steel in its back, the international community would step in to ensure respect for the election result. Gbagbo is no doubt still stunned to find himself facing trial in The Hague before the International Criminal Court.

The shemozzle in the Gambia is another example of the effect of elections in Africa. The day before the Trump inauguration, there was supposed to be an inauguration in the Gambia, mainland Africa's smallest country, which is surrounded by Senegal. The long-serving president, Yahya Jammeh, lost the election to Adama Barrow but refused to step down. Barrow ran to Senegal for help, and the African Union, which has of late taken a very hardline position against losing incumbents who refuse to leave, told Jammeh that he was no longer accepted as president. For the results of the election to hold, Senegal had to threaten to intervene militarily. In the meantime, people fled the capital, Banjul, and tourists who hold up the economy were flown out. Elections in Africa are not a celebration of democracy but have far too often triggered a national crisis.

Rather than lose an election, many incumbents decide to steal one instead. Manipulating election results is one way to stay in power, and tinkering with the constitution is another common ploy. In the West African country of Burkina Faso, President Blaise Campaoré had been in power since 1987, when he led a coup in which the then incumbent was killed. Campaoré slowly transformed himself into an elected leader of a pseudodemocracy and competently played the regional-statesman and bulwark-against-terrorism cards. In 2014, his twenty-seventh year in power, he decided that Burkina Faso could not function without him, and he set about changing the constitution to rid himself of the inconvenient provision on term limits. To his surprise, the "square people" came out in force and would not go home until he fled the country.

The significance of the developments in Côte d'Ivoire, the Gambia, and Burkina Faso goes well beyond the situation within those three countries. At the time of the events in Abidjan, capital of Côte d'Ivoire, Africa was anticipating a couple dozen elections over the coming two years. If the Gbagbo precedent had been allowed to stand, there is little doubt that the numerous incumbents facing elections would have paid careful attention. In light of the success in defeating and arresting Gbagbo, others took note. In the 2012 presidential election in neighboring Senegal, amid controversy over the constitutional validity of a third term for incumbent octogenarian president Abdoulaye Wade, opposition candidate Macky Sall defeated the incumbent, who decided to ignore his family's entreaties and go quietly.

And the events in Burkina Faso will also be examined closely in other African capitals where incumbent presidents face the end of their term limits—the countries affected are Benin, Burundi, the Republic of Congo, the Democratic Republic of Congo (formerly Zaire), Liberia,

Rwanda, Sierra Leone, and Tanzania. Some, such as President Joseph Kabila of the Democratic Republic of Congo, have already begun maneuvers to change the rules; others are considering their options. Now they have to factor in the Burkina Faso precedent, and hopefully they will go quietly into the night as did old Abdoulaye Wade. But the realist in me fears that many of them will try to fight to the bitter end to stay in power; that Africa has not quite yet escaped authoritarianism.

In Asia

The frail frame of student leader Joshua Wong in Hong Kong explaining the end of his hunger strike on doctor's orders and lamenting the lack of any concessions from China made for a pathetic picture. But also a heroic one. Wong and his 2014 umbrella revolution protestors, more "square people," proved to the world a fact that many people already know yet needs further emphasis: Chinese rule in Hong Kong has limited legitimacy. Yes, Hong Kong is reconciled to being part of China, but its people want China to stick to the deal that convinced them to accept China; the famous one-country, two-systems deal that should allow Hong Kong to govern itself. When locals elect politicians not to Beijing's liking, Beijing finds ways to expel them from the chamber. Why is China being so stubborn? Because to allow democracy in Hong Kong will allow people in China to hope for democracy in China itself, and that is a hope that the Chinese Communist Party will do all in its power to supress.

It is easy to conceptualize China hovering menacingly over Hong Kong, a part of China, but it is not as easy to accept that China also hovers over the balance of Asia. Yet that is the very argument I tried to unpack in a previous book,[8] in which I posited that until a civilizational consensus in favor of democracy forms in Pacific Asia, or East Asia, in both China, as the core state, and among its neighbors from which it continues to require fealty, it will be difficult if not impossible for any country in the region to consolidate its democracy. I further noted the irony that while the problem in Pacific Asia lay with the core state, the problem in South Asia was the opposite. The core state, India, has resolutely adopted democracy, but all the countries on its peripheries are struggling to follow its example. And when it comes to Central Asia, with the honorable exception of Mongolia, the former Soviet republics have simply localized the former Soviet systems of government though now shorn of any form of ideology. What seemed a few short years ago to be a march toward democracy is now looking like a more hesitant lurch. The process of democratization in Asia has not reached critical mass.

Given the pleasing direction of events in Myanmar, it may be worth devoting a little space to further analysis. Burma was my second posting and remains the most memorable.* It is visually stunning, from the glorious decaying colonial capital of Rangoon to the thousands of temples of Pagan, right down to the timeless villages where the most common metal was the gold leaf for the tiny stupas on top of each hill. As a diplomat, I lived a privileged existence among a handsome and mostly gentle race of people. Our house sat precariously on a hill with the Shwedagon Pagoda visible from the upstairs windows. At the base of the hill was a little village. One day the cook reported that the garden goose had been stolen. A couple days later, the gardener apprehended the thief, a boy from the village, and brought him to me for judgment. My five-year-old daughter was watching the proceedings, so I puffed myself up to my haughtiest to deliver my Solomonic wisdom. Did the boy know the goose belonged to this house? Yes. Did he realize that the goose protects us from snakes? Yes. Did he sell the goose to the local restaurant? Yes. Did he give the money to his family? Yes. Very well, I sentenced him to come to our house every day after school for one month and assist the gardener. I turned to my daughter to see if she had drawn any lessons from this fine display of summary justice. "But papa, he stole the goose, he should be helping the cook, not the gardener."

Myanmar has undertaken an electoral do-over. Elections were held in 1990 and 2015 with basically the same result—a victory for Aung San Suu Kyi and her National League for Democracy. But whereas the military annulled the 1990 result, imprisoned the victors, and ruled as despots, it accepted the 2015 result. Does this mean all is well? Certainly not, but it does open the door to the possibility that Myanmar can now debate and decide on key aspects of its future. Social science employs a concept of "path dependence" that argues that future decisions are conditioned by the path that has brought the society to that decision point. Societies remain in the grip of their respective histories. This is obviously true, but trite in its obviousness. Some may interpret path dependence as an almost fatalistic adherence to stay on the same path. Democracy, however, provides the possibility of a fork in the road. It allows a society to blaze a new path. In the case of Myanmar, the underlying question is whether the Burman people, the majority group of central Myanmar, are prepared finally to shed their sense of colonial victimhood and build a democratic state for all its people.

---

*I will use the place names employed at the time when discussing the past and the present names when discussing the current situation.

Some countries seem rather easily to shed their colonial suffering while others cling to it. One of the qualities to be admired in Vietnam is its capacity to live in the present even though it has every reason to wallow in the past. Of course it has its museum of American war atrocities, but unlike the North Korean version that uses that name, the Saigon version is called the War Remnants Museum. Dien Bien Phu, the Ho Chi Minh Trail, and the Tet Offensive are all in the past, and leaders worry that young people are insufficiently mindful of them. The national psyche has somehow moved on. For some reason Myanmar has not moved on. Before the British onslaught, Burma thought of itself as the regional hegemon. In the 1760s the Burmese king invaded the neighboring kingdom and sacked its capital, Ayutthaya, forcing the construction of a new capital in Krung Thep (Bangkok). Over the next one hundred years the British defeated these regional hegemons in three wars, each leading to the annexation of more territory, until there was nothing left of the Burmese throne. In the course of a couple generations, the Burman people became outcasts in their own country as the British favored other ethnic groups such as the Karen and the Shan and opened the country to outsiders, leading to migrations from Bengal, India, and other parts.[9] This is the trauma that today's Myanmar has not shed. The results can be quite odd.

When decolonization allowed Burmans to regain control, the early period of engagement with the world quickly gave way to withdrawal. The rightful place of the Burmans could now be restored. In Ne Win's long period at the helm it led to autarky and a continuing battle with the minorities at the peripheries of the country. The military leaders that followed him continued these policies, sprinkled with the occasional cease-fire and one-sided peace plan. But the international pariah status attached to the military forced them into the uncomfortable embrace of the Chinese. One reason the military accepted the process leading to the 2015 results is that this Chinese embrace was deeply unpopular. Finding an accommodation with minority groups was the challenge faced by newly independent Burma in 1948 and remains the same challenge facing newly democratic Myanmar today. There is plenty of blame to go around for the inability to find compromises so far, but a key question is whether the Burman majority is prepared to forgo Burman majoritarianism. The treatment of the Rohingya, the least respected of the minorities, does not augur well for a national reconciliation.

I served in Rangoon in the mid-1980s. I returned briefly in 1996 and in 2013. The visit in 1996 was depressing. I was at the time posted as ambassador in Vientiane, Laos, and I found a spare long weekend for a quick visit to Yangon. On the flight, I realized that my plans of visiting old friends and acquaintances were futile. The military authorities had issued my visa and would know I was coming. I had to work on the assumption I would be followed, and anybody to whom I spoke would come under suspicion. So I spoke to no one and spent the three days glumly walking around the tourist sights I had seen so often. My visit in 2013 was exhilarating. A strange reversal had occurred. In freewheeling Bangkok, one had to be careful with every spoken word lest one fall foul of the draconian *lèse-majesté* laws ostensibly protecting the throne but in reality being used as a political weapon. Whereas in Yangon, everybody was in a frenzy of discussion and debate about the future. The main question was how far the tolerance of the military would extend. The locals were hoping the military coup precedent from Thailand would not be followed.

In Chapter 7 I will have some more to say about Asia, with a particular focus on Thailand, once the poster child of democratization and now returning to a paternalistic form of military dictatorship. In contrast, Indonesia is now the transition country showing the greatest progress, though enormous problems remain.

In Latin America

In contrast to Asia and Africa, there is a stronger argument to be made for the acceptance of democracy as the default form of government in Latin America. The major countries of Latin America that serve as role models for others, Argentina, Brazil, Chile, and Uruguay, are strengthening their democracies and building a culture of democracy among its peoples. Colombia and Peru may not be too far behind now that the insurrections are being resolved. Costa Rica can also join this group and serve as a role model for its far less successful Central American neighbors. Mexico is now also beginning to behave more like a democracy, demonstrating the political dividends delivered by the North America Free Trade Association (NAFTA). NAFTA triggered a growth in the size and assertiveness of the middle class, which has demanded more accountable government. And there are a number of strong democracy contenders in the Caribbean, led by Barbados.

We nevertheless need to resist the enticing allure of triumphalism. Latin America faces twin challenges. The first is the existence of a regional challenger to the market-based model of democracy. Cuba has bravely assumed the role of democracy's *bête noir* for over half a century. For most of that time it was backstopped and bankrolled by the Soviet Union, but in the past twenty-five years it has maintained its socialist posture on its own. It has had some financial assistance from Venezuela and some unintended assistance from the United States, whose ill-conceived embargo of Cuba—which may soon finally begin to be removed under a more enlightened policy—is the key plank holding up the legitimacy of a Castro regime built on resistance to its powerful neighbor.

The Castro model of socialism, with its notable showcase success in the fields of medicine and sport, has a particular salience in Latin America because it dovetails with two major currents of Latin American politics. One is populism. Latin America is the one region of the world where this term does not have a pejorative connotation. In its appeal to the oppressed and marginalized, populism can at times draw from the rhetoric of the Cuban regime, and politicians sprouting populist lines can start to sound almost Fidel-like. The other major current flows from the region's Bolivarian traditions of struggling against oppressors. Cuban rhetoric loves nothing more than portraying itself as part of a liberation process, though so many of its people are chained either literally or in poverty. Brazil's Lula and his successor Dilma Rousseff, Bolivia's Evo Morales, Ecuador's Rafael Correa, and, of course, Venezuela's Nicolás Maduro, successor to Hugo Chávez, all happily draw from this leftist rhetoric; other politicians in the region will follow suit if the rhetoric might lead to electoral dividends. Venezuela is a special case and will be examined in greater detail in Chapter 7.

Latin America's second challenge may be even more difficult to deal with than Cuban-style anti-imperialism. The region spent its first few European settler centuries in denial of its nativist origins and is only now coming to grips with the reality that its pre-Columbian nations have not disappeared but have been transformed into blighted and angry communities. Democracy is giving these communities a voice it was previously allowed to project only through the mediation of the Catholic Church. The indigenous voice has a unique perspective. At times it is admirable and visionary, as in its conception of humankind's relationship with the Earth, a symbiotic relationship requiring stewardship, not ownership, of land. But at times it is harsh and discordant when it expresses its patriarchal traditional origins. Latin America needs to deliberate and negotiate itself through indigenous assertiveness and come to some sort of broad consensus. Bolivia, Colombia, and Mexico as well as much of Central America will host the sharpest debates, which only democratic systems will be able to accommodate.

In the Arab World

It is in the Arab world, however, that democracy is getting its ugliest black eye. Although the Arab world was the last region to climb aboard democracy's bandwagon, the Arab Spring phenomenon demonstrated that Arabs, whether from North Africa, the Gulf, or the Levant, felt the same way about their political impotence as did people in the rest of the world. In this respect, Arabs are no different. But one key difference has been the lack thus far of successful transitions to democracy in the Arab world. Iraq took the democracy baton from the American and allied occupiers and turned it into an instrument to get even with their former sectarian overlords. Egypt took the shortest glimpse at the incompetent Muslim Brotherhood government before deciding it would prefer to return to military authoritarianism. Yemen is succumbing to sectarian and tribal conflict. And Syria has descended into such a hellish civil war that the prospects of any sort of democratization process in that country will be left for future generations.

I recall the great hopes with which we approached the Arab Spring. The Egyptian partner of the UN Democracy Fund at the time was an admirable group called the Cairo Institute for Human Rights Studies. We co-hosted a conference in Cairo in 2011 full of well-meaning statements and debates, drawing from transition stories in other parts of the world and trying to entice the locals to adapt and apply what we pompously called "lessons learned." The conference even attracted Islamist scholars and politicians, whose very participation in what we again so pompously called "deliberations" was seen as a positive sign. I certainly headed to the airport with a warm glow, rationalizing away all the ugly warning signs—the anaemic economy, the slow death of the tourist industry (apart from a busload of sun-worshipping Russians—the god Ra would be pleased; I was the only other tourist at the pyramids one morning), and the reality that foreigners were dealing with a tiny band of the educated urban elite but that the future of Egypt would be decided by others. The real action was happening elsewhere. In the mosques in myriad villages a completely different discourse was taking place. It was about traditionalism, patriarchy, and fear of change all dressed up in a package entitled Islam. While our little conference promised glorious uncertainty and messy politics for ever more, the message in the mosques was about eternal harmony and justice on Earth if only everyone would completely submit to the Islamic version of the Deity. While we struggled to put together the tens of thousands of dollars for the conference and then dutifully reported the results and rigorously accounted for every cent in audited accounts poured over by our funders, hundreds of millions of dollars of Wahhabi money from Saudi Arabia and Qatar poured in to the mosques without the slightest oversight or publicity.

Add to this an inappropriate electoral system, deep uncertainty about the rules of the game, and no history of democratic participation, and it should have come as no surprise that Egypt ended up with President Morsi of the Muslim Brotherhood. A year of chaotic government was brought to an end with a military coup that, to my distress, even those educated urban elites in Cairo supported. The Cairo Institute could now return to the role it grew comfortable with: ineffectual criticism of a military regime. But some nasty surprises would come its way as General-cum-President, Sisi would direct his anger at the civil society world just as much as at the Brotherhood. By the end of 2014 the Cairo Institute was moving its offices to Tunis.

Which leads to the one point of hope in the Arab world—maybe Tunisia can negotiate its way to some sort of successful democratic transition. There are other candidates, but none has positive prospects. Lebanon and Jordan are caught in the Syrian maelstrom. Algeria is still in recovery from its long and deadly civil war. Morocco cannot become a democracy if the royal family continues to dispense only teaspoons of power while avariciously eyeing large dollops of the economy. And so the Arab Spring has come down to the fortunes of a single small country.

Conclusion

The post–Cold War democratic triumphalism has turned out to be mainly hot air. Some of the individual claims from that triumphalist rhetoric were valid. The Soviet system was unproductive and unsustainable. So the Soviet alternative ideology vanished. But with the exception of Cuba, no countries in the global South had really bought into that ideology. It was not the Marxism that the autocrats were interested in but the Leninism. It was the centralized control, the absence of contestation, and the obvious flow-on benefits of corruption these factors allowed that captured the interest of leaders of so-called Socialist countries. These same leaders would happily bray in favor of capitalism if they could hold on to their existing Leninist privileges.

The "end of history" claim that democracy with a market economy is the best system humankind has invented is also generally true. But the list of caveats is long and daunting. The caveats deal with institutional architecture and the difficulty of making electoral, representative, and oversight institutions work effectively. They deal with the need for rule of law and constitutionalism leading to human rights, which is the bedrock on which the institutions are built. They deal with the public conversation and how it can be dominated by illiberal or simply profit-seeking voices. And they deal with the generations-long need to build a culture of democracy. So, identifying the "enemy" (Soviet ideology) and the "solution" (market democracy) is only the starting point of a long process.

Turning, however, to the governance outcomes of the transition era, we can identify a few broad categories. There is, of course, the dominant political party outcome where the harried and hopeless opposition is mere ornamentation. Central Asia has a clear liking for this outcome, but southern Africa is no stranger to it either. Then there is what can perhaps be described as the census outcome, where ethnicity or religion or language determines political allegiance and the supposed democratic system simply becomes the new forum to fight age old quarrels. Lurking in the shadows is the Islamist theocratic outcome with its fraught relationship with democracy. Perhaps most damaging of all is the feckless pluralism outcome where political parties are weak, civil society is fractured, theocracy lurks, and the military watches warily as ultimate kingmaker. These may not be the final outcomes—they may perhaps be way stations on the road to democracy—but at this point, they are not inspiring confidence.

After transition, the next magic word is *consolidation*. Like good art, one knows it when one comes across it. There are definitions of *consolidation* that help narrow the issues. Huntington's test is that consolidation comes after two turnovers of power following free and fair elections.[10] This has the advantage of being a simple quantitative test. Reality, however, has defeated Huntington's test in various places, with turnovers of power but no democracy in sight. Juan Linz and Alfred Stepan's "only game in town" test is far more helpful.[11] It posits that democracy has consolidated when no significant political groups wish to jettison it for another system. But there is a suspicion of circularity in this test. Significant political groups wish to retain the system in which they are significant. That system may just as well be feckless pluralism.

And thus in the quarter-century since the end of the Cold War, democracy regressed from an attractive system broadly demanded all around the world to one of caveat emptor. Buyers needed to beware of illiberal outcomes, indecisive elections, failed and stalled transitions, power delegated electorally to leaders who then behave like autocrats, falling living standards, the perils of people power, and other democrazy outcomes. While there are examples of nations successfully traversing these hazards, they tended to be in the minority, making the buyer even more wary. The frustration we are all experiencing is in witnessing how tentative and tenuous are many of the supposed transitions to democracy. This loss of democratic soft power need not be fatal if there remains the shining city on the hill toward which people wish to climb and if the consolidated democracies continue to radiate soft power. But rather than witnessing this outcome, we are witnessing the resurgence of autocracy.

Notes

1. Thomas Carothers, "The End of the Transition Paradigm," *Journal of Democracy* 13, 1 (January 2002): 5–21.

2. Roland Rich, *Parties and Parliaments in Southeast Asia: Non-partisan Chambers in Indonesia, the Philippines and Thailand* (London: Routledge, 2013), chapter 5.

3. Krishna Kumar (ed.), *Postconflict Elections, Democratization, and International Assistance* (Boulder, CO: Lynne Rienner, 1998).

4. Roland Rich, "Crafting Security Council Mandates," in Edward Newman and Roland Rich (eds.), *The UN Role in Promoting Democracy: Between Ideals and Reality* (Tokyo: United Nations University Press, 2004).

5. Mwesiga Baregu, "From Liberation Movement to Ruling Parties in Southern Africa," in Chris Landsberg and Shaun McKay (eds.), *Southern Africa Post-Apartheid? The Search for Democratic Governance* (Capetown: IDASA, 2004), pp. 92–103.

6. Fareed Zakaria, *The Future of Freedom: Illiberal Democracy at Home and Abroad* (New York: W. W. Norton, 2003).

7. Guillermo A. O'Donnell, "Delegative Democracy," *Journal of Democracy* 5, 1 (1994): 55–69.

8. Roland Rich, *Pacific Asia in Quest of Democracy* (Boulder, CO: Lynne Rienner, 2007): 69.

9. Richard Cockett, *Blood, Dreams, and Gold: The Changing Face of Burma* (New Haven, CT: Yale University Press, 2015).

10. Samuel Huntington, *The Third Wave: Democratization in the Late Twentieth Century* (Norman: University of Oklahoma Press, 1993).

11. Juan J. Linz and Alfred Stepan, "Toward Consolidated Democracies," *Journal of Democracy* 7, 2 (1996): 14–33.

4

Autocrats Are Resurgent

The *Times* of London named Vladimir Putin the 2013 "Person of the Year." To be the person of the year is not the same as winning the Nobel Peace Prize. It is not about virtue; it is about influence. The reasons given by the *Times* concerned Putin's success in Syria, where he propped up Bashar al-Assad and deflected US influence; his meddling in Ukraine, demonstrating that it is far easier to destabilize a country than to develop it; and his propaganda coup in giving asylum to the whistle-blower Edward Snowden, thus shining a torch on American diplomatic perfidy. But Putin's even more far-reaching success is the way he has rehabilitated authoritarianism.

Before coming to Putin's contribution, it is important to examine some of the ways in which the global political economy supported authoritarianism. This is not an issue that can easily be delineated into black and white. The forces at play are vast and complex and have varying effects. But we can discern several of them. Clearly, the Cold War was a comfortable era for autocrats. An uncomfortable period followed in its demise, but many autocrats managed to traverse it nevertheless. The resource curse is a cause of corruption, but it also bolsters authoritarianism. The prominence of oil and the world's dependence on it was well demonstrated by the Arab oil embargo, the effects of which endured for decades. And China's entry into the world economy also had major ripple effects, many positive, some less so.

End of Cold War Blues

The immediate post–Cold War period was a harsh time for autocrats. A totalitarian regime with an enormous army and possibly a usable nuclear weapon was able to ride it out. One of the great tragedies for the long-suffering people of the Democratic People's Republic of Korea, a.k.a. North Korea, is that the international community is more comfortable with the status quo than with the risk of change. The DPRK is an embarrassment to China partly because it reminds China of its Maoist days and partly because the constant threat of war is not good for business. But China would rather deal with the DPRK under the Kim dynasty than with a united Korea under US protection on its borders. The United States has already fought one war to a stalemate on the Korean Peninsula and has no appetite for another. The DPRK is an insult to American values and principles but is not a realistic direct strategic threat. The status quo, wrapped up in criticism and rhetoric, will work fine. The most surprising force for the status quo is South Korea. There is a sense among its people that a duty is owed to their siblings and cousins of the North to rescue them from the worst human rights abuses being perpetrated on the planet.[1] But there is an even stronger undercurrent of the enormity of the task. Before even coming to the military issues, the sense in Seoul is that South Korea is neither wealthy enough nor sufficiently committed to emulate Germany at the end of the Cold War, when it absorbed the German Democratic Republic. The comparison is daunting because East Germany was the wealthiest and most advanced of the Warsaw Pact countries; and even after trillions of Euros were spent and a generation has passed, the East is not yet fully integrated, though enormous strides have been made. The Democratic People's Republic of Korea is no German Democratic Republic. All the two have in common is the misnomer "Democratic" in their names. The DPRK is a failed society where the nomenklatura prey on the rest; where the gulag is enormous and entry to it is capricious at best; and where starvation is the rule, not the exception. The people of South Korea do not have the courage to take on this challenge even if their nation could overcome the military barrier. The DPRK is therefore in its own category.

For those without the capacity to practice totalitarianism and without the geopolitical calculus in favor of the status quo, the post–Cold War period was one of adaptation to the end of history paradigm. The earliest manifestation of the passing of authoritarianism as the norm came in South America in the 1980s. Huntington describes this as part of the third wave of democratization, but it is probably more accurate to see this period as a transition from the end of fascism and the successful implantation of democracy on the Iberian Peninsula, which greatly influenced Latin America. Thus did the major countries of the continent—Argentina, Brazil, and Chile—turn to democracy. The timing was often triggered by local factors, coming early in the 1980s in Argentina because of the loss of military prestige caused by the disastrous Falklands War in 1982, and coming late to Chile because of the towering figure of Augusto Pinochet, whose extended presidential term was finally rejected in a referendum in 1988. Latin America set its course for democratization, and authoritarian regimes were thereafter on the defensive, with only Cuba—though soon impoverished by the loss of Soviet subsidies—sticking to its ideological guns, and Venezuela under Chávez seeking a new path bolstered by oil revenues.

Eastern Europe was directly affected by the end of the Cold War, the collapse of the Soviet Union, and the loss of legitimacy of Soviet satrap regimes. In May 1989, Hungary dismantled its Iron Curtain border with Austria, incidentally allowing thousands of East Germans in their Trabants to take this circuitous route to West Germany. The Berlin Wall and the Iron Curtain, ostensibly defensive measures, were clearly shown to be prison walls eloquently displayed for the world to see by the escaping East Germans. Erich Honecker was replaced by an East German Politburo colleague, but his successor would soon have no state to head. Poland's Solidarnosc trade union was legalized in 1989, and thereafter it was only a question of time before it formed the government and then captured the presidency for Lech Walesa. In Bulgaria, Todor Zhivkov was removed that November by his colleagues, who themselves would only survive two more months in power. A wonderful lightly fictionalized account of Zhivkov's 1992 trial was written by Julian Barnes under the title *The Porcupine;* in it, Zhivkov gives as good as he gets in the cross-examination. Then to Romania where within one week in December 1989, the Ceauşescus were heckled by a crowd of supposed supporters, then went on the run and were soon captured, put on trial, and executed. The hardline Czechoslovak regime would also fall.

I had the great privilege to be head of the section of the Australian foreign ministry that dealt with Eastern Europe during this period.[2] The foreign minister was Senator Gareth Evans, and for personal and political reasons he wanted to be, and be seen to be, in the middle of the action. So we organized an immediate tour of the region to include triumphant stops in Berlin, Warsaw, and Budapest. He called me to his office and complained that Prague was not on the itinerary. I explained that Prague was still governed by the old guard, but he dismissed this "quibble" and insisted that the itinerary include this beautiful city. So, I called in the ambassador of Czechoslovakia and advised him of the minister's wish for a working visit to Prague without any pomp and ceremony. The ambassador asked the purpose of the visit, and I formally handed him a list of Czech human rights defenders under threat from the authorities. A few days later the ministerial party was hobnobbing with allies, old and new—arm in arm with Chancellor Helmut Kohl to cross the Berlin Wall, in a bear hug with Lech Walesa in Warsaw, and warmly welcomed in the stately parliament building in Budapest. Not more than twenty-four hours before the party was due in Prague, the Czech government fell and Vaclav Havel became acting head of state. Gareth Evans was the first foreign minister to be received, and that evening he and Havel went to jazz clubs to the wee hours. So much for my diplomatic caution. I was breathing a huge sigh of relief when the ambassador of Czechoslovakia asked to see me. He had with him the same *bout de papier* I had handed over and said he would like to go over the list. "The first name on the list, he is our president. The second name on the list, he is our foreign minister..." *und so weiter.*

In Yugoslavia the end of Cold War stasis forced the country to examine whether the marriage of its constituent parts should be dissolved. The elites of three generations of Yugoslavs had accepted the progressive concept of the union of southern Slavs and had intermarried and migrated to each other's cities. In fact, when the country fell apart its president, prime minister, and foreign minister, based in Belgrade, were all Croats. The rural folk had not bought into it nearly to the same extent. It was not the concept of the union of southern Slavs that was the problem, it was Tito-style authoritarianism. Those most successful at challenging it were the nationalist demagogues appealing to their heartlands, inevitably leading to the violence that would follow. The union of southern Slavs would eventually be replaced by a new concept more in keeping with our global village, the European Union, and to qualify for membership, democratization would eventually come— though not before much blood was shed.

The message to the autocrats of the former Soviet empire was clear: the game had changed irretrievably. Where civil society was strong, where the international community cared, and where countries had some history and culture of democracy to fall back on, the institutions of genuine democracy were slowly but surely erected. The Baltic States fell into this category, as did most of the states of central and southeastern Europe. Even where these factors were not present, as in most of the newly independent former Soviet Republics, the old autocrats nevertheless had to pretend to respect multiparty democracy, pretend to hold free and fair elections, and pretend to respect human rights. The pretense is not without utility, as it necessarily creates a space in which courageous opponents of the regime can dare speak up, but after a couple of decades of this pretense we need to face the reality that there has been little progress toward democratization in the former Soviet Union. As will be noted later in this chapter, the Putin factor means that even the pretense is now no longer particularly necessary.

Southeast Asia also felt the winds of the end of the Cold War. The Philippines anticipated the inevitable when it finally turned on Ferdinand Marcos. Thailand went on a binge of deliberative democratization caused by the shock of military coup leaders spilling the blood of student protesters in 1991. The end of unquestioned US support for the Thai military brought about by the end of the Cold War also played its part. Suharto would last a few more years in Indonesia but would fall in the 1998 financial crisis, when he lost face in succumbing to the forces of international economic pressure—a phenomenon that would not have been allowed to play out in the Cold War years. There were nevertheless significant holdouts. Vietnam and Laos would continue on their Leninist way, hoping that government-managed capitalism would bail them out. Cambodia's Hun Sen would play the democracy game but with a crooked deck and resort to force as necessary. Malaysia and Singapore continued their experiment with soft authoritarianism, allowing wide economic freedom with limited political freedom.

The end of the Cold War would also have its effects in southern Africa, where the apartheid regime no longer could count on its anticommunist card to win a trick. The release of Nelson Mandela from Robben Island prison would lead to sweeping changes and set an example for the rest of the continent. The countries of the East African community have taken some steps toward democracy, as have some West African countries, including Ghana and Senegal. The African Union has been emboldened to step up its rhetoric and actions in favor of democracy.[3] But as noted in the previous chapter, we are not there yet.

The Arab world seemed strangely impervious to the winds of change. The third wave would not reach its shores until 2005. Its autocrats soldiered on. A mix of anticolonial resentment that continued to simmer, a vague promise of pan-Arabism, leftist rhetoric in the form of socialist concoctions such as Baathism, and all-purpose opposition to Israel sustained the autocrats long after their Cold War patrons lost interest in proxy ideological battles. Of course, nobody lost interest in Arab oil, which provides a powerful explanation of external meddling long after the ideological rationale receded. And it provides a more convincing explanation of American intervention in Iraq than the three reasons serially cobbled together at the time. When the Arab Spring occurred it became clear that the people of the Arab world were not rejecting the invitation to join the democratization party, they were just latecomers. Yet the hold of authoritarianism has endured, with Egypt providing the best example of the return of old-style military government, sustained this time not by the Cold War but by the war against terrorism.

Enter OPEC

Waning democratic soft power contributing to the autocratic resurgence has already been discussed. There are other influences moving the pendulum in that direction. Turning from soft power to the more traditional hard power, one of the key tools has always been economic pressure in the form of incentives, disincentives, and *diktat*. In the post–World War II period, the wealthy first-wave democracies controlled the levers of economic power. They established and controlled the Bretton Woods institutions that set down economic orthodoxy and enforced it with loans and advice that borrowers had little choice but to take and accept. They controlled the rules of international trade not only because of their dominance in GATT (the General Agreement on Tariffs and Trade, predecessor of the World Trade Organization) but because of the size and wealth of their consuming markets. Thus, to be granted most-favored-nation status, or to be given a fat quota or a low tariff, were all means of exerting influence. And finally, the wealthy democracies controlled that post–World War II invention that came to be known as official development assistance (ODA), to be discussed in detail in Chapter 9.

There has always been some level of resistance to the economic hegemony of those wealthy democratic countries that banded together in a study group in Paris, known as the Organization for Economic Cooperation and Development (OECD), the Development Assistance Committee (DAC) of which is the high priest of ODA orthodoxy. One pole of opposition was the Soviet bloc, which created its own economic world among its acolytes, the Council for Mutual Economic Assistance (CMEA). But the CMEA was such a flimsy imitation of the OECD that it attracted little influence beyond its own members. A more powerful intellectual competitor comprised the formerly colonized countries that banded together as the Non-Aligned Movement (NAM, now with 120 members) in 1961 and that had a strongly overlapping manifestation in the multilateral arenas as the Group of 77 (G-77, now comprising more than 130 countries), which sprang into existence at a UN conference in 1964.

Different interpretations of the OECD's and Bretton Woods' worldview on trade, aid, and development emerged from the NAM/G-77.

Some proclaimed that the colonial economic relationships continued to hold sway in a neocolonial model. Others developed dependency theories of how the international capitalist system was simply a means of keeping developing countries within the OECD orbit and dependent on OECD countries' economies. Subaltern theories emerged from the subcontinent explaining how colonial countries chose local successors to continue to reflect their perspectives rather than those of the teeming voiceless. Some argued that ODA should not be seen as a voluntary gesture owned by the donor but rather as legal reparations for colonialism and therefore owned by the aggrieved party and owed by the donor. Discomfiting though these theories may have been, their influence was limited and perhaps had its most significant articulation in the adoption of the UN General Assembly's resolution on the "Permanent Sovereignty over Natural Resources" on December 14, 1962, by eighty-seven votes in favor to two against, with twelve abstentions.[4]

Theoretical discussions and UN resolutions may not have direct impacts, but they prepare the ground for other forms of action by providing the justification for unorthodox policies challenging the status quo. They therefore played some part in the first major noncommunist challenge to the OECD world's economic hegemony, the 1974 Arab oil boycott against countries that supported Israel in the 1973 war, including the United States, Western Europe, and Japan. The Organization of Petroleum Exporting Countries (OPEC) supported this boycott, forcing gas prices to rise from $3 to $12 a barrel.[5] The negative impact on the economies of oil-importing countries was immediate. An important new economic actor had entered the field to disrupt the status quo.

The Western world soon absorbed the oil shock and adjusted their economies to higher energy prices, a process that would later make alternative energy far more competitive. Sadly, it was the developing countries that suffered more deeply from the oil shock as the terms of trade did not allow them to absorb the energy costs into their raw material and agricultural exports in the same way as the industrialized countries could in relation to their exports of elaborately transformed manufactures. The result was a not-uncommon decision among governments of developing countries to subsidize energy costs, causing long-term disruption to their economies and creating an impossible political situation, as any attempt to cut the subsidies would lead to riots.

The embargo demonstrated the primacy of oil in the world economy; any country that exported it came under a different set of requirements. The major producers of the Persian Gulf region got a pass on issues of democracy and corruption. A country such as Venezuela could embark with impunity on a course of redistribution and retribution through plebiscitary democracy. Angola, Gabon, and Nigeria were above reproach. Russia could indulge its new czar. High oil prices excused all sins. Lower prices and structural changes through the green economy plus carbon era throwbacks such as shale oil are today putting all these calculations under review.

Enter China

The next major resource issue was the commodities boom of the first decade of the new millennium. The entry of large countries into the international manufacturing economy, mainly China but also India, Brazil, and others, created high demand for commodities and forced up their prices, reversing what had been a steady decline in the terms of trade for raw materials. But few countries were able to exploit this momentary advantage, and those that did, such as Australia and Canada, were already likely to be developed nations.

The key phenomenon changing the world economy is China's emergence as a major player. In relation to the global South, China has become Africa's largest trading partner, with two-way trade growing from US$10.6 billion in 2000 to US$166 billion in 2011 and foreign direct investment increasing thirty-fold between 2003 and 2011, from US$491m to US$14.7 billion.[6] Alongside the growth of the commercial relationship has been a growth in development assistance. The figures are not as clear-cut, but China's ODA is between $5 billion[7] and $7 billion[8] annually, more than 50 percent of which goes to Africa. As to the future, China has pledged $60 billion for Africa's development, and though this figure may not ultimately be realized, it still leaves China as a major source of Africa's development funds.[9]

"China's development aid programmes are depicted in some quarters as a challenge to Western-style good governance, and the protection of human rights and democracy."[10] Indeed. China is still in the early infrastructure and basic human needs stage of its development assistance process. It studiously avoids explicit conditionality in relation to governance and human rights. While the usual altruistic rhetoric is bolstered by a discourse of solidarity with developing countries among which China claims membership, it is also undoubtedly true that there is a realist element in its ODA to strengthen a relationship with the continent from which China derives a vast amount of its resource needs. This simply mirrors the realism of other donors.

Whether strategically planned or not, China's entry as a major aid player (it would rank about sixth among OECD donors) but not following the DAC playbook has at the very least changed the perception of the universality and inevitable applicability of democracy and human rights values as universal values. A refusal by the World Bank to support a loan guarantee for a new dam on environmental or social equity grounds will have the foreign minister of the requesting government on the next flight to Beijing to put forward the same request. China knows a lot about building dams and in all likelihood would accede to such a request and have a Chinese company in the new market in no time flat.

The absence of explicit conditionality is a great comfort to aid-receiving governments but a severe reversal for their people. Receiving governments can take refuge in the fiction of absolute respect for sovereignty and the convenience of noninterference in the internal affairs of another country to plan economic projects without the need to consult aggrieved locals affected by the project. And receiving governments need have no fear of Chinese money going to civil society or to academic institutions interested in contestability of policy positions because that is not the Chinese model. Defying its own heritage of meritocracy in scholarly pursuits, the Chinese model accords to the sending government the gatekeeping and patronage of approving scholarship winners.

Explicit conditionality may not appear in aid documentation, but there is clearly implicit conditionality. It is the export of China's model of economic growth; a Leninist, corrupt, top-down, expert planning version that treats people paternalistically at best and expendably at worst. Civil society has no role to play in this model. Contestability, if it takes place at all, is behind closed doors and probably among different government factions wishing to maximize their own benefit. The result is indifference to regime types in the receipt of Chinese aid. Case studies point to examples of China shoring up autocratic regimes in Angola, Democratic Republic of Congo, Sudan, Venezuela, and Zimbabwe.[11] In other words, China's rise is good for authoritarianism.

Does the Chinese model have soft power? Undoubtedly. Lifting hundreds of millions of people out of poverty in the space of one generation is an unprecedented achievement worthy of the highest praise and respect. This is so even if the main policy step by the Chinese government was simply to let go and allow people to thrive without government interference. This is so even if the kudos should be shared with the United States and Europe, which opened their markets to Chinese products, thus creating the conditions to trigger the economic take-off. And this is so even if the system of governance China developed proves ultimately to be unsustainable. But it is a limited and constrained soft power. It is the soft power of admiration, not emulation.

It is difficult for people around the world to wish to emulate what they see in China. Only India can truly compare itself to China in size, population, and civilizational pedigree. More important, China has traditionally adopted an attitude of exceptionalism as the Middle Kingdom and required those around it to demonstrate subservience through tribute processes. It may subscribe to the international rhetoric of sovereign equality, but it does not behave accordingly, as the littoral countries of the South China Sea know full well. Indeed, one commentator has described China's international conduct as "autistic" because of an inability to empathize with the sentiments of others.[12] One can admire the genius and accomplishments of an autistic nation, but this is a long step from wishing to emulate it. What remains is a detached form of admiration by the people. But from the point of view of governments, Chinese soft power has strong emulation qualities. It puts central authority in a position of primacy. It relegates people to the status of objects of government action. It establishes leadership impunity. What is being emulated, as I noted earlier, is a Leninist, corrupt, top-down, expert dominant version of governance. More will be said about this model in Chapter 9.

Putin Pounces

Accidental leader though he may be, Vladimir Putin wants to be the czar. It is not too difficult to see the world through his eyes. Russia has been the heart of an empire for over a millennium. Each time it was destroyed, the empire was resurrected in a different name but with the same czarist leadership: Ivan the Terrible, Peter the Great, the Romanovs, Lenin, and Stalin. The collapse of the Soviet empire did not mean the form of the state or its leadership system need necessarily change. Indeed, one reason for the fall of the Soviet empire was the lack of czarist-style leadership. The denunciation of Stalin's crimes by his successor, Nikolai Khrushchev, in 1956 was also a denunciation of absolutist leadership, which thereafter acted as an element of constraint on the Politburo. A type of sleepy nomenklatura collective gerontocracy evolved. Under stress, however, the pendulum had to swing back to the Politburo's youngest member, Mikhail Gorbachev. He had the great distinction of recognizing how untenable were the government and economic systems of the Soviet Union, but he lacked the strength to reform them. Boris Yeltsin was prepared to let go of the far reaches of the empire so that he could hold on to the leadership of the heartland, Russia. But his hand-picked successor believes the end of the Soviet Union was a geopolitical disaster.[13] He wants the empire back, and he understands that empires must be ruled by czars.

Why did democratization fail so miserably in Russia? A response may be drawn from comparing events in two similarly governed countries, Poland and Russia, which both attempted what is called "big bang" transition, eschewing any notion of planned sequencing of the different steps toward democratization and instead changing everything at once. Poland succeeded while Russia failed. Of course, the differences between the two countries are significant, and it is in the search for these differences and their impact on democratization that lessons may be found, but their important similarity was that they were transitioning from the same command economy, authoritarian leadership, secret police–disciplined system that their people had lived under for several generations. What are the distinctions that allowed Poland to succeed? There are at least four issues here.

First, Poland had no issue with "stateness." The nation was forged in the furnace of being between Germany and Russia. Its borders may have changed over the years, but it knew itself to be a nation-state. Russia has a long and proud cultural history, but it remains unsure whether it is a nation or an empire. By definition, an empire cannot be a democracy to all its people. Second, Poland has a long history of being part of Europe, including some experimentation with democratic structure and culture. It could thus negotiate its way back to a former path. Russia is still debating whether it is part of Europe and has no previous path to democracy toward which to return. Third, and a corollary of the second point, foreshadowed membership by Poland of the European Union acted as an inducement to adopt conduct, including democratic practices, required for membership. No such invitation has or will be extended to Russia. And finally but perhaps most significant, Poland had a thriving form of civil society in the ten-million-member trade union Solidarnosc. This realm of society between the family and the state is a necessary aspect of democracy, allowing society to deliberate and act authentically. Russia has never had civil society, and its current embryonic urban manifestation is under constant risk of attack or takeover by the state.

Big-bang democratization can work if the conditions for it are present. Poland has demonstrated its success. But big-bang democratization in Russia was a boon only for the oligarchs and the autocrats who now rule Russia. Perhaps the missing ingredient is time. Perhaps Russia will eventually develop civil society, an open society, tolerance of minorities, and responsible international conduct, at least toward other democracies. But there are precious few signs of this at present. It leads to the conclusion that the concept of "transition to democracy" is an inappropriate one for an entity such as Russia because so many other steps need to be taken before democracy even looms on the horizon. It needs to deliberate on its status—state or empire? It needs to deliberate on its geography—European mainstream or oriental autocracy? Russia easily let go of utopian communism, but it is holding fast to realist Bolshevism, a crude form of cultural majoritarianism intolerant of all others. Russia needs to negotiate its way from Bolshevism to a far more open society. Sadly, there is a catch-22 in this analysis: *only democracies* demonstrate the capacity to deliberate and negotiate such national transitions.

Clearly, Putin is not the person to lead the deliberative revolution Russia needs. He wants the old Soviet empire back but without the inconvenience of an ideology to shape policy. Yet, without a utopian ideology to inspire people within the empire and beyond, as communism did in its early years, Putin has had to look for other justifications for his rule. Samuel Johnson is to be thanked for the apt adage "patriotism is the last refuge of a scoundrel" and how well it applies to Putin. Lacking ideology or a vision for the future of his country, Putin has turned to the scoundrel's playbook with a vengeance. Patriotism comes in many flavors. Some, like the enhancement of soft power by holding a successful Olympic Games and winning lots of shiny medals for the Motherland, are legitimate—though, as Sochi showed, expensive. Subsequent events have added the taint of doping to tarnish the soft power gloss. But even an event as large as the Olympics only lasts a few days. It can hardly sustain the sort of patriotism that Putin requires to justify his excesses. For that, one needs to turn to less savory manifestations of patriotism and its more political arm, nationalism.

A particularly macho form of nationalism that clearly appeals to Putin's personality and works well to galvanize popular sentiments is irredentism. Wanting an empire may be termed imperialism, but wanting little bits of it back is closer to irredentism. The Soviet Union was a polyglot empire where Russians lived in the outlying republics and Caucasians and Central Asians traveled to the heartland, not to mention Stalin's grotesque attempts at geographic ethnic engineering. So when these internal administrative borders became international borders with the collapse of the Soviet Union, some ethnic heterogeneity was left behind within each new nation-state. This is a common manifestation of the end-of-empire phenomenon. It can lead to people from the core state becoming subjects of new entities, as occurred to the millions of Hungarian speakers in Romania, Serbia, Czechoslovakia, and Ukraine upon the demise of the Austro-Hungarian Empire. Or it can leave large communities of colonially imported foreign workers in newly independent states, such as those from the subcontinent in Myanmar and Fiji, as happened with the end of the British Empire. The solution to the resulting problems lies in respect for human rights, and it is not unusual for a country of origin to become a champion for the human rights of its minorities abroad.

Human rights is a shallowly understood concept in Russia. Putin wishes it to mean supporting the human rights of Russian speakers in foreign lands. It thus lends itself as a policy to rouse nationalist feelings and justify "strong" leadership. Military threats or action are corollaries of this form of nationalism. Thus, a favorite tactic has been destabilizing recalcitrant neighbors under the guise of protecting Russian speakers in those countries. The list to date is not inconsiderable: Transnistria in Moldova, Abkhazia and South Ossetia in Georgia, and Crimea and Donetsk in Ukraine. One can add to that Russian support for Armenia's occupation of Nagorno-Karabakh under a clash-of-civilizations rubric whereby Russia takes on the mantle of defender of Christendom.

Karl Marx famously described religion as the opiate of the masses, and Putin has taken this critique and turned it into a tactic. As far as the Orthodox religion is concerned, Russia can certainly aspire to world leadership. Privileging religion also fits neatly with ideas of traditionalism, exceptionalism, and victimhood, three aspects of Putin's appeal to the Russian faithful. According to this mantra, Orthodoxy represents true Christianity and has therefore always been under attack from decadent Western Christianity. This fits in with the view of Russians that Putin favors as sentimental big-hearted people, unlike those cold, calculating, and acquisitive Westerners. There is little doubt that this worldview appeals to certain segments of Russian society; babushkas, Cossacks, and oligarchs. While it is a deeply reactionary perspective with no vision of the future, it has the advantage that an attack on one's enemies such as Mikhail Khodorkovsky or Pussy Riot can be portrayed as a defense of traditional Russian values.

An important step in the process is to control the media so as to control the message. Implementation was not difficult; Putin could use state assets or oligarch assets to take charge of all the main electronic and print media channels. But Russia has a long samizdat tradition, and it has migrated to the Internet. To control content on the Internet, Putin first had to whistle up the old enemy—the CIA—and accuse it of using the Internet to destabilize the Motherland. He then simply reverted to his defense of tradition and used arguments such as the obligation of the state to protect children from pornography. The result is that the state has the power to block any website and any social networking site. Russian laws target popular opinion, and any blogger with more than three thousand readers must register with the state.

Yet even with all these propaganda controls and assets, Putin considered that he needed to shore up his support by appealing to one of the basest aspects of human society; contempt for those that are different. One of religion's core tasks is to teach people to love one's neighbor. One of government's most sacred roles is to protect the weakest in society. Putin turned these concepts on their heads by arguing that homosexuality was contrary to Russian heritage and should barely be tolerated. Putin sees Western society's acceptance of homosexuality as yet another sign of decadence and thus a weakness that can easily be attacked. Rather than taming Bolshevism, in this case it is encouraged—the "us" being "normal people" and the "them" being gays. The actual Russian law is about homosexual propaganda, but the broader signal it gives is clear.

One final Putin tactic needs examination because it has become quite influential: the attack on civil society. Civil society represents the antithesis of all that Putin stands for. It has no antecedent in Russian history. It is by definition independent of government. Its members are notoriously difficult to control. And, as the comparison with Poland demonstrates, it is a necessary attribute of a democracy. Putin readily identified its weakness—its not-for-profit nature, which makes civil society dependent on contributions from others, domestic and international. In wealthy societies with charitable and philanthropic traditions, civil society can survive and indeed thrive. In poor countries and countries with little tradition of civil society, it becomes much more difficult to survive. One response to this situation has been the channeling of aid funds to and through civil society—annually from OECD countries, some $20 billion in official development assistance as well as a further $32 billion raised from private sources.[14] This instinct was extended to the countries of the former Soviet Union to assist in their democratic transitions, led by the pioneering work in this region of George Soros.

By working through civil society, a donor can get a big bang for the buck. Civil society organizations (CSOs) contribute significant voluntary time and generate great enthusiasm. Contributing to local civil society is also a means to attain local expertise. Contributing in a period when democracy's soft power was at its height ensured a major response from local civil society. Accordingly, a relatively modest investment in supporting champions of democracy brought weighty results. Results, of course, would not be possible without that level of local enthusiasm, without an issue drenched in soft power, and without local champions who are expert in the politics of their own countries. Transitions to democracy cannot be purchased by foreign funds, but they can be encouraged and supported through this form of international solidarity.

Putin saw things differently. Being an old KGB hand, he knows that money is one of the tools available to any intelligence outfit. Why deal with the complexities of reality when a facile conspiracy is easily at hand? And thus was born the myth that the color revolutions, in particular the Orange Revolution in Ukraine and the Rose Revolution in Georgia, were purchased by the CIA. From the perspective of Putin and his cohorts, investing in foreign civil society was "creating destabilizing revolutions in other states as a means of serving (Western) security interests at low cost and with minimal casualties."[15] The response was not difficult to find—cause the foreign funding to dry up, attack civil society leaders, and entice parts of civil society to accept Russian government funds. A clever twist was to require any CSO that received foreign funding for "political work" to register as a foreign agent.

It also follows that as an old KGB hand, Vladimir Putin would think it a standard operating procedure to advance Russia's interests by assisting an American presidential candidate more favorable to Moscow by hacking the Democratic National Committee and releasing the email dump just in time to compromise the 2016 Democratic Convention. Ironically, Richard Nixon tried to do something similar forty years earlier.

Follow the Leader

In crafting these responses, Putin established an alternative governance model quite different from the one being propagated by the Western aid industry with its emphasis on contestation, transparency, accountability, and alternation of power. The Putin model, which he has called Sovereign Democracy, has none of these and also dispenses with ideology and instead relies on tradition, religion, and nationalism as the pillars on which to build a support base. If this proves insufficient, find enemies within (gays) and beyond (Western perfidy and destabilization) to consolidate one's hold on power. Attack critics as if they are personal enemies but do so ostensibly in defense of tradition, religion, and nationalism. It certainly helps to have an economy dependent on government-controlled resources where access to wealth flows from access to government, but even poor countries can use available resources such as condition-free aid, control of land, and control of boundaries to help finance this governance model.

Who is following the leader? One method is to stick to the rhetoric of liberal democracy while quietly building the means of control à la Putin. A debt is therefore owed to the prime minister of Hungary, Viktor Orban, for having the courage to articulate his vision of Hungary following in the steps of Putin: "I don't think that our European Union membership precludes us from building an illiberal new state based on national foundations."[16] His models are Russia, China, and Turkey. Orban's speech was not captured surreptitiously as, for example, the "47 percent" speech that ended Mitt Romney's chances of victory; rather, the Orban video was posted on the government website. Here then is a telling sign of the decline of democracy's soft power and the rise of Putin's influence. Hungary is in a surly mood, having championed the breakaway from the Soviet sphere and reconstructed its former democratic political parties only to fall foul of the 2008 global financial crisis, which seemed to eat away all the progress made in the previous years. It is that surly mood that allows for politicians such as Orban to succeed. Hungary is an important test case. Will it return to European individual and cosmopolitan values, or will it plummet down the Putin path? Poland is also beginning to show some illiberal tendencies.

Being organized, opinionated, and independent of governments, civil society is almost by definition a thorn in the side of incumbents. As I have noted, civil society is probably what constituted the difference between success and failure in the democratization processes of Poland and Russia. And as also noted earlier, a recent trend in ODA is to channel funds to and through civil society. It is understandable that some governments will see civil society as a critic, a competitor for donor funds, and a threat to their autocratic instincts. The result is the use of government power to try to control civil society. In a study entitled *Defending Civil Society*,[17] the International Center for Not-for-Profit Law (ICNL) and the World Movement for Democracy secretariat listed the different ways that this has been done:

- Barriers to entry
- Barriers to operational activity
- Barriers to speech and advocacy
- Barriers to contact and communication
- Barriers to assembly
- Barriers to resources

Russia has rules in support of most of these barriers, as do dozens of other countries in the world. But Russia's recent introduction of the "foreign agent" rule is a good way of gauging its influence because of this law's specificity and originality. Orban referred directly to it as a good policy. Malaysia is now considering its introduction. Some Central Asian autocracies are following suit, including Kyrgyzstan, the nation thought to be the most liberal in Central Asia. Egyptian authorities said anyone who protests against the army will be regarded as agents of foreign powers. The ICNL/WMD study and similar studies, such as the Civicus annual *State of Civil Society Report*,[18] point to some fifty countries taking measures to limit and control civil society.

Another strong indicator of Putin's influence will be to monitor the growth of anti-gay laws now that he has validated this practice. From the perspective of politics, gays are an easy group to attack. They are rarely strongly organized because they are often unwilling to declare and defend themselves. Attacks on gays fit neatly into the Putin tradition-and-religion playbook. It can even have a nationalistic overtone, as in former president of Iran Mahmoud Ahmadinejad's ignorant comment that there are no gays in Iran.

Putin has become an influential figure. He has provided autocrats around the world with a model and a playbook of how to stay in power, marginalize opponents, and woo supporters. Putin's influence is a challenge to democracy and a fillip for autocrats. But Putin is not the only challenger. Democracy promoters argue that it is a concept as universally applicable as that of human rights, that it is not a Western value but a universal value, and that there is no other system that can lead to sustainable peace and development. Yet there are two other powerful ideas today that pose a serious challenge to those claims.

Notes

1. United Nations Office for the High Commissioner for Human Rights, *Report of the Commission of Inquiry on Human Rights in the Democratic People's Republic of Korea*, 2014, http://www.ohchr.org/EN/HRBodies/HRC/CoIDPRK/Pages/ReportoftheCommissionofInquiryDPRK.aspx.

2. See Roland Rich, "Recognition of States: The Collapse of Yugoslavia and the Soviet Union," *European Journal of International Law* 4, 1 (March 1993): 36–65, http://ejil.oxfordjournals.org/content/4/1/36.full.pdf+html.

3. See, for example, African Charter on Democracy, Elections and Governance, http://www.ipu.org/idd-E/afr_charter.pdf.

4. UNGA Res 1803 (XVII), http://legal.un.org/avl/ha/ga_1803/ga_1803.html.

5. David Frum, *How We Got Here: The '70s* (New York: Basic, 2000), p. 318.

6. Africa Research Institute, *Between Extremes: China and Africa,* Briefing

Note 1202, October 2012, http://www.africaresearchinstitute.org/files/briefing-notes /docs/Between-extremes-China-and-Africa-P2E56236DQ.pdf.

7. Yun Sun, *Africa in China's New Foreign Aid,* White Paper (Washington, DC: Brookings Institution, July 16, 2014), http://www.brookings.edu/blogs/africa-in -focus/posts/2014/07/16-africa-china-foreign-aid-sun.

8. Naohiro Kitano and Yukinori Harada, "Estimating China's Foreign Aid 2001– 2013," *JICA Research Paper 78* (June 2014), http://jica-ri.jica.go.jp/publication /assets/JICA-RI_WP_No.78_2014.pdf.

9. David Dollar, *China's Engagement with Africa—From Natural Resources to Human Resources* (Washington, DC: Brookings Institution, 2016).

10. Zhou Hong, "China's Evolving Aid Landscape: Crossing the River and Feeling the Stones," in Sachin Chatuvedi, Thomas Fues, and Elizabeth Sidiropoulos (eds.), *Development Cooperation and Emerging Powers: New Partners or Old Patterns?* (London: Zed, 2012), p. 157.

11. Austin Strange, Bradley Parks, Michael J. Tierney, Andreas Fuchs, Axel Dreher, and Vijaya Ramachandran, *China's Development Finance to Africa: A Media-Based Approach to Data Collection,* Working Paper 323 (Washington, DC: Center for Global Development, 2013), http://www.cgdev.org/sites/default/files/chinese-development -finance-africa_0.pdf.

12. Edward N. Luttwak, *The Rise of China vs. the Logic of Strategy* (Cambridge, MA: Belknap, 2012).

13. Vladimir Putin, Annual Address to the Federal Assembly of the Russian Federation, April 25, 2005, http://archive.kremlin.ru/eng/speeches/2005/04/25/2031 _type70029type82912_87086.shtml.

14. OECD, *Aid at a Glance: Flows of Official Development Assistance to and Through Civil Society Organizations in 2011,* October 2013, http://www.oecd.org /dac/peer-reviews/Aid%20for%20CSOs%20Final%20for%20WEB.pdf.

15. Anthony Cordesman, *Russia and the "Color Revolution,"* Center for Strategic and International Studies, May 28, 2014, http://csis.org/publication/russia-and -color-revolution.

16. Zoltan Simon, "Orban Says He Seeks to End Liberal Democracy in Hungary," *Bloomberg News,* July 28, 2014.

17. International Center for Not-for-Profit Law (ICNL) and World Movement for Democracy Secretariat, *Defending Civil Society,* 2d ed. (Washington, DC: World Movement for Democracy, 2012), p. 14, http://www.icnl.org/research/resources /dcs/DCS_Report_Second_Edition_English.pdf.

18. Civicus, *State of Civil Society Reports 2016,* http://civicus.org/index.php /socs2016.

5

China Is a
Formidable Competitor

It is evident that the phenomenon of China's economic suc-
cess achieved under a system that does not even purport to be democratic poses a challenge and a dilemma for supporters of democracy.
Even as Fukuyama was crafting his "end of history" theory, China was
undermining it. But undermining a theory is far easier than construct-
ing a new one, and it remains unclear just what China's achievements
mean in political terms. It clearly means something pretty significant,
and both critics and admirers are paying close attention. The question
this chapter poses is whether China has invented a viable alternative to
liberal democracy.

China's Achievements

A good place to start is the following mash-up of China's official propaganda on the occasion of the new millennium:

> Along with the coming of 2000, the PRC had undergone a glorious yet
> tortuous course of 50 years, amid great changes in Chinese society. Before
> the founding of New China in 1949, China's highest yearly outputs of
> major industrial and agricultural products were 445,000 tons of yarn, 2.79
> billion meters of cloth, 61,880,000 tons of coal, 320,000 tons of crude oil,
> 6 billion kwh of electric energy production, 150 million tons of grain, and
> 849,000 tons of cotton. Since the founding of New China, especially in
> the 21 years after the start of the reform and opening to the outside world
> in 1978, China has made great achievements in economic construction
> and social development. In 1999, the GDP was 8,205.4 billion yuan, an

increase of 6.4 times over 1978, at constant prices; the outputs of some major industrial and agricultural products, such as grain, cotton, meat, edible oil, coal, steel, cement, cloth and TV sets, leapt from a backward position to first place in the world . . . and basically realizing modernization in the mid-21st century, [with] the GDP per capita reaching the level of the moderately developed countries, and people living a well-off life.[1]

Should we contest the figures? No, it's all true. And the Western-dominated World Bank can confirm it:

Since initiating market reforms in 1978, China has shifted from a centrally planned to a market based economy and experienced rapid economic and social development. GDP growth averaging about 10 percent a year has lifted more than 500 million people out of poverty. All Millennium Development Goals have been reached or are within reach.[2]

China's achievements are remarkable by any measure. The term *unprecedented* has become somewhat hyperbolic, and rarely does its use mean that there has never been such a development in the past, but in relation to China's development, *unprecedented* sounds grudging and inadequate. Nothing in world history comes even close to the feat of lifting half a billion people out of poverty in one generation. Regardless of one's view of China and its government, it stands to reason that a system that can achieve this result has some significant positives going for it. Any democratically elected government with this curriculum vitae would expect the public to shower it with kudos and votes. Yet, acknowledging a phenomenon as significant is not the same as knowing what that significance may be. It has more than one component, and it can be viewed both in terms of what it is and what it isn't.

China Is Not a Democracy

China has not had the temerity of two if its authoritarian neighbors, Laos and North Korea, to employ the term *Democratic* in its name. It is the People's Republic of China, not the Democratic People's Republic of China. But reading the 1982 Constitution suggests that China is in theory a democracy and that it has a multiparty system in which individuals can stand for election and vote freely. Turning once again to state propaganda:

The Constitution guarantees the fundamental rights of every citizen, including the right to vote and stand for election, the freedoms of speech, of the press, of assembly, of association, of demonstration and of religious belief. Citizens' freedom of the person is inviolable, as is their right to protection from unwarranted intrusions into their personal dignity and the sanctity of their homes. Freedom and privacy of correspondence are protected by law. Citizens have the right to criticize or make suggestions to any state organ or functionary, and the right to supervise them.[3]

Here one needs to give cynical realism its full play. Every word in this paragraph is a half-truth at best and probably better described as false. Citizens have certain rights unless the authorities believe they do not deserve them. They have a right to vote in meaningless elections and to stand for election at the village level but then to be sabotaged if they win and authorities do not like them. They have the voice freedoms unless they criticize the party and the political system, and they are in greatest danger if their criticisms are effective. They have the privacy freedoms unless the authorities consider these citizens to be dangerous to the party's continued incumbency. They are free to send petitions to Beijing, but woe betide those who attempt to attract publicity to their grievance. In sum, China does not respect human rights and is not a democracy.

What about those vaunted village elections where more people vote than in either the United States or Europe? The optimistic view had been that this was a first step toward a gradual upward creep of democratization in China. There is a certain logic in the theory of democratic transitology of beginning the learning process at the lowest level of governance, especially if the process does not follow a revolutionary regime change. The idea is to start the process of democratic acculturation by voting for local representatives who are often personally known to the voter and to discuss issues that have direct personal salience to local people. In theory, this should allow the voter to better understand the process in which she is engaged and to appreciate its value. Having understood this value, it is not too difficult a step to move to the next layer of government and apply the system of open elections there before finally allowing national leaders to be directly elected in open, free, and fair elections. Though not buying the inevitability of democratization in China, many observers nevertheless were keen to see village elections as an excellent first step.

Now that several decades have passed and these elections have been studied closely, a more realistic perspective is emerging as to the true nature of village elections. They are a mess, they are consciously designed not to articulate to national elections, and, in many cases, they are a sham. Elections in the first two decades (the 1980s and 1990s) were often rigged by local party elites. After a change in the electoral processes in 1998, the conduct of elections has improved and the capacity of local authorities to fabricate the result has diminished, but this opened the way to the more usual democratic abuses: vote buying, bribery, patronage politics, gangsterization of politics, and ascriptive voting. One effect of the loss of faith in elections is apathy, not uncommon in democracies, with the direct result that many elections do not achieve the required 50 percent voter participation and are thus ruled invalid. Another is the unrelenting influence of the party, whereby the senior official successfully runs for office, leading to the very common result of holding both elected office and party appointment concurrently.[4] Very convenient.

Had village elections been successful, one could have anticipated that the resulting governance structures would have resolved some problems and lessened the number of protests and petitions; but neither of these impacts has come to pass. Party officials have also been resolute in delinking village elections from other aspects of governance in China and in rejecting any parallel with the color revolutions in Europe and elsewhere. In the eyes of Chinese officialdom, village elections were an experiment to see whether participation by local people in local governance might limit the rampant corruption that was beyond the reach of party headquarters. It was never an experiment in democratization.

The major remaining question about village elections is whether they may yet have some unintended consequences. Have they inspired a sense of individual rights among local people? Can there yet be some examples of local people electing a champion who stands up to the party and its depredations? And if so, will Chinese-controlled social media allow this sort of news to spread? In other words, is there some possibility of democratic blowback?

Needless to say, no Chinese leader is advocating a change in the political system, though some occasionally speak about reform. It is difficult to know whether calls for reform or its most common articulation, anticorruption, is a genuine systemic comment or a short-term campaign against a political enemy. Conflict is inherent and inescapable in politics, and in open democratic systems it is given structure and articulation, allowing the voter ultimately to decide. But that does not mean that the stab in the back, the slanderous whispering campaign, and the big lie have been eliminated from democratic politics. It does mean that these tactics are more likely to be revealed by the supposedly ever-vigilant media and thus less likely to be employed. But these sorts of tactics are the only means by which personality and policy conflict are dealt with in a closed Leninist system. So let's not expect any grand visions of systemic political change coming from Chinese leaders.

For such visions, one needs to turn to fallen political leaders. But in China, former leaders tend to fit into two categories. Either they become elder statesmen who are routinely consulted (and, not inconsequentially, whose families continue to have their commercial and political interests protected) or they are purged and, often, imprisoned. In neither case is it likely that the public will have access to a tell-all reflection of their time in politics that is so common and often commercially lucrative in democratic countries. But there is one towering exception. Zhao Ziyang was the Chinese premier at the time of the Tiananmen demonstrations in 1989. He opposed military action against the demonstrators and was therefore purged and spent the balance of his life in seclusion in a form of house arrest. Zhao Ziyang was ousted by Jiang Zemin, who is now himself being indirectly purged in the form of the prosecution of his three acolytes, Zhou Yongkang, General Xu Caihou, and Bo Xilai. It turns out that Zhao did not go down quietly. He secretly produced a memoir, speaking into tapes that were then smuggled out of China and published several years after his death.[5] Here are some extracts:

> In fact, it is the Western parliamentary democratic system that has demonstrated the most vitality. This system is currently the best one available. . . . Based on this, we can say that if a country wishes to modernize, not only should it implement a market economy, it must also adopt a parliamentary democracy as its political system. Otherwise this nation will not be able to have a market economy that is healthy and modern, nor can it become a modern society with a rule of law. Instead it will run into the situations that have occurred in so many developing countries, including China: commercialization of power, rampant corruption, a society polarized between rich and poor.[6]

Zhao is realistic as to the likelihood of this happening quickly if at all in China but, importantly, he posits two critical milestones on the journey to democracy—to allow other political parties to compete for power and to allow a free press. A quarter of a century after his downfall, these two milestones are neither in sight nor even on the far horizon. To advocate the former is tantamount to sedition and will invite upon the advocate the full panoply of criminal enforcement options. There might be slightly more tolerance of the latter if framed in the context of whichever current anticorruption campaign is currently afoot. As things stand, Zhao's vision is lonely and quixotic.

Some have therefore looked for a halfway house. Because the current leadership of China has abandoned communism and lionized Confucianism, one idea is to draw on a Confucian idea—the examination. The idea is for a House of Exemplary Persons; rejecting the acceptability of open national elections in the near term, its proponents argue instead for a system of examinations for a seat in a "meritocratic legislature." According to this view, a Confucian examination process will have popular credibility because of its cultural acceptability.[7] Perhaps, but don't hold your breath.

Authoritarian Resilience

China is nowhere near becoming a democracy. The party may have abandoned Marxist ideology but it holds fast to Leninism, whereby the party is the sole font of authority and will not brook any formal form of opposition or even an effective form of criticism. Nevertheless, a quarter of a century after Tiananmen and the fall of the Berlin Wall, the regime endures.

China is not the only authoritarian country to endure. Repression, a favorite tool of authoritarian rule, can take different forms. The sort of totalitarian repression practiced by the Kim dynasty in North Korea is effective by forcing the vast majority of the population to concentrate on the daily grind of survival and give it no capacity to think of ways to organize itself for regime change. This leaves the threat to Kim as coming only from the small privileged class of party and army personnel and their families. This threat has been handled by the occasional purge and the constant flow of privileges to the ruling class. Ironically, the greatest threats to the Kim dynasty would come from either a policy of liberalization undermining totalitarian control or from further isolation from the world, undermining its economy and thus the regime's ability to deliver privileges to the chosen few.

At the other end of the repression spectrum one finds the soft authoritarianism of countries such as Malaysia and Singapore. This mixes crony capitalism with large dollops of economic freedom, which is particularly appealing to their industrious peoples. It also allows a certain degree of political freedom, considerable free speech, legally recognized opposition groups, and a fairly free civil society. But the constant threat looming over these freedoms is the reality of state-sanctioned repression through the criminal and civil codes. Both regimes are well-armed with the legislation of repression, some leftover from the British colonial era.

A publication that proves to be critical, effective, and popular will soon lose its license to print. When it goes digital, it will soon start experiencing technical difficulties from the government-owned or -controlled telecoms. When it overcomes these it will lose its advertisers, each strong-armed by the government. Ultimately it will go cap in hand to George Soros, thus "proving" the government's point that it was part of a foreign plot all along. An individual who proves to be an effective communicator and rabble-rouser will learn about the extent of the public nuisance laws and eventually the sedition laws. And the individual who gains sufficient international notoriety as to make the use of sedition laws unattractive to the regime will soon be bankrupted in a libel case brought by one of the leaders, generating massive penalties imposed by the supposedly incorruptible bench. And woe betides the electorate that has the temerity to elect opposition candidates. It will soon find government services no longer being delivered and development projects drying up.

China, along with Laos and Vietnam, is trying to move from the Pyongyang model to the Singapore precedent. China is the most advanced along the path. It makes perfect sense. The enormous battalions of bureaucrats that are needed to maintain a machine of totalitarian repression is expensive and unproductive. It can now be cut down to more manageable size. The official elite still need to be coddled, but, by freeing up the economy leading to the consequent growth in the size of the pie, the politics of distribution can be significantly enhanced. Economic freedoms will benefit and therefore appeal to both the urban middle class, whose only choice once was for which state-owned enterprise they would work, and to rural people once held captive in collective farms. Yet the machinery for repression still stands, though it is applied more sparingly and selectively. The limits may shift subtly depending on who is being purged and which anticorruption campaign is currently afoot, but anyone who criticizes the party's legitimacy knows that there is a good chance that the state will come a-knocking.

The difficult question in authoritarian resilience is how these regimes have been able to manage liberalization but prevent government overthrow followed perhaps by democratization. There is a sturdy collection of academic opinion on this point. A common explanation centers on the capacity of an authoritarian regime to buy popular support through public largesse, made possible by a readily available resource such as oil. This certainly applies to some regimes but is not as helpful in relation to China, which is a net importer of these resources. A more relevant issue concerns elite cohesion, which is the most common explanation posited in relation to Malaysia. Accordingly, the incumbent Malay political elite, aided and abetted by a self-selected group of Chinese and Indian political figures, have been able to maintain high-level stability at the helm of dominant political parties in coalition by using the powers of incumbency to marginalize opposition while deciding tricky issues of succession and distribution of spoils behind closed doors. When Anwar Ibrahim, a senior member of the cabal, upset this arrangement by splitting off and challenging the regime, elite cohesion was maintained by using the criminal law to humiliate and marginalize him.

Elite cohesion has an intrinsic explanatory attraction because its opposite, fractiousness and public squabbling, is an obvious explanation for loss of public confidence. But while elite cohesion may be a necessary part of the explanation of authoritarian resilience, it cannot be a sufficient reason. Managerial competence is another common explanation. This is the explanation often favored to explain the economic success of the authoritarian regimes of South Korea and Taiwan in the take-off stages of their development. It turns on the ways the regimes were able to co-opt the business community to support the government, often in return for favorable industry policies. It also looks at competent management and improvement of health and education services. And it deals with the issue of adaptability to changing circumstances, both domestic and international. Clearly, this explanation sits well with the China situation. But the problem with the managerial competence explanation is its relativity. *Competence* needs definition. Is it competent to grow the economy at the cost of the environment? Is it competent to grow the pie but ignore its division? Is it competent to hold the economy hostage to the needs of the *chaebols* (in South Korea) or the state-owned enterprises (in China)?

The most pleasing explanation of authoritarian resilience in China is the one that turns on the capacity of the regime to institutionalize the processes of government. It centers on establishing a more predictable and stable rules-bound system, a division of responsibilities among qualified managers, greater meritocracy in the selection of those managers, and regularity in the functioning of governance structures. By institutionalizing a large set of decisions affecting ordinary people and thus making them more transparent, understandable, and predictable, China has earned a degree of the broad popular legitimacy it lacked when it was governed by leaders who would govern through sudden massive campaigns with volatile and invariably negative outcomes. Institutionalization also took the pressure off the senior leaders in Beijing to decide *everything*. They could now delegate thematically and geographically to comrades running functioning systems with standard operating procedures that produced many sensible outcomes. Institutionalization sat well with the orderliness and meritocracy of Confucianism, and it was not long before Confucius trumped Marx. But not Lenin!

Institutionalization is rule *by* law. It has the advantages of being written down and understandable and of therefore adding a large element of predictability in citizens' interactions with government. It is infinitely preferable to the uncertainties of Maoist rule by the leader's whim. But it falls a long way short of rule *of* law. Taking a functionalist definition, I have previously listed the components of the rule of law comprising the following six requirements:[8]

1. Judicial independence protected in a basic instrument such as the constitution and acted upon by the judiciary.
2. An executive arm of government accepting that it is subject to laws, increasingly including, in the era of globalization, international law.
3. Procedural fairness in the making of laws, delivery of justice, and enforcement of laws, including such concepts as equality before the law and application of natural justice.
4. A significant degree of effectiveness of the law, an expectation of its enforcement, and a reliance on its provisions.
5. A significant level of predictability of the law, and a public that understands the likely consequences of unlawful acts.
6. Public acceptance of the legitimacy of the legal processes, often achieved through longevity.

Chinese rule by law is unencumbered by these six inconvenient requirements of rule of law. The courts are not independent. The authorities need not be subject to law. The elite will always have preference. The law may be effective and often predictable, but so might its unrestrained repressive aspects. The public will accept rule by law as an improvement, though many will crave rule of law.

Institutionalization takes China a long way down the path of regime resilience. In the relatively short term at least, it is a workable system producing impressive results, and it reflects credit on its architects.

Does Resilience Imply Endurance?

Resilience describes a current state; it is based on previous evidence. *Endurance* looks at a future state; it is based on analysis of that evidence.

While a quarter of a century after Tiananmen is not a particularly long time, that period provides sufficient evidence of regime resilience. Yet there is no consensus that resilience implies endurance, and indeed there is a robust body of assessment arguing against regime endurance.

Just about all those who doubt the capacity for endurance of the Chinese regime point to the fact that many authoritarian regimes have looked strong before their collapse. Collapse is imminent, they continue to argue. It is one of the attributes of an authoritarian regime to do all in its power to give the impression of implacable durability. Military parades showing off the latest armaments are a common device. Having the leadership associate itself with international political celebrities is another. Major ribbon-cutting events at home or abroad constitute yet another theme— and when the authoritarian regime is too poor or incompetent to deliver ribbon-cutting-worthy infrastructure, the leaders are shown inspecting progress and invariably giving "essential direction" to the project.

Needless to say, this durability impression rests less on regime achievements and much more on propaganda. It was how the military ruled Myanmar. It can easily be applied to Muammar Qaddafi's Libya. And in the case that haunts China, there is a strong argument to be made that the Soviet Union fell into this category. So we need to take the propaganda trappings of durability with a large dose of skepticism. And it is true that regimes may unexpectedly collapse even when giving the impression of permanence. But the imminent-collapse argument is not without problems. One problem is that it is logically undeniable. Twenty-five years from now with no change in governance in China, the same argument can still be made and still have the same degree of validity. The argument therefore can only be sustained after the regime collapse event. Before the regime collapse event, however, analysts can only consider the relative strengths of achievements versus propaganda and weigh their impact on the public acceptance of the regime. Clearly, China knows all about propaganda and uses it widely in both old-fashioned ways, such as patriotic billboards, and new-fashioned ways, in having tame bloggers and tweeters sing the regime's praises and demonize its enemies. But as I pointed out at the beginning of this chapter, the regime has plenty by way of achievement to back its claims to resilience and endurance. The imminent-collapse argument does little to advance the general understanding of this issue.

A more sophisticated set of reasons against regime endurance is put forward by Minxin Pei.[9] He argues that corruption is an inevitable by-product of this sort of regime and will eventually dissipate any legitimacy it may have; that the regime has been remarkably successful at co-opting different segments of society into the system but that it has come to its limits in this regard; and that factionalism will emerge, leading to unpredictable outcomes.

David Shambaugh, long in the more conservative school of sinologists, recently changed his mind and joined the collapse prognosticators.[10] He bases his view on the following points. Money and people are fleeing China, not trusting the regime and expecting worse to come. Repression is getting worse, in particular with the officially sanctioned attack on "universal values" leaving Chinese political orthodoxy as the only acceptable discourse. Propaganda is losing its power of persuasion in an increasingly sophisticated society hooked into the global discourse, even though the great firewall of China tries to limit that access. Corruption is endemic and structural, with the corollary that anticorruption campaigns are in truth political purges. And, perhaps most devastating of all, reform is simply not working.

If there is one thing on which regime supporters and critics will agree it is that corruption is a problem in China. President Xi Jinping's current campaign has since the start of 2013 seen over 200,000 officials punished, including three dozen ministers, provincial leaders, or top executives at state-owned companies.[11] Xi's rhetoric sees corruption as not only a threat to legitimacy but also a break on efficiency and development. Xi's politics sees corruption as a very convenient way of neutralizing his political enemies. Those arguing against regime endurance have a far more fundamental critique—corruption is the inevitable result of the union of Leninism and capitalism. Leninism provides the uncontested grip on power that gives its incumbents and their families a privileged position to exploit the wealth-creating capacity of capitalism. The privileges come in many forms. Appointment to various positions is a privilege of leadership, and with the continuing vast role of state-owned enterprises this is a traditional route to power and wealth. Licenses in the form of permissions or contracts with the government are another privilege of power that can be used for family wealth creation. Information privy to the government may well be used for wealth creation. And of course there is impunity, which, unless one falls politically foul of President Xi, can protect corrupt officials from the selective arm of the law.

In fact, the Chinese system falls squarely within the famous Klitgaard formula defining corruption:[12]

$$C = M + D - A$$

Corruption equals Monopoly plus Discretion minus Accountability

The Leninist system gives the party a monopoly by definition. It may not exercise its monopoly in decisionmaking on all occasions or issues, but it can if it so wishes. The vast remaining elements of the command economy provide the regime with plenty of discretion on the use of state resources. And the lack of rule of law means that ultimately there is no accountability. Klitgaard's formula has been criticized, as is to be expected from any attempt to reduce such a vast enterprise to a single formula, but that does not mean the formula is wrong, only that it may not be comprehensive. It is quite revealing that the Chinese system fits so neatly within its terms.

Conceding the accuracy of the corruption critique, is this regime disease one that is necessarily politically mortal, or can society live with ongoing corruption morbidity? At this stage one would have to say that the evidence points to the morbidity outcome. Every society has corruption. The aim of successful societies is to keep corruption to tolerable limits. The level of tolerability is dependent on social expectations, and expectations are in turn dependent on the level of satisfaction with one's lot, which is in turn shaped by the path one has traversed. This suggests that the objective for the Chinese leadership is to ensure that corruption does not become a regime-ending issue through two strategies: first, continue to provide rising standards of living, displaying regime competence and effectiveness; and second, continue anticorruption drives, including prosecution of the occasional big fish to demonstrate that something is being done. This combination of performance legitimacy and well-publicized anticorruption drives has served as an effective pressure valve in the past, and there is no reason to believe that it will not continue to do so in the future.

Without the capacity to demonstrate political legitimacy through regular elections, China needs to demonstrate it by other means. One such method has been the co-opting of significant sectors of society into the Leninist-capitalist system. The transformation of large swathes of rural folk into urban dwellers has assisted the party in targeting them with new educational options whereby the number of tertiary education graduates quintupled between 1997 and 2009.[13] The economy produced sufficient jobs in the export-led sector, and the party increased its membership—the key to personal success—by around one million per year. The party has even been able to manage the growth of civil society, occasionally offering public funds for tasks associated with social safety nets while using the criminal law to attack those considered too effective politically. The unrelenting persecution of the Falun Gong group demonstrates the length the authorities will go to crush perceived threats, and clearly other parts of civil society could not do otherwise but take careful note. Critics argue that there are clear limits to this co-opting capacity and that China has reached those limits.

These arguments might be seen as aspects of performance legitimacy. University degrees are only valuable where they lead to good jobs or opportunities. Industries employing workers need to remain viable in terms of the quality of the products and the environmental impact of their processes. Party membership only remains valuable where it offers the realistic possibility of privileges. While there may well be limits to co-optation, there is no reason to believe that China has reached those limits. The leadership has been agile in trying to move the economy toward a codependence on exports and domestic demand. The environmental damage caused by low-quality growth has been demonstrated to government and people alike, and there has been important remedial action, which might slow down the level of environmental degradation. The quality of products is also a matter well understood by the government and public alike after such episodes as the melamine in milk scandal in 2008. Again, the Chinese government has the capacity to improve its oversight processes. Finally, it is unlikely that the privileges associated with party membership will dry up significantly. The more likely outcome is that those attracted to membership will not be the best and brightest individuals, who might prefer their chances seeking opportunities independently in the private sector. Instead the party might attract the ambitious but less competitive segment of society. Does this not, however, also hold for liberal democracies, where the best and brightest do not necessarily gravitate to government service? Once again, there is no reason to believe that the successful practice of co-opting large groups into the system cannot be maintained into the future.

Pei's final critique concerns the inevitability of factionalism in a closed political system. Factionalism may take different forms of articulation but invariably reflects aspects of the division of spoils. Policy factionalism might simply point to which sectors will benefit from government priority and whose interests will be affected. Succession factionalism will turn on which group will have the greater privileges within the system. Without the rigor of elections weeding out actors, closed political systems must find ways of purging or appeasing them. The critics argue that this is an unsustainable process. The case of neighboring Myanmar provides a good example of unsustainability. Battered by sanctions and a comatose local economy, the military elite could not grow the pie. Without the economic wherewithal to appease all factions, there was a need to prioritize within the elite; and the public purging of the family of former leader Ne Win demonstrated that this was the only tactic left to the regime. The choice was to continue to purge parts of the elite as the economy sustained ever fewer or to let go of absolute power and attempt another course. They chose the latter.

But China is not Myanmar. It has shown a great deftness in the mix of "purge and appease" policies in the past, and there is little reason to doubt its capacity to continue to do so. Yet again, this argument turns on the regime's performance legitimacy and its ability to grow the pie to give itself appeasement options.

I have also suggested a psycho-social reason why the Chinese regime has entrenched itself but will have difficulty sustaining its governance formula into the future:

> The reason the Chinese formula has worked to date may, however, be specific to a certain time period. After the famines and poverty under Mao, the Chinese people were very grateful for a period of pragmatism and realism. After watching the Soviet Union's collapse, and the collapse of living standards accompanying it, Chinese reformers understandably gravitated more towards gradual change than "big bang" upheaval. The generation that lived through the Maoist period will be very happy for Deng's cat to catch the mice regardless of its color. But the generation of spoilt "young emperors" living through the period of material opportunity will be far more demanding.[14]

These young emperors, the products of the one-child policy, will make economic and political demands. Having grown up with greater access to news and opinions, they will have a different set of premises on which to base their conclusions. They will have the powerful example of Taiwanese democracy to consider and thus banish arguments that democracy is not culturally suited to the Chinese people. This was particularly evident in 2012 in the course of the presidential elections in Taiwan. Chinese propaganda invariably equates elections with conflict and lack of harmony, but those in China following the Taiwanese elections commented heavily in social media on certain features such as the fact that one of the two leading candidates was a woman, Tsai Ing-wen; the graciousness of her concession speech when she congratulated President Ma Ying-jeou on his victory; and the joyful victory speech by the future president standing in the pouring rain with his supporters. Nothing as exciting or admirable occurs in Chinese politics.

This all means that the bar is higher, the demands more acute, and the means of success more difficult. But it does not mean the bar is too high or the demands too lofty or the means of success too difficult. It still depends on performance.

How Relevant Is Culture?

Now that the Asian values debate has died down, commentary on it is no longer seen as advocacy. The Asian values debate took a kernel of truth and tried to build it up into a bulwark against the application of human rights in Asian autocracies. It died because Asian people, as opposed to certain Asian leaders, showed no interest in pursuing this line of reasoning and sensibly took for granted that universal human rights do and should apply to Asian peoples along with everyone else. The kernel of truth is not about values that some Asians might hold that no other peoples hold, but about values that might be given higher priority in Asian societies than in others. It is therefore about degrees, not absolutes. And attitudes toward the issues it focused on were never seen uniformly in either Asian or non-Asian societies. There is always overlap between societies as well as differences within societies.

With these caveats in mind, the kernel of truth in the Asian values debate concerned attitudes toward issues of individuality and communitarianism, rights and duties, savings and consumption, discipline and creativity, and the degree of conservatism in relation to authority. Attitudes to these big issues in life vary within societies and indeed within families. And one can examine the literature of different societies to come to the realization that individuals struggle with these questions and will come to differing answers given different circumstances and different times in their lives.

There is little point in unpacking these issues to examine the amount of overlap and the degree of difference between societies' attitudes. To begin with, there are limited tools for this task. Asian values proponents relied on intuitive knowledge and observational generalizations. In the hands of a skilled ethnographer, long-term observation is a powerful tool. In the hands of a politician, these sorts of generalizations carry the suspicion of being self-serving. Opinion polling is becoming a useful tool as societies become accustomed to the practice and where longitudinal results allow for tentative conclusions as to the direction of opinion formation. But it is of limited value where freedom of speech is not respected and where the populace has accordingly developed acute self-censorship habits. Opinion polling has the advantage of quantifiability, which is considered ever more essential in American social science, though even in this case the problem of identifying a representative sample on which to base that number is becoming acute. But there is little point in playing with numbers based on opinions that are expressed but not genuinely held. There is no control process for self-censorship.

The key issue about culture is not its immutable impact on politics but the speed with which it is changing and the direction it is headed. The concept of culture as a constant, forever fixed in society, is clearly false in ever-changing advanced societies but was given some credibility by the early anthropologists in relation to primitive societies. Bronislaw Malinowski involuntarily invented long-stay ethnography when, as a subject of the enemy Austro-Hungarian Empire during World War I, he was not allowed to return to Europe and was in effect banished by the Australian government for the duration of the war to the Trobriand Islands, in what is today Papua New Guinea. His methods were followed by others, resulting in a series of ethnographic studies describing various primitive peoples living in a balanced and timeless social structure with fixed cultural beliefs. Basically, the ethnographers did not stay long enough. All cultures change to adapt to changing environments and circumstances. All culture is negotiable.

China never particularly bought into the Asian values debate. One reason is that the concept of "Asia" is foreign to Chinese historical understanding of the world, which simply has China as the middle kingdom and makes little distinction between the various tributaries and barbarians beyond the gates. Indeed, the term *Asia* is a European construct because "the idea of Asia or the Orient is an artefact of the European imagination"[15] and no Asian languages prior to European contact had a word for "Asia." But the Chinese leadership was not blind to the advantages the concept bestowed on its advocates. What we are seeing in China today is a similar tactic being played out with Confucianism as the new version of Asian values.

Viewed from the perspective of modern politics, Confucianism embodies a list of useful attributes: from antiquity, deeply ingrained, not a religion, and establishing no religious cadre. Add to that list a feature of all broad moral philosophies—malleability. As scholars over the years have demonstrated, one can find varying interpretations of Confucianism, providing rulers with a useful menu from which to select. In Maoist times, Confucius was reviled and seen as a throwback to a despised past and a hindrance to building a new China. In the Deng era things started to change. In 1984 the China Confucius Foundation was established in Qufu, and in the following year, the China Confucian Study Association was established in Beijing, both as nationwide organizations.[16] In 1994 the International Confucian Association was founded in Beijing and held its inaugural conference to celebrate the 2,545th anniversary of the birth of the sage, at which the keynote speaker was none other than Singaporean prime minister Lee Kuan Yew, the lead booster of Asian values.[17] The best evidence that Confucius has been fully rehabilitated is in the establishment of the Confucius Institute in the early years of this century. By 2012, the Confucian Institute had 400 establishments in more than 100 countries, with a Chinese central government budget of $200 million (an amount that needs to be matched by host universities).[18] Rather than the European model of a stand-alone office situated downtown, the Confucius Institute model is more modest and, perhaps, more effective in the longer term by being part of a university. It nevertheless discharges the same role as the European counterparts, enhancing the nation's "soft power."[19] At home, Confucianism is put to a different use, as outlined by Chris Patten: "It is usually Confucius who is taken as the fount of Asian distaste and disregard for liberal values. Confucius, it is said, emphasized order, hierarchy, self-discipline, and obedience. . . . Confucius was largely ignored in his lifetime, at least by those whom he would have liked to serve politically, and was then placed on a pedestal by Chinese emperors who promoted his ideas as a convenient official cult."[20] Which takes us full circle to the current Chinese leadership.

While Confucian thinking may well be ingrained in Chinese culture, it cannot successfully be used to sideline all other influences. To examine a particular society's culture is to enquire how it is responding to its particular environment and circumstances. As environment and circumstances can never be constants, culture is by definition always in flux. But some societies change very slowly, and some long-standing aspects of culture may be more difficult to change than others—one example is the culture of patriarchy, which will be discussed in Chapter 8. Perhaps the most radical form of change is the drastic change in lifestyle and relationships that occurs when individuals change from living in close-knit and traditional rural social structures to the far more atomized urban environments. In 2009 the number of people living in urban areas in the world (3.42 billion) surpassed the number living in rural areas (3.41 billion). The global trend is toward an urban culture having many features in common. The urban human will no longer live by the seasons but by the various clocks dictated by business hours, the opening of stock exchanges, and the timetables of trains. The urban human will drift away from the extended family toward the nuclear family or even living alone. The urban human will be better educated, more activist, more critical, more demanding, and more discerning than her rural counterpart. Urban cultures will converge, though they will never become identical, and will continue to be influenced by the path from which they came, even if only in traces.

The global trend in urbanization is strongly reflected in China. China's urban population more than doubled in the two decades after Tiananmen to surpass the 50 percent mark, and China's leadership announced an urbanization target of 70 percent by 2025. China can therefore be expected to be a leading generator of urban culture in the future. Returning to the question in the subtopic, it follows that it is not Chinese culture that is the relevant variable but urban culture. Chinese characteristics of urban culture, including Confucian thinking, will still be traceable and perhaps even influential on the rate of change but will not in and of themselves be determining factors. To return to a replay of the Asian values debate through the new emphasis on Confucius is therefore beside the point. A better question concerns the relationship between urban culture and democratization. Urban culture is clearly propitious for modernization, and many theorists see modernization as the key to democratization. This is the issue that will be tackled in Chapter 7.

End of Chinese History?

Fukuyama's thesis would be seen as particularly jarring in a country with five thousand years of recorded history. Like everybody else, people in China care about what will happen tomorrow and live with the normal immediacy of life. But their country's long history and its ups and downs tend to make them focus on longer historical timeframes. In support of this proposition, one need not rely on the apocryphal tale of Zhou Enlai saying it was too soon to tell the results of the French revolution—he was speaking in 1972 to Richard Nixon about the student revolution of 1968, not the revolution of 1789.[21] Anyone who has dealt with China is aware that people view Chinese history in terms of dynasties, epochs, and centuries. For many Chinese people, the "end of world history" in Fukuyama's meaning came with Confucius. The concept of having recently arrived at the best governance formula would strike many people in China as the intellectual equivalent of a cargo cult.

Democracy has its champions in China, mainly in the academic and civil society world. It has two restive autonomous areas, Hong Kong and Macau, which have been bitten by the democracy bug. It has strong role models in Taiwan and South Korea to foreshadow a possible path to democracy. And it has at least one former leader advocating this path. Democracy is therefore an option, but at this stage one would have to say it's an unlikely one. Any theory of the inevitability of the democratization of China would founder on the jagged rocks of today's reality. That reality shows that China is developing an alternative governance model based on performance legitimacy bolstered by episodes of officially inflamed nationalism. The Leninist single party is an indispensable part of the model. Elite cohesion will attempt to be maintained by continuing to grow the pie and thus give the party the option of purging some while appeasing others. Rule by whim has been replaced by a far more predictable and palatable process of rule by law, but it remains far from the rule-*of*-law concept that is mutually constitutive with democracy. The Chinese system is clearly resilient, and it shows every sign of also being durable. It may not be admired by people around the world, but it provides a pleasing model for nondemocratic governments. China's Leninist capitalism is clearly a challenger to liberal democracy.

Notes

1. China Daily, *China in Brief*, 2000, http://app1.chinadaily.com.cn/highlights/ChinaInBrief/economic_d.html.

2. World Bank, *China: Overview,* 2016, http://www.worldbank.org/en/country/china/overview.

3. Constitution of the People's Republic of China, Chapter II: The Fundamental Rights and Duties of Citizens, http://www.npc.gov.cn/englishnpc/Constitution/2007-11/15/content_1372964.htm.

4. Baogang He, *Rural Democracy in China: The Role of Village Elections* (London: Palgrave, 2007).

5. Zhao Ziyang, translated and edited by Bao Pu, Renee Chiang, and Adi Ignatius, *Prisoner of the State: The Secret Journal of Premier Zhao Ziyang* (New York: Simon and Schuster, 2009).

6. Ibid., p. 270.

7. Daniel Bell, *China's New Confucianism: Politics and Everyday Life in a Changing Society* (Princeton, NJ: Princeton University Press, 2008).

8. Roland Rich, *Pacific Asia in Quest of Democracy* (Boulder, CO: Lynne Rienner, 2007), p. 86.

9. Minxin Pei, "Is CCP Rule Fragile or Resilient?" *Journal of Democracy* 23, 1 (2012): 27–41.

10. David Shambaugh, "The Coming Chinese Crackup," *Wall Street Journal,* March 6, 2015.

11. *The Economist,* "No Ordinary Zhou," August 2, 2014.

12. Robert Klitgaard, *Controlling Corruption* (Berkeley: University of California Press, 1988).

13. OECD, *Education Indicators in Focus*, 2012, https://www.oecd.org/edu/50495363.pdf.

14. Rich, *Pacific Asia in Quest of Democracy,* p. 285.

15. Grant Evans, *Asia's Cultural Mosaic: An Anthropological Introduction* (Singapore: Prentice Hall, 1993), p. 1.

16. Li Tianchen, "New Trends in the Studies on Confucius and Confucianism," *Culture Mandala: The Bulletin of the Centre for East-West Cultural and Economic Studies* 3, 2 (1999): article 6.

17. Reg Little, "Confucius in Beijing: The Conference of the International Confucian Foundation," *Culture Mandala: The Bulletin of the Centre for East-West Cultural and Economic Studies* 1, 2 (1995): article 4.

18. Ingrid d'Hooghe, *China's Public Diplomacy* (The Hague: Netherlands Institute of International Relations Clingendael, 2015).

19. Ibid.

20. Christopher Patten, *East and West: China, Power, and the Future of Asia* (New York: Times, 1998), pp. 140–141.

21. Richard McCregor, "Zhou's Cryptic Caution Lost in Translation," *Financial Times,* June 10, 2011.

6

Jihadism Is Posing a New Challenge

This chapter deals with religions in general and Islam in particular. It is not about terrorism. Terrorism is a symptom, not a cause. Terrorism is a nasty irritant, but it is not a life-threatening danger to any society unless we make it so. The cause of most of today's terrorism is jihadism, and it is this phenomenon that is worthy of a closer look. It can only be examined as a challenge to Islam, which in turn can only be understood within a broader study of religion. From the perspective of this book, the germane issue about jihadism is its rejection of democracy and the nation-state.

Religion and Democracy

For the social scientist, there is a nagging doubt about the value of generalizations in this field. Societies differ markedly from each other. They have different geographies and different histories that are the drivers of change. They often have different beliefs and values. And there are clearly no pre-ordained paths for them to follow because in a sense they each make it up as they go along. But to take this doubt to its logical conclusion is to create a devastating vacuum. To say everyone is different and every step is new is to see the world as unknowable, unpredictable, and beyond comparison. While there are often surprising events, more often than not developments are consistent and expected. Let's face it, everybody makes basic generalizations to make sense of everyday life. Further, there would be no social science scholarship without generalizations.

They are necessary components of any system of understanding society. The problem can be rephrased as the need to understand the limits of generalizations and the need to look at predictability from the perspective of likelihood rather than certainty. Armed with this context, religion can better be discussed and the issues generalized.

The relationship between democracy and religion is tricky. There clearly needs to be some sort of modus vivendi between democracy and religion given the significant influence each has on society. But the relationship is not simple, partly because religions cannot be said to be democratic institutions and indeed may not see democracy as in their interests. In search of an accommodation, it is necessary to unpack a few basic aspects of religion from the political or sociological perspective. The first important premise is that religious dogma is necessarily unreliable. The world has seen hundreds of mutually contradictory religions—one god or many, this prophet or that, a certain belief or another. The chance that the dogma of one of these hundreds of religions is correct while all the others are wrong is unfathomably infinitesimal. While practitioners might look to hermeneutic interpretations to justify their acceptance or otherwise of democracy, logicians cannot. The content of religious texts is therefore inherently irrelevant and is a hindrance to the understanding of the role of religion in relation to society and democracy. What texts say is irrelevant, but what people who profess belief in those texts do is very much a matter worthy of study.

The majority of people in the world profess to belong to a religion, whereas only a small percentage has the courage to adopt agnosticism or atheism. So the role of religion may well be significant. Examining the majority that profess belief in religion, many if not most do so for reasons of ascription and identity rather than blind belief in religious dogma. Accordingly, religion is one of those attributes ascribed to a person at birth, which is then often followed by religious instruction and the practice of religious ritual. And religion is a key means of identification, sometimes but not always reinforced by other identifiers such as race and language. Indeed, where there are no racial or linguistic distinctions, religion usually is the key means of identification. Ascription and identification are often linked and strengthened by external indicators of religion—dress, dietary taboos, hirsuteness, and certain idiosyncratic conduct.

Ascriptive allegiances are particularly convenient for those claiming political leadership of a community defined by ascription—religion, race, language, displacement, or other form of inheritable minority or distinctive status. There is necessarily a common enemy—the other or others. Membership is not easily dispensed with, as it is cemented by the glue of allegiance to family. Orthodoxy invariably comes with a code of physical identification making it that much more difficult to relinquish. Ascriptive communities do not spring up easily or quickly; they usually claim distinctive creation myths and a heritage stretching back to time immemorial. Ascriptive communities can be seen as responding to certain evolutionary societal needs for security, cooperation, and connectedness. For leaders, these are captive communities. Leaders derive status, importance, and material benefits from their positions. They can tax or tithe, often select to their desires for marriage or sex, and wield influence by interpretation of texts and judging purported infractions. Leaders of ascriptive communities are unlikely to find it in their interests to submit to the vagaries of democracy.

Those with a blind belief in dogma or an unquestioning belief in and no identification beyond their own ascriptive communities will find it difficult to deal with the culture of democracy. Many people, however, are able to break free of their ascriptive allegiances, and modern urban environments have facilitated this form of liberation. But this is not a situation that can be rendered in clear black and white. There are many shades of gray. There are many way stations between uncompromising belief and quietist tolerant belief in a particular religion; and between total adherence to the sanctity of traditional community beliefs and accepting its place as one of many faiths within a multicultural society. It is in this gray area that democracy can find a place, and it is in the black-and-white world of absolute certainty that democracy is starved of the oxygen of deliberation and contestation that it needs to survive.

One important tactic that was developed to allow for the modus vivendi between democracy and religion is the accidental invention of secularism, constitutionally enshrined by the Founding Fathers. America was settled by victims of religious intolerance. Its first settlers were deeply religious communities that had not been allowed to practice their faith freely in their lands of origin. Their religions were invariably minority religions at odds with mighty state religions. Many religions, claiming absolute truth, have little choice but to be evangelical on the grounds that not to be so would be uncaring of the unbelievers. And it is more than likely that if any of the early minority religions of North America were able to transform itself into a hegemonic state religion, it would have done so. But it was tough enough maintaining orthodoxy within one's own community and plainly impossible to force that orthodoxy onto outsiders scattered in the American vastness. Accordingly, the religious communities of this new world took the pragmatic view that each should be allowed to practice its own religion and that no single religion should dominate the others. This brilliant realist acceptance of the situation in the new world in which they had settled was eventually given expression in the First Amendment to the US Constitution, which famously articulated the key proposition of secularism when it stated:

> Congress shall make no law respecting an establishment of religion, or prohibiting the free exercise thereof; or abridging the freedom of speech, or of the press; or the right of the people peaceably to assemble, and to petition the Government for a redress of grievances.

Far from being a protestation of atheism, as is mistakenly believed or mischievously misinterpreted in parts of the world, secularism is a means of defending religious practice by safeguarding it from the state or from other religions. Secularism is not antithetical to the practice of religion but allows it to fit within the practice of democracy. For this reason it has been adopted in one form or another in countries around the world. The dividing line between church and state is not always without various historical inconsistencies. For example, Britain's constitutional monarch is the head of a state religion, which means, according to the official monarchical website:

> In the United Kingdom, The Queen's title includes the words "Defender of the Faith." This means Her Majesty has a specific role in both the Church of England and the Church of Scotland. As established Churches, they are recognized by law as the official Churches of England and Scotland, respectively. In both England and Scotland, the established Churches are subject to the regulation of law.[1]

But the website goes on to say that "the principle of religious toleration is fully recognized both for those of other creeds and for those without any religious beliefs."

Another apparent anomaly is the fact that one of Germany's principal political parties is the Christian Democrat Union (CDU). The post–Wolrd War II establishment of the CDU needs to be seen in its historical context. One reason for the rise of Adolf Hitler was the division of political party support among Christians between Catholics and Protestants, thus weakening what should have been a strong Christian voice against Hitler. The establishment of the CDU was intended to bring all Christian voices together in one political party that would henceforth act as a bulwark against extremism.[2] Thus, while its adherents may be motivated by

Christian ideals, the CDU does not privilege any one church and, indeed, is dedicated to secularism and modernity.

Turning to another great democracy, India, one also finds a major political party, the Bharatiya Janata Party (BJP), the current incumbent, apparently based on a religion, Hinduism. Although Hinduism is clearly the majority religion in India, there are also many millions of adherents to other religions, including Islam, Buddhism, and Christianity. For example, there are as many Muslims in India as in Pakistan. So is this party practicing ascriptive politics based on a crude majoritarian calculus? Not according to its platform, which claims that "Hindutva [BJP's underlying philosophy] is a nationalist, and not a religious or theocratic, concept" and which quotes a Mahatma Gandhi saying, "There is in Hinduism enough room for Jesus as there is for Muhammad, Zoroaster and Moses." Of course, this does not guarantee that some adherents and even leaders will not fall back on crude majoritarian tactics, but it is important to begin with the premise that this is not the party's philosophy or stated intention.

One therefore can find in successful democracies different ways of accommodating religious aspects of society without religious leaders also being political leaders or religious laws being national laws. As was noted earlier, in one example a sovereign must be of a particular religion and is given a religious title ("Defender of the Faith"), but this does not translate into direct political power. There are also the examples of political parties on two continents that may be inspired by certain religious ideals but nevertheless behave in secular ways by not trying to impose their religious views through political means. Are these examples useful in relation to finding an accommodation between democracy and Islam?

The Arab and Islamic Worlds in Context

Why is the Arab world of particular significance to the international community and to the issue of democracy? After all, the combined population of the nations comprising the Arab League is only 370 million, which amounts to only about 5 percent of the world's population. Oil is, needless to say, an important part of the response. But even when the oil runs out, the Arab world will remain significant. One reason is because developments in the Arab world suggest that there might be a viable alternative to democracy.

The third wave of democratization that gathered force with the fall of the Berlin Wall was the first truly global wave. Its waters washed over Asia, Africa, South and Central America, and of course Eastern Europe. Central Asia did not feel much of an effect, with the notable exception of Mongolia, which continues to hold fast to democracy. Central Asia had to deal with "desovietization" as well as issues of national identity and the collapsing CMEA economic system. Central Asian countries have no history of civil society formation or multiparty contestation, and it is perhaps explicable that there has been a continuation of authoritarian government though events in Kyrgyzstan in 2010 demonstrated that Central Asia's people may yet demand democracy.

The other region initially unaffected by the third wave was the Arab region. One can construct elaborate explanations for this Arab exceptionalism going back to the Ottoman Empire and the subsequent colonial divisions and spoliation, but the popular uprisings of the Arab Spring that burst forth in Tunisia in late 2010 and spread to half a dozen other Arab states suggested that Arab people were not exceptions to the rule but simply late to the party. From the perspective of the universal value and applicability of democracy this level of Arab demand filled an important lacuna. The Arab region is significant because it completes the universal picture of all or parts of every region and every civilization turning to democracy.

But as I noted previously, the main demand of the Arab Spring demonstrators was not democracy but dignity. Many saw these as broadly overlapping terms or even synonyms. The democracy support community certainly adopted this perspective and poured resources into the Arab world in support of its thesis. That thesis is well-founded only if there is no competing ideology that also promises to deliver dignity. But there is another ideology promising dignity. Islam is that ideology. In this regard, the term *ideology* is more appropriate than *religion* because, as will be discussed, Islam is focused not only on one's spiritual fulfillment but also on one's temporal existence. Like other utopian ideologies, Islam promises a system of law and government that will bring perfection in this world.

The question of the Arab peoples' demand for democracy remains open. If it turns out that it is democracy that they are ultimately after, then the value seen in democracy is truly universal and the task before the nations of the world is to work hard to turn that value into a working and sustainable system that delivers strong (though far from perfect) outcomes. But if the people of the Arab world turn to Islam as their form of law and government, then democracy cannot be claimed to be the universally desired system. Democracy may not be utopian, but it does see itself as universally applicable, so for an entire region of the world to hold out is a significant detriment.

The discussion thus far has dealt with the Arab world, which for ease of reference can be defined as the twenty-two nations of the Arab League. Within the world of Islam, however, this is a minority. There are well over one billion Muslims outside the Arab League nations. They comprise the majority in several large non-Arab nations—Indonesia, Pakistan, Bangladesh, Iran, Turkey, Afghanistan, and Malaysia—and several former Soviet republics. Using the Freedom House guide, none of these countries, nor any from the Arab League, are seen as "free," though several are in the "partly free" category and hold competitive elections.[3] Iran also holds elections, but the religious establishment has the discretion to disqualify candidates, and even once in office, ultimate power resides with the religious hierarchy; this makes Iran a theocracy and clearly "not free." Afghanistan is in the midst of a continuing civil war and is also "not free." None of the former Soviet republics are "free." The remaining countries are all "partly free" and therefore more interesting from a democracy perspective.

Pakistan and Bangladesh have been holding elections for many years, and they are often meaningful and expressive. But the military has cast a constant shadow over both countries by either violently taking over or exercising a type of veto power. Pakistan is on the verge of its own civil war, which is ongoing in the tribal areas bordering Afghanistan and whose tentacles are reaching into the cities. Interestingly, the cause of the current chaos is not democracy but Islam. Pakistan is inextricably tied to Islam because the partition of the British Raj created Pakistan as an expressly Islamic state to distinguish it from India. One interpretation of Pakistan's current travails is that it cannot form a social contract as to the meaning of what it entails to be an Islamic state. Bangladesh's problems have more to do with an irreconcilable form of winner-takes-all partisanship that has a political grip over the nation, but we are also currently seeing an ideological wing of Islam casting its shadow over the country.

Indonesia and Malaysia have also been holding elections for many years. In the Suharto period of Indonesia's modern history, elections were used not as a means to determine leadership but as a formal celebration of existing leadership. In the post-Suharto era, elections have come to have far greater significance, and the election in 2014 of Joko Widodo as president marks the first election of a post-Suharto politician and a final break from that period of Indonesian history. There are several Islamic political parties in Indonesia, but they are having difficulty exerting any great significance in political decisionmaking, though if the wearing of head scarves by women is an indication, Islam is certainly having an increasing social impact.

Malaysia has not had a change of government at the federal level since independence, more than half a century ago. Practicing a type of consociational politics bolstered by soft authoritarianism, the United Malays National Organization (UMNO) together with its Chinese and Indian coalition partners has won every national (but not every state) election. Unlike Indonesia, where some 90 percent of the population lists itself as Muslim, only about 60 percent of Malaysians call themselves Muslim, and the divide is bolstered by ethnic divisions in that the non-Muslim community is primarily of Chinese or Indian ancestry. For much of its history, Malaysia's major opposition party has been the Parti Islam Se-Malaysia (PAS), which sought to challenge UMNO in the Malay Muslim heartland. The result has been a contest between the two Malay parties as to which is the more faithful guardian of Islamic law and values. The dilemma for both parties is that the further this pushed them toward the Islamification of society, the more difficult it was to gain non-Malay support. Anwar Ibrahim and his Justice Party has tried to trump the existing discourse through appeals to democracy and anticorruption with considerable but not decisive success.

Turkey also presents an interesting case study in the place of Islam in politics. For several generations Turkey followed Kemal Atatürk's vision of becoming a modern secular European nation, with the military in the vanguard of this movement. In 2001, Recep Erdoğan, a popular mayor of Istanbul who had fallen foul of the military, established the Justice and Development Party, which swept into office the following year on a platform of reform, anticorruption, and support for Islamic ideals. After some legal squabbling, Erdoğan regained his right to run for office and became prime minister. Ever since, Turkey has been conducting a national conversation, expressed in words and votes, about the place of Islam in society and politics. Having put down the 2016 coup, Erdoğan is consolidating his power and his Islamic vision for Turkey.

In several non-Arab countries with a Muslim majority holding competitive elections, Islam has become the central issue in politics. In Pakistan it is central to national self-identity. In Turkey it centers on the social mores of society and the degree to which Islam will be their arbiter. In Malaysia it expresses itself as a means of winning the Malay vote between two Malay parties, both bidding to be seen as the true champions of Islam. Yet it could not be said that in any of these three large countries there is mainstream support for Islam as an ideology to govern the country. It is more about changing the look and feel of society, displaying indices of piety, and fighting Western permissiveness. Support for Islam the ideology comes from the Arab world.

Islam as Ideology

At what point does a religion cross the threshold and become an ideology? Both religion and ideology can be defined as a set of beliefs and theories to explain the world. Religion does so by reference to a god or gods or some other superhuman being that has a critical role in the explanatory narrative. Further to its set of beliefs, ideology has a vision for the whole society and a means to arrive at this vision. Religions usually list prescribed and proscribed conduct that will please this god. The wider the prescriptions and proscriptions, the closer religion comes to ideology. That is because ideology complements its set of beliefs with its own set of prescriptions and proscriptions to achieve its goal. Whereas religion may satisfy itself with individuals' spiritual well-being, ideology is necessarily interested in temporal matters. Perhaps all religions began as ideologies but gradually moved their sphere of influence toward the spiritual and away from the temporal.

The key distinction then is the breadth of the set of prescriptions and proscriptions, the set of conduct that is *halal* or *haram*. Beginning with the most common, many religions have food taboos as this is an easy way to distinguish one set of believers from the others and also imposes a certain discipline on the religious community. Another common code of conduct concerns dress as, again, this is important to distinguish believers from the others. It also allows for certain gender biases to be given scope, a subject that will be discussed in Chapter 8. Because religions need to sustain themselves on this Earth, it is common for them to have certain taxing power (tithing) though with limited enforcement capacity. It is also common for them to have gatekeeping rules to allow believers to enter or former believers to leave the religion. These conversion and apostasy rules can be a source of conflict in society.

The main friction point between religion and secular society concerns family law. Family law covers the rites of passage—birth, initiation, marriage, death—and various aspects of life associated with these, such as divorce, inheritance, and adoption. The battle between secular society and religion traditionally has centered on the extent to which religion and religious hierarchy will govern the family law aspects of life and whether the state will establish a parallel and competing structure. One of the key distinctions between Christian and Muslim society concerns the degree to which the latter allows a far wider role for religion in family law. While religious governance of family law may well lead to injustices and gender bias, it does not in itself cross the threshold to ideology. Admittedly, a very broad interpretation of family law imposing rules on whom one is allowed to see and to be seen by, on limitations on mobility, on the proscription of certain cultural products, and on the conduct of personal and business affairs comes close to an ideological view of the world in its effects on those subject to its jurisdiction; but in general, family law is the traditional field of battle between religion and society. Of course, this is a distinction based less on logic than on history and practice. An argument might be advanced that the family is part of the private realm and thus should not be governed by the institutions of the public sphere, but this distinction is becoming ever more difficult to sustain. If there is one important lesson feminists have taught us it is that the personal is political. Until recently, the arc of history has been toward the limitation of religious rules on society even in relation to family law. But has that arc reached its zenith?

Religion becomes ideology when it advances well beyond family law to other aspects of life. When it purports to be the arbiter of what is criminal, it has crossed the line. When it asserts control over enforcement of rules, it has crossed the line. When it claims relations with outsiders can only be viewed in a religious context, it has crossed the line. And when it insists on applying its dogma literally to establish society's rules, it has clearly crossed the line.

Most Muslims wish to contain the struggle of their religion to the confines of the spiritual and the family. Most Muslims recognize national authority and accede to its laws. Most Muslims view the world as a collection of nation-states. Most Muslims are tolerant of other religions. For most Muslims the public conversation concerns the reach of religion on matters of family law but not beyond. For most Muslims, the sort of accommodations that other religions have concluded in their societies—concerning political parties based on religious ideals but not dogma and symbolic public positions being held by co-religionists— would be satisfactory.

Jihadism

The jihadis are not like most Muslims, and their worldview has crossed the threshold from religion to ideology. Jihadis are not reformers. They are not pragmatists. They are not fatalists patiently awaiting theistically driven developments. They may not be united and there may be tactical difference among them, but the jihadis have a fully formed worldview, a utopian goal, and a clear means of getting to it—jihad. There was once a definition of *jihad* as a personal battle for self-improvement, but the insistent howls of the political jihadis have shouted down that meaning.

Today the only commonly understood meaning of *jihad* is pitiless armed struggle to reestablish the caliphate and bring peace and harmony to a Sunni Islam world.

In 2014 a well-armed group of jihadis took control of a significant parcel of territory in Iraq and Syria and declared the Islamic Caliphate. This was a sign of confidence verging on bravado and also a propaganda message to all Muslims that the Mohammedan vision (as interpreted by the jihadis) was not a theoretical construct but an exciting and current project. What does a caliphate entail? The constructive response is that it entails a return to a mythical time a millennium and a half ago when for a fleeting moment Mohammed established paradise on earth. The deconstructive response is a little more complicated. The caliphate is a rejection of the nation-state. It is a rejection of the construction of the international community based on the Treaties of Westphalia in the seventeenth century whereby the local secular prince would have the sovereign right to govern (that is tax, conscript, and impose his religion on) the people within the confines of the territory he controlled. This European invention paralleled the rise of colonialism, which saw it ultimately imposed on the rest of the world such that today there are some two hundred sovereign states. The caliphate is a rejection of those two hundred states. The caliphate is also necessarily a rejection of the international system constructed by those two hundred states. It is necessarily a rejection of international law, the inescapable building blocks of which are sovereign states. It is therefore also a rejection of the thousands of treaties concluded and the international organizations constructed by those sovereign states. That is why communications between the jihadis and the rest of the world are so stilted. The world talks about humanitarian law and Geneva Conventions; the jihadis talk about the Koran and tales of Mohammed and his companions.

Along with the rejection of the international system is the rejection of legislated law. This is a sweeping rejection applying to all positive law from the constitution down to enabling regulations, because such laws are human-made and therefore necessarily imperfect whereas Koranic law was written by god himself through the hand of the illiterate Mohammed and is therefore perfect by definition. Between these opposing views there can only be a dialogue of the deaf. All the virtues that modern society might see in the passage of laws—the debate over options, contestation over different policy visions, deliberations about likely outcomes, eventual adjudication by skilled and dedicated jurists, compassionate enforcement by a caring government—are to the jihadis simply evidence of such laws' imperfection.

Democracy fares no better in the eyes of the jihadis. The first reason is that democracy and sovereignty remain "joined at the hip."[4] This is because every democracy needs to be able to identify its demos through a census and registration process within a defined territory. And because the world is currently organized in a system of some two hundred sovereign states, it is within each of those states that the institutions of democracy are constructed. Many Arab Islamist movements, such as the Muslim Brotherhood in Egypt, Hamas in Gaza (a part of a putative state), and Ennahda in Tunisia, have accommodated themselves to this reality and found doctrinal interpretations that justify the decision to form a political party and run for office in elections within a sovereign state. The main doctrinal support for democracy in the Koran flows from the use of the term *shura,* meaning consultation in a single passage.

The jihadis distinguish themselves from these Islamists by rejecting democracy on a number of grounds.[5] To begin with, democracy is a human-constructed system, not god-made, and therefore not acceptable to those who follow god's will (as they see it). The rejection of the sovereign state also logically leads to the rejection of that institution to which it is joined at the hip. And it is the embrace of the politics of a sovereign state through participation in democratic processes that has caused the great rift between the jihadis and nationalist Islamist movements. Going beyond the doctrinal issues, however, the jihadis see in democracy only the theoretical rationalization for the autocracies that dominate the Arab world and for the states of Europe and America that support them. Grievance is the fuel that propels jihadis, and the conflation of democracy with the policies of the states they despise is a convenient way of tarring the concept with the brush of grievance.

As noted in Chapter 1, Jihad has certain attractions. Doctrinally, it is simple to understand. The world it describes is one of black and white, right and wrong, allowed and forbidden, *halal* and *haram.* There are no difficult gray areas. Tactically, jihad is particularly convenient. After all, when god has established heaven on earth and shown the path toward it (jihad), nothing can stand in the way. Everything done to progress along that path is justified. Concepts such as human rights or humanitarian law are simply seen as imperfect and inferior positive law at best, and the tricks of the enemies of god at worst. Emotionally, jihad is exciting. The concept of a soldier of god has been a recruiting tool for millennia. Why spend years studying, then competing against many others, while often being discriminated against, simply to achieve a boring middle-class existence when the prospect of adventure in the service of god beckons? Simple, convenient, exciting; no wonder thousands of Muslims from all over the world including Western countries are flocking to the Levant in the service of jihad. Of course, those thousands of jihadis constitute the smallest fraction of the Muslim world. The vast majority of Sunnis understands the reckless folly of the jihadi mission. They understand that it will fail to live up to the impossible rhetoric. They are embarrassed and discomfited by an ideology that tries to turn the clock back a millennium and a half. But as in any large group there will be some who stand outside the bounds of group constraint. That is the catchment area jihadi recruitment targets.

Is there a competing political movement that stands in the way of jihad? On the battlefield, jihadis may win or lose various skirmishes, but the war can only be won within the Muslim world as a whole and the Arab world in particular. The bitterness of the feud between jihadis and the Arab nationalist Islamists is a sign that this is the key friction point of the war. Both groups are fueled by similar grievances and appeal to similar disaffected individuals. The nationalists have chosen to accept the modern world as it is, including the existence of sovereign states over which they wish to exert influence. On the whole the Arab nationalist political movements have heeded the call of the mid-twentieth-century Egyptian Muslim Brotherhood to work peacefully. Success in peaceful political contestation through incumbency and the patronage and policy power it confers would be the best argument in the contest against the jihadis. But democratic success is always compromised. There is forever the fear of losing the next election. There are always the constraints on action imposed by positive law, by querulous civil society, and by the international community. Democracy cannot lead to utopia, though it can avoid dystopia. Yet even this constrained form of success has eluded the Arab Islamist parties. Hamas in its frustration has turned to armed conflict, the result of which can only be loss and further grievance. The Egyptian Muslim Brotherhood won office but governed incompetently. A democratic system should have been allowed to operate and to punish that government at the polls, but instead the army stepped in, and one effect may be to push the Brotherhood to violence. Ennahda holds out some prospect of democratic success and is the role model for finding an accommodation between Islam and democracy in the Arab Sunni world.

Wahhabism

Developments in the Arab world are far more influential than developments in the Muslim world as a whole. While Islam has pretensions to be a global religion and, indeed, *the* global religion, it is an Arabic-language religion—as god wrote the Koran in Arabic—and this establishes the Arabic-speaking people as its privileged members. It follows that Arabs do not consider the non-Arabic speaking countries as particularly interesting or relevant as role models. John Stuart Mill counselled to only compare like with like, and it is human nature to focus on difference. Racial, ethnic, and linguistic differences trump religious similarities. Political developments in Indonesia and Malaysia or Pakistan and Afghanistan are not followed closely in the Arab streets. Politics in Turkey are of greater interest given the Ottoman connection to the Arab world and Turkey's role as a regional hub. Thus, while academics and commentators may look to precedents of Islamic accommodation with democracy in places such as Indonesia and Turkey, most Arabs do so only fitfully.

The types of Islam being practiced are also quite different within and outside the Arab world. Southeast Asian Islam, for example, is hardly seen as relevant to the Arab world because it is famously syncretic.[6] In this region, Islam was an accretion on previous religious practices and was happily blended into them. The Talibanization of Afghanistan and perhaps even Pakistan is of more interest to traditional communities, though it has very little to attract sophisticated urban Arabs. Wahhabism is the Islam that is making waves in the Arab world. The impact of Wahhabism can be measured in monetary terms: "Estimates of Saudi spending on the funding of Muslim cultural institutions across the globe and the forging of close ties to non-Wahhabi Muslim leaders and intelligence agencies in various Muslim nations that have bought into significant elements of the Wahhabi worldview range from $75 to $100 billion."[7]

I recently taught a short course at a university in Najaf, in southern Iraq, a city that prides itself on being the birthplace of Shiite Islam. It seemed far removed from the chaos in other parts of Iraq, and the city had a strong sense of community. I was struck by the commonly repeated analysis from academics and clergy that all the problems of the Arab world flow from Wahhabism. The problem was not the Sunni branch of the religion but, in their view, the Wahhabi sect. A few years earlier I had been giving a talk in Tunis, capital of Tunisia, and in the discussion that followed, several people talked about the destabilizing tactics of the Saudi and Qatari governments in propagating Wahhabism in Tunisia. One participant lost his temper, asking, "Why do these people want to impose a Bedouin religion on me? I am a city person and I will follow Islam as a city person." There is considerable truth in this accusation. Wahhabism is the biggest part of the problem of jihadism. The problem flows from the notion of "purity" propagated by Wahhabism. It is, on reflection, an absurd concept in relation to any religion. Religion is a function of human society, and it cannot logically exist in a "pure" form. Furthermore, it leads to the struggle against impurity, from which concepts such as *takfir* flow. *Takfir* is the accusation that because of his or her conduct the accused has turned away from Islam and should be treated as an apostate, for which some believe capital punishment should apply. So to the Wahhabi worldview, a rejection of this Bedouin sect is apostasy.

Whether jihadis trace their doctrine to Wahhabism or not, jihadism flows directly from its concepts. That does not necessarily mean that the Saudi government is supporting jihadism. In fact, Saudi Arabia is a victim of jihadi terrorism. But jihadism draws doctrinally from Wahhabi ideology and financially from private Gulf money, itself generated by oil. Wahhabism is based on a simplistic concept to return to "pure" Islam. It is an attempt to turn back the clock 1,400 years to the time of the Prophet. It draws on the religion's creation myths and takes them literally. It is necessarily intolerant of any other strand of Islam. Jihadism has borrowed these concepts and in many ways is a purer form of Islam than the Saudi Wahhabi version, which has partly accommodated itself to the modern international community. Jihadis accuse the Saudis of being impure, demonstrating the plasticity of the concept of purity.

The Wahhabi push for Islamic purity, patriarchy, and asceticism has had limited influence in Southeast Asia but far greater impact in Pakistan and Afghanistan, where it provides a major means of schooling. The closest Sunni Islam comes to a ruling hierarchy is the Wahhabi establishment in Saudi Arabia, and, bolstered by Saudi wealth, Wahhabism is able to exert influence in the Sunni world. As noted, it has a tense relationship with jihadism, with which it shares doctrinal similarities but with which it differs on the issue of sovereignty. Saudi Arabia's social contract is to grant the Saud family the right to govern while allowing an unfettered Wahhabi monopoly on religious issues. The problem with this social contract is its imprecision. Problems of governance can be papered over while wealth is generated from oil. Mismanagement and corruption can be forgiven when there is so much to go around. Whenever the Saudi authorities are confronted with public disquiet, they merely shower more money on Saudi citizens. The problem arises more acutely over the other part of the social contract: religious issues. How broadly does this term extend? It extends to teaching Wahhabism all over the Muslim world. It extends to funding groups that share Wahhabi ideals. And there is no doubt in my mind that it extends to funding jihadism. Once again, the common denominator for success is oil—all that funding must come from somewhere.

Which leads me to a sour piece of optimism. Jihadism is weak in numbers and influence, and so it must resort to the weapon of the weak, terrorism. Ideologically and financially jihadism is largely fueled by Wahhabism. Wahhabism's global influence flows from oil. When that oil stops being pumped because the world recognizes that to protect the planet the oil reserves must remain stranded, Wahhabism will slowly but surely lose its global influence. Jihadism will lose its principal patron. And terrorism will recede.

Conclusion

The ideological choices facing the denizens of the Arab streets are not particularly attractive. Democracy is losing its soft power and is associated with Western permissiveness, including homosexuality. The type of liberal constitutionalism in support of democracy has fewer and fewer adherents in part because of the conflation of this Western developed system with unpopular Western policies. The political parties that champion this system are particularly weak and only have a hope of success in Tunisia. In Egypt, for example, the champions of democracy gravitate toward civil society rather than politics and therefore have the more limited role of carping from the sidelines.

Islam is the force that motivates people in the Arab world today. The expression of Islam in politics takes several forms. From democracy's perspective, the most hopeful path is the acceptance by Islamic political parties of the institutions of democracy and perhaps eventually the culture of democracy. Various Islamic parties agreed to play by the rules of the game, but the results have not been positive. The Islamic Salvation Front in Algeria was a straw in the wind. It won local elections and began the process of learning how to govern at the local level. In 1991 it won national elections, but before it could take the reins of government an army coup, with tacit Western support, toppled it, leading to a decade of bitter civil war. The next great chapter was written by the Muslim Brotherhood in Egypt, with very similar results as in Algeria though Egypt has thus far avoided civil war. Once again, only Ennahda in Tunisia shows some promise of finding an accommodation between Islamism and democracy.

Inertia is often a popular choice and, it can be argued, has been the dominant choice in the Arab world for many decades. Inertia means rule by either kings or generals. Many people in the Arab world will laud the stabilizing role of monarchy. It is the system in use in much of the Gulf, in Jordan, and in Morocco. A distinction needs to be made between the royal families of the Arab world and the constitutional monarchies of northern Europe. A couple of little anecdotes may illustrate the issue. Many years ago, as a junior diplomat in Paris, I accompanied the Australian ambassador to Rabat, where he presented credentials to King Hassan II. We were not to wear suits, national dress, or even evening dress for the occasion. The Moroccan embassy in Paris (from where many ambassadors are accredited to Morocco) gave me a sheet of instructions explaining that we had to hire tails and top hat for the ceremony. We were dressed to the tails, but the Chief of Protocol who accompanied us to the palace was in his military whites. What struck me most that day were the hundreds of male courtiers sitting on the floor along both sides of the long corridors in their comfortable *jalabiyyah*s playing with their prayer beads and doing strictly nothing. It would have looked the same hundreds of years ago. Now fast-forward to a few years back in Oslo where I found myself in a delegation accompanying Ted Turner, who dropped in on the palace to say hi to his old yachting buddy, King Harald V of Norway. In fact it was Queen Sonja who gave us the tour of the palace. What stands out in my memory was a rather tetchy explanation by the queen of how mean the parliament was being in denying her the funds to replace the tatty curtains. Thus can one witness the difference between the medieval monarch and the modern constitutional monarch.

They may address each other as brothers and sisters, but they are different species. The northern European constitutional monarchies are true figureheads. Their political power is minimal. Importantly, they have little or no private wealth and are dependent on the public purse. In return they provide an important service as role models, national representatives, and chief mourners in national tragedies. The Arab royal families are executive rulers or hold a veto power on government decisions. Far from being poor, they are the wealthiest families in their kingdoms, and they use their political power to protect and indeed increase their wealth. While they retain this wealth, they cannot be transformed into northern European–style constitutional monarchs. Inertia means remaining under this type of feudalism, with royal paternalism being the best possible outcome. The Jordanian royal family seems at first blush to be the exception, but when I tried to discuss this with civil society colleagues in Amman, they went into silent mode, so perhaps we should leave a question mark there.

Are the generals different? They may begin their tenure as popular heroes preaching pan-Arabism or Baathism or simply anticolonialism, but they invariably fall into the pharaonic mindset and begin to resemble kings. They prefer dynastic politics, with the best example being the Assads in Syria. They rule through absolutism, with the best example being Qhaddafi in Libya. They develop megalomania, with the best example being Saddam in Iraq. These are the precedents open to Abdel Fattah el-Sisi in Egypt, along with three other pharaonic former military figures—Gamal Abdel Nasser, Anwar Sadat, and Hosni Mubarak.

A rejection of greedy monarchs or absolutist generals should lead to democracy. But with its soft power in retreat, militant Islam becomes a viable alternative. Compared to the deeply unattractive Wahhabi Bedouin style of Islam, the tribal mentality of the Afghani and Pakistani Taliban, and the failed attempts to govern by nationalist Islamists, modern jihadism as practiced by al-Qaeda or the Islamic State has its attractions. It attracts adherents because of its simplicity, convenience, and excitement. A disaffected Arab youth with few prospects, little hope, and many grievances will see the jihadi project as the adventure of a lifetime. And so will Muslim youths in the Western or Russian worlds, especially if they are already on the wrong side of the law. Through the eyes of many young people, jihad is far more appealing than democracy.

Notes

1. Royal Family webpage, "The Queen, the Church and Other Faiths", https://www.royal.uk/queens-relationship-churches-england-and-scotland-and-other-faiths.

2. CDU, "History of the CDU," http://www.cdu.de/partei/geschichte.

3. Freedom House, *Freedom in the World,* 2014, http://freedomhouse.org/report-types/freedom-world#.U_Nz5PldVlo.

4. Laurence Whitehead, "State Sovereignty and Democracy," in Peter Burnell and Richard Youngs (eds.), *New Challenges to Democratization* (Oxford: Routledge, 2010), p. 27.

5. Nelly Lahoud, *The Jihadis' Path to Self-Destruction* (London: Hurst, 2010). In particular, see the chapter entitled "Why Jihad and Not Democracy."

6. Merle Ricklefs, *Mystic Synthesis in Java: A History of Islamization from the Fourteenth to the Early Nineteenth Centuries* (Norwalk, CT: EastBridge, 2006).

7. James M. Dorsey, "Creating Frankenstein: The Saudi Export of Wahhabism," 2016, http://mideastsoccer.blogspot.sg/2016/03/creating-frankenstein-saudi-export-of.html.

7

Where Does the
Middle Class Stand?

This chapter will gallop through some theories of democratization. These are not theories of democracy, which is a field approaching philosophy, but theories of why and how countries become democracies—a subject anchored in the political science literature. The question is not without significance. Figure 2.2 listed all the democracy support institutions; these groups must rely on some sort of theory of democratization to guide and sustain their work, whether they articulate the theory or not. *Theory* can be a terrifying word. To a layperson it seems to denote complicated formulae with Greek letters, the sort of thing Sheldon from *The Big Bang Theory* would write on his whiteboard. But *theory* is simply another word for *causation*—what caused this to happen? What caused these countries to become democracies? The complication does not flow from the concept of causation with which everybody is comfortable, but from the difficulty of determining causes given the vast number of inputs in the process of democratization and the long length of time for those inputs to have their causative effects. The difficulty lies in sifting through what is causation, correlation, or simply coincidence. *Theory* implies a certain amount of generalization to determine the main cause or causes of democratization.

Three Theories of Democratization

The dominant theory of democratization is modernization theory, which will be the subject of the next section. It might be useful, however, to look at a few competing theories to determine the place of modernization theory and the weight it should be accorded. Examining theories is also important because good policy flows from good theory. If a policy wishes to have a certain effect, then one needs a theory of how to cause that effect.

The first and easiest to deal with is E. E. Schattschneider's theory that "political parties created democracy and modern democracy is unthinkable save in terms of parties."[1] This sentence seems strangely ahistorical. In the early years of American democracy, the concept of political parties or factions was frowned upon. Legislators were intended to be individuals voted in by their peers because of their high moral and intellectual standing and were expected to vote their conscience at all times. Banding together among like-minded representatives was seen as akin to cheating. But this idealized form of representative democracy could not withstand the forces of modern history, in particular the movement of Europe's social tectonic plates caused by Marxism. Whereas political cleavages in pre-Marxist times may have been dominated by religion, language, and locality, the Marxist analysis established the far more fundamental owner-worker cleavage, which would dominate politics for the next century and beyond. One of the manifestations of the Marxist cleavage was the emergence of massive workers' parties, which then had to be matched by parties supporting the owners of capital often arguing their case on the basis of conserving existing structures, institutions, and ideals. The workers' parties developed the "cradle to grave" mentality of seeking to improve the lot of their supporters in every aspect of social and public life. They developed political platforms and the party discipline necessary for its delivery. Conservative parties had no option but to try to match their political savvy and enthusiasm.

In this sense, political parties created the democracies with which we are now familiar. Political parties created democracy as we know it. And because nearly all the democracy support institutions come from countries where democracy follows this logic of political parties, it is a major part of their mission to help nurture political parties so that they in turn can establish democracies in the image of the donor democracies. One problem associated with implementing a program based on this theory is that countries in the global South have not traversed the Marxist revolutions in the same way Europe did. The political parties created in the global South are based on the worker-owner cleavage only rarely; rather, they tend to be based on the pre-Marxist cleavages of religion, language, and locality. A possible exception may be the political parties that sprang from successful national liberation movements, many of which professed a certain Marxist bent. But experience has shown that these parties are more focused on the logic of incumbency and all its trappings than any policies they may have professed during the struggle.

Looking at the empirical evidence, the towering example of a political party from the global South that built democracy in its country is the Congress Party of India, established in 1885 and still competing for power but prepared (with one exception, during the 1975–1977 state of emergency) to alternate and allow others to step in where the electoral results so dictate. On the flip side, one can look at the political parties emerging from national liberation movements in southern Africa. There may be progress toward democratization in these countries, but in some two hundred years of the combined independence or postapartheid period covering almost thirty elections, there has been no alternation in power in Angola, Botswana, Namibia, Mozambique, or South Africa.[2] Needless to say, the same is true of Zimbabwe, where Robert Mugabe and his party have ruled since independence and where his wife is showing every sign of taking over from the nonagenerian.

Another relevant issue concerns changes in the role and makeup of Western political parties in recent times. In short, parties are losing partisans, and the era of the massive cradle-to-grave political parties seems to be over.[3] Indeed, there is a suggestion that in recent times political parties are being supplanted by political movements, a more amorphous and transient phenomenon. Are the democracy activists therefore promoting a model that no longer exists in their own countries? Or has the nature of membership and support evolved to more fluid twenty-first-century forms? Perhaps the best conclusion is that the empirical evidence is mixed, but without necessarily endorsing Schattschneider's theory, one can conclude that political parties are an essential element in a functioning democracy. Indeed, my own study of three attempts to take political parties out of parts of parliaments demonstrated the futility of this exercise, as parties will either infiltrate or isolate the nonpartisan chambers.[4]

The next theory of democratization concerns human rights. The official literature of the UN and the major Western countries treat democracy and human rights as coterminous—inhabiting the same space and having the same boundaries. They are seen as mutually reinforcing and essential components of each other. Democracy needs the freedoms protected by human rights, and human rights are best protected and promoted in democracies. Each concept has its set of supporters, and it is an unfortunate feature that these communities are at times in competition with each other, vying for status and resources. The theoretical competition turns on the issue of causality while nearly all articulation follows the official "coterminous" line.

The basic principle of democracy flowing from human rights is set out in Article 21 of the Universal Declaration on Human Rights, which describes "the will of the people" as "the basis of the authority of government" and calls for that will to be discerned through "periodic and general elections." Observation of this principle—put in binding treaty form in Article 25 of the 1966 International Covenant on Civil and Political Rights (ICCPR)—establishes the procedural mechanisms that allow democracy to flourish. It was not until 1996 that the United Nations Human Rights Committee, a body of experts established under the ICCPR, adopted General Comment 25 elaborating on the rights enshrined in Article 25.[5] The General Comment's interpretation of Article 25 represents a considerable strengthening of the democratic ideal. Applied correctly, its provisions would ensure free and fair elections. It requires freedom of expression, assembly, and association (paragraph 12); enshrines nondiscrimination with respect to the citizen's right to vote (paragraph 3); rejects any condition of eligibility to vote or stand for office based on political affiliation (paragraph 15); calls for voters to be free to support or oppose the government without undue influence or coercion of any kind (paragraph 19); and requires states reporting under the covenant to explain how the different political views in the community are represented in elected bodies (paragraph 22). General Comment 25 provides the jurisprudence that gives teeth to the covenant's obligation to hold "genuine periodic elections." It establishes a checklist that, if followed, will result in a functioning electoral democracy—and, if combined with adherence to the other obligations in the basic human rights treaties, a functioning liberal democracy.

In 1999 and 2000 the principal UN human rights body adopted, though far from unanimously, two resolutions on the "right to democracy" and the "consolidation of democracy." Resolution 47 of 2000 advanced the matter by describing the right to vote as "a free and fair process . . . open to multiple parties," thus establishing that single-party polities could not possibly be democratic. It must be said that the argument in favor of human rights as the way to democracy has not been particularly vigorously advanced since these resolutions were passed and has run into academic opposition.[6] One reason that the democracy community has not particularly pursued this argument is that it would be self-defeating from a resource mobilization perspective—if human rights necessarily lead to democratization, then let's spend money on promoting human rights rather than democracy. From a theoretical perspective the problem of causation remains unresolved. Rather than one causing the other, perhaps both result from a different cause or set of causes?

The third theory has a longer pedigree because it flows from the observations of Alexis de Tocqueville when he traveled around the New World in the nineteenth century.[7] Tocqueville recognized the importance of associational energy in the America he visited in the 1830s, seeing it as a key requirement for democracy. Unlike the Europe from which he came, where communal life was organized either by the nobleman or by a deeply hierarchical church, associational life in the New World was spontaneous and self-generating. It is the fact that this organized realm of public life is dependent neither on the family nor the state that gives it its particular character of building the social capital on which democracies thrive. Even in the early days of civil society, within the wide variety of social and cultural groups, there emerged advocacy organizations with specific policy goals and an evolving tool kit of actions to achieve their policy outcomes. Perhaps the best known early international campaigns by civil society groups were the generation-long campaign to abolish slavery in the mid-nineteenth century and the campaign for women's suffrage in the late nineteenth century. While the term *human rights* had not yet been formalized and popularized at that time, the assertion of individual—and later collective—rights continued to be the galvanizing issue for civil society in the twentieth century.

The prototype and role model for the modern international advocacy civil society organization is Amnesty International, established in London in 1961. It opened branches in many other countries in the world, and its US branch became a powerhouse, going from 3,000 to 50,000 members between 1974 and 1976.[8] The next galvanizing issue on the world stage grew out of the seminal 1972 Club of Rome report, *The Limits to Growth,* which alerted international society to the impending threats to the environment and led to the establishment of new international civil society actors such as the World Wildlife Fund and Greenpeace. Those organizations joined their first-generation counterpart, the International Union for the Conservation of Nature, established in 1948 and composed of both governments and civil society. The ability of such groups to tap into deeply held concerns of large groups of people was the basis of their success and provided an important means of popular participation on these key issues beyond the strictures of party politics. International CSOs gave voice to these concerns, and people moved by these concerns gave money and time. While the model was not new, the professionalism that came with scale, the sophistication of the messaging, and, eventually, the use of mass media and social media were certainly new elements that elevated the reach and significance of the CSOs.

Domestic CSOs have operated since Tocquevillian times, but the success of their international counterparts led to a blossoming of their numbers and effectiveness. In the 1980s the number of domestic CSOs in the global South could be counted in the hundreds. Today they need to be counted in the millions. Even in a country as politically constrained as China there are estimated to be some two million CSOs, of which only a small percent is registered.[9] The growth of civil society has led to the acceptance by most major international actors that civil society sits alongside government and business as the sectors that share prime responsibility for policy determination. This can be seen from the growth of CSOs as UN partners in recent years. Article 71 of the UN Charter allowed for nongovernmental organizations (NGOs) to enter into consultative status with the UN, and more than four thousand groups enjoy this consultative status.[10]

The institutions of democracy that need to be built include representative assemblies, independent judiciaries, competent oversight agencies, and militaries under civilian control. These can be seen as the "supply" side of democratization, and it is understandable that the bulk of the democracy support effort has focused on these institution-building aspects. But the supply-side investment will not yield the required dividend without being shaped by and responsive to the "demand" side of democratization. The demand side requires participation by citizens in various ways—voting, supporting political parties, patronizing mass media, and speaking out as civil society. It is in this role of shaping the institutions of society that civil society can be seen as a means of democratization.

The empirical evidence in support of a civil society theory of democratization received a considerable boost from Robert Putnam's work in Italy.[11] Putnam's intelligent oxymoron, *social capital,* has already been mentioned. His proposition that societies with strong horizontal social bonds are more likely to be successful at building democracy provides direct support for the civil society theory. In an earlier chapter the comparative cases of Poland and Russia were discussed and the conclusion reached that the key distinction that allowed Poland to succeed was the strength of its civil society. A similar argument might be hazarded in a comparison of Tunisia and Egypt, the former having a viable civil society sector while the latter's was limited to a small corner of the elite. From the policy perspective, the civil society theory of democratization provides for the clear strategy of funding and strengthening civil society in countries attempting to democratize. It is the theory on which the UN Democracy Fund bases its work. And this leads to an interesting backhanded piece of evidence in support of the theory. The Putin-led attack on civil society as a means of averting democratization and its adoption by other autocrats demonstrates that Putin and his ilk endorse the theory. It is a viable theory with empirical underpinning and is perhaps the major alternative to modernization theory.

Modernization Theory

Modernization theory is the dominant theory of democratization. An underlying premise of the theory is the now widely accepted linkage between economics and politics. Marxism established this premise. The development of modernization theory in relation to democracy comes from Seymour Martin Lipset, whose 1963 book *Political Man* argued that economic development sets off a series of profound social changes that favor democratization and proposed that the more well-to-do a nation, the greater its chances of sustaining democracy. The engine driving these social changes is the middle class growing ever larger with prosperity and more demanding commensurate with its size and influence. The middle class would build democracy. Fukuyama is today the leading academic voice of modernization theory, and he put it this way: "What the Marxists called bourgeois liberal democracy is really what seems to lie at the terminus of this historical process of modernization."[12]

Several years after Lipset published his book, Barrington Moore wrote *Social Origins of Dictatorship and Democracy* (1966), which adopted the same underlying premise but examined the issue not from the perspective of the largely urban middle class but from the perspective of the farmer's relationship with agricultural land. His conclusion was not dissimilar to Lipset's in that small-holder capitalist agriculture, resolving issues of labor and commodity prices through demand and supply without undue political interference, would lead to market-based democracy. It must be said, however, that Moore's thesis is more convincing in relation to the origins of dictatorship and how it is facilitated by feudal or "serf"-like agricultural relationships.

It is not an exaggeration to say that these ideas changed popular notions of politics. One no longer had to be a Marxist to accept the determinative quality of economic relationships to political outcomes. Politics was seen as far more than the debates in the Federalist Papers or the various declarations of rights, it was mainly about wealth: how it was produced and how it got divided. Like all great ideas, their simplicity and explanatory power eventually make them commonplace understandings. The "end of history" thesis follows this path and is about both liberal democracy and the market system.

The Lipset thesis was specifically about democratization, and half a century later there are a number of useful empirical examples to examine. Needless to say, the countries of Western Europe and North America as well as Australia and New Zealand fit the thesis neatly. Intuitive understanding was given useful quantitative support in a study by Adam Przeworski and his colleagues that found "once a country is sufficiently wealthy, with per-capita income of more than $6,000 a year, democracy is certain to survive, come hell or high water."[13] This has been referred to as the point at which democracy becomes impregnable, but it is not an argument that any country with this level of wealth must necessarily be a democracy, and there are several that are not. It is an argument about impregnability, not transition.

In relation to transition, the Asian Tigers—South Korea, Taiwan, and probably Hong Kong if it had a free choice—are textbook examples of a growing middle class becoming wealthier, more assertive, and ultimately rejecting authoritarian rule and demanding the establishment of democracy. Similar arguments could be made in relation to several Latin American countries, including Argentina, Chile, Mexico, Uruguay, and perhaps Brazil. These are powerful examples of a common process of transition that is internally led by assertive voices, often belonging to civil society, that owe their capacity to focus on such demands by the relative wealth they have accumulated. And it establishes a path that others will admire and try to emulate.

It is clearly not the only path to democratization. India is a committed democracy that, for all its many faults, is developing a culture of democracy and robust institutions in support of that culture. It comes nowhere near the per capita wealth of the nations listed in the previous paragraph. India's massive diversity condemns it to practice democracy because no other system is conceivable. Indonesia may be following the same "no alternative but democracy" path.

At the other end of the scale there are the wealthy Gulf countries that are not democracies and where there seems to be little demand for it. Perhaps it is because their economies are dependent on a single resource and the nation's wealth has not been built by millions of individual entrepreneurs. The same reason cannot be given in Singapore, which has never seen a change in government. This city-state is an outlier.

Modernization theory focuses on market-based wealth generation and its impact on politics. It suggests that a focus on modernization through economic uplift is a surer path to democratization than the seemingly more direct initiatives such as assisting political party development or funding civil society initiatives. If correct, the great test will be China, a country with a fast-rising per capita income. And if China does democratize, then the credit will partly go to those Western countries, the United States in particular, that opened their markets to Chinese products, allowing economic takeoff to occur.

One of the sly attractions of modernization theory is that it turns Marxism on its head. For Marx, it is the exploited classes that will turn on the owners of capital and overthrow the system. Thus, according to Marx, it is the working class that is the transformative class in society because its only viable strategy is to destroy the exploitative status quo. The Marxist prescription requires revolution followed by the construction of a new classless society without private property. It conjures images of wild mobs throwing cobblestones and setting fire to the pillars of capitalism.

Modernization theory downplays the role of the working class and highlights the constructive energies of the middle class. The role of members of the working class is to escape their low economic strata through their own efforts in a society open to economic opportunity and mobility; in other words, to become members of the middle class. The role of the middle class is to gain wealth, education, and influence and to become assertive and demanding in support of a system that will facilitate that process. The images conjured are of attending town hall meetings, holding peaceful protests, organizing workshops, and joining political parties—or more recently, civil society organizations. According to modernization theory, the middle class has taken the place of the working class as the transformative element in society, and, happily, the transformation is not necessarily accompanied by violence.

This is a pleasing perspective, and it might help explain why modernization theory is the dominant theory of democratization. As I noted earlier, it rests on solid empirical support. In these examples, middle-class interests and democratization were seen as synonymous. The theory rests on an assumption that advancing middle-class interests will necessarily flow from democratization. But what happens when the disadvantaged classes buy into the rhetoric of democracy and attempt to use its possibilities? What happens when rural people and recent migrants to the cities decide not to wait until they have attained middle-class status before asserting their political voices? What happens when they elect their champions, who then institute policies that favor the disadvantaged classes rather than the urban middle class? In effect, these people are adopting aspects of modernity though they do not fit neatly within modernization theory. Will the middle class continue to support democracy in those circumstances?

The answer to these difficult questions need not be based on theory or conjecture. There are ongoing examples to study and from which to draw tentative conclusions.

Thailand

Thailand is a country of considerable significance. It is not simply because it has a population of nearly seventy million, that its per capita income is almost $10,000, or that it has the tenth-highest international tourist arrivals in the world. Thailand is significant because it was never colonized. Though both the British in Burma to the West and the French in Indochina to the East exerted significant influence, Thailand retained its monarch and its sovereignty. This makes it rather unique in the global South, almost like a control case in a vast colonial experiment. And it is an important regional country as the hub and one-time hegemon of mainland Southeast Asia. That is why Thailand's process of democratization is so critical; it comes very much from within.

For seven centuries, Thailand was ruled as an absolute monarchy. A small group of Western-educated intellectuals and military officers calling itself the People's Party put an end to it in 1932 and instituted a system of constitutional monarchy with government supposedly alternating based on election results. The following sixty years in Thailand tells a story of coups and constitutions peppered with occasional elections but mainly dominated by the military and its puppets. Thailand has had twenty constitutions in eighty-five years.[14] Whether called "interim" or "permanent," nearly all these constitutions were intended to serve the interests of the strongman of the day. There are, however, several exceptions: the constitutions of 1946, 1974, and 1997. The 1946 Constitution was drafted in a brief postwar period of liberalism and allowed multiple political parties to operate freely. But with the ink of the constitution hardly dry, the then king, the late King Bhumipol's older brother, died from a single gunshot wound to the head in circumstances that remain unexplained to this day, and neither the government nor the constitution would last much longer. The Nixon Doctrine of 1969 put Thailand on notice that the future may not simply be business as usual in terms of the United States acting as the military's backstop. As in

Western capitals, students were on the streets demanding reform. King Bhumipol decided to get involved, and he convoked a national convention to act as an electoral college for the selection of a 240-seat National Assembly tasked with drafting within six months a permanent constitution "that would reflect the socio-political aspirations of the people." But the political architecture ushered in by the new constitution did not deliver the hoped-for stable and competent governance, and a 1976 coup put an end to this joint effort by the king and the people.

The 1997 Constitution was an attempt to learn from the failed attempts at liberal constitution drafting and, this time, put in place a basic law that would not only live up to its name as a permanent constitution but would change the very nature of Thai politics. Borrowing from the 1974 episode, the document was drafted by a 99-person committee, three-quarters of which were by way of self-selection and then internal election on a provincial basis, leading to one representative from each of the seventy-six provinces joined by twenty-three experts selected by parliament from nominations submitted by universities. The result was a document of extraordinary length—336 sections with 40,000 words—that elaborated a system with a strong executive overseen by citizen participation and by an innovative fourth branch of government assuring oversight of the executive, all guarded by a directly elected senate of nonpartisan individuals of high merit.

The 1997 Constitution was a triumph of the growing middle class that saw Thailand as a sophisticated country with an important role in the global economy needing high-caliber political leadership, which the military could no longer provide. The 1997 Constitution was a triumph of deliberation over vested interests as it attacked issues such as money politics, economic privileges, and centralized decisionmaking. The 1997 Constitution was a model of middle-class led democratization attempting to reform institutions, banish the military from politics, and change Thai political culture all at once. It might have worked if it had been given time to embed itself and allow the newly established bodies to build up self-confidence and expertise, but in 2001, Thaksin Shinawatra was elected prime minister in a decisive victory and soon overpowered the complicated embryonic system built by the constitution.

Thaksin was not a veteran politician like his predecessors and many of his competitors. He had entered politics in the mid-1990s as one of Thailand's richest businessmen, having emerged from a Chiang Mai family of Chinese immigrants who had succeeded both in the silk business and in local and national politics and having spent his early career in the police, where he rose to the rank of lieutenant colonel and married a general's daughter. His business success was the result of a series of concessions from the government of the day, initially in leasing computers to the police and operating paging services and eventually moving to mobile telephony and managing Thailand's satellite communications. He thus became a communications mogul and Thailand's richest man, and accordingly, he was courted by the various political parties. I recall a talk he gave in this period to a group of Southeast Asian parliamentarians at a workshop co-hosted by the Centre for Democratic Institutions that I then headed. Thaksin was brash and bright and revelled in his image as the outsider businessman. He had paid the television stations to cover the event, and clearly our workshop was merely the prop to cover his pitch to the television audience. When it came time to respond to detailed questions from his regional peers, he simply referred them to one of his expert employees accompanying him. In this period he floated from one political party to another, his choice resting on whether it was assigned the communications portfolio in a coalition government rather than on anything in its policy platform. Like many before him, Thaksin entered politics to protect and increase his wealth. He eventually decided this could best be accomplished by forming his own party.

In winning the 2001 election, Thaksin used some standard techniques and also some innovations. He used his wealth to lure incumbent parliamentarians from other parties and to attract strong new candidates. But he also used his wealth to establish a mass party that would soon have some eleven million registered members. The membership did not come from the urban middle class but rather from more rural communities and urban migrants from these communities. In so doing, Thaksin accidentally became the standard bearer for Isarn, the populous north and northeast of Thailand, with its twenty million Lao-speaking people who had always lived in the shadow of Bangkok's elites. Thaksin also developed policies attractive to his new party members, including subsidized doctor's visits, loans to villages, and improved marketing of rural products. The Bangkok middle class dismissed these policies as mere populism, but an economic assessment by a reputable commentator after two years of implementation gave these policies a good report card.[15]

In the five years after his initial election, Thaksin achieved unprecedented political results. In the 2005 election his party won a majority in its own right. He infiltrated, subverted, or otherwise emasculated the oversight branch of government and its Senate guardian. He did not succeed in deepening his relationship with the king, but he successfully courted the queen and the heir. Perhaps most threateningly, Thaksin was

overseeing a changing of the elites and menacing various economic pre-
serves. And, of course, his Shin Corporation was becoming ever more
powerful and wealthy. Because Thaksin threatened Bangkok's elites, its
network monarchy,[16] and its middle-class supporters, the coup that was
considered a part of Thailand's past returned in 2006 to oust him and
force him into exile. A new constitution was drafted with the hope that
subsequent elections would return the country to the trusted Bangkok
elite, the so-called network monarchy.

Coups do not resolve political problems; they simply incubate them.
Thailand's subsequent history has been a battle between Thaksin's supporters adopting the color red, and the anti-Thaksin forces adopting the
king's color of yellow. The red forces win the battles of the ballots, but
the yellow forces win the battles in the courts, in the media, and for the
hearts and minds of the urban middle class. The courts, seen as the
king's new champions, have repeatedly tried to undermine the results of
ballots by deregistering Thaksin's political party, which simply forces it
to adopt a new name, and by dismissing its leaders from office, which
leads to an exercise in musical chairs.

The problem is that in a democracy, ballots are ultimately decisive,
and so to get rid of Thaksin's influence in Thailand, Thaksin's opponents also had to get rid of democracy. The 2014 coup simply proved
that the 2006 coup had been ineffective. Incompetent military leaders
are back in power, but far from seeing the Bangkok middle class
protesting on the streets, it is sighing a deep sense of relief at getting rid
of the standard bearer of those country bumpkins from the north. As
each argument used to discredit ballot results, including that Thaksin's
victories were achieved by vote buying, is shown to be irrelevant or
false, the middle class and its champions have started to abandon the
idea of democracy as the appropriate form of government for Thailand.

In the case of Thailand, the question as to whether the middle class
is necessarily in favor of democratization, as modernization theory
would have it, can confidently be answered in the negative. In a situation where the less privileged strata of society seize on the opportunities
presented by democracy to elect their champions and to implement their
policies, the middle class will revert to protecting its interests in any
way it can. If jettisoning democracy is called for to protect these interests, so be it.

Thailand is exceptional in the historical sense that it was never colonized. Does that lead to a conclusion that Thailand's individuality
explains its actions as idiosyncrasy and therefore of little comparative
value? There might be some support for this argument in the unusual

nature of the nation's devotion to its king. The late King Bhumipol Adulyadej was the world's longest-reigning monarch, having ascended to the throne in 1946 as an eighteen-year-old. He reigned over the nation through good times and bad, at times involving himself in matters of state but usually content to maintain a dignified silence and work through his network of officials and supporters. Longevity, dignity, and modesty may be explanations of why he became so popular. The anti-Thaksin forces have invariably tried to portray their battle as defense of the king, and this clearly has salience with some segments of the public, including the middle class. Without taking a position on the honesty of this portrayal of the red-yellow conflict, it is a valid argument in favor of the idiosyncrasy argument. But to test its idiosyncrasy we need to ask whether there may be other examples of middle-class ambivalence toward democracy in other countries.

The following sections of this chapter are not intended to be comprehensive analyses of the countries under consideration. Some basic contextual information is necessary, but the thread that is being followed is the attitude and role of the middle class in particularly trying circumstances. Admittedly, the thread is not always easy to discern as forces rarely self-identify with the broad brush of being "middle class" but the key to this identification is the examination of the groups being opposed who happen to be in the majority. Following the thread provides an indication of where the middle class stands when democracy traverses difficult times.

Venezuela

Hugo Chávez was elected president of Venezuela in December 1998, two years before Thaksin's election as prime minister of Thailand. The two politicians are quite different creatures; Thaksin coming to power as Thailand's richest tycoon, Chávez emerging from the military as an admirer of Fidel Castro. The two countries are quite different as well; Thailand being a globalized entrepôt economy with a massive tourism sector, Venezuela being dependent on oil exports. Both countries are similar in that they have been moving, though with considerable hiccups in Thailand, toward government decided by free and broadly fair elections. They are also both similar, as with many other countries in the world, in having large groups of people who see themselves as disadvantaged and shut out from the wealth of the country.

Chávez appealed to those disadvantaged groups to gain power through free and broadly fair elections. He stayed in power until his death in 2013, winning his fourth term (having previously successfully conducted a referendum abolishing term limits) while on his deathbed in 2012. In fact, elections in Venezuela have been very frequent in the Chávez era, with four presidential, four regional, three legislative, two municipal, and one constitutional convention election as well as six national referendums. Chávez won them all with the exception of one referendum in 2007 and a loss of seats in the 2010 constitutional convention election, where he nevertheless retained a majority. This self-confidence through the power of the ballot led to one of the many descriptions of the Chávez system as plebiscitary democracy. It mirrors Thaksin's confidence in falling back on the strategy of calling an election to resolve a deep political problem.

Chávez's ability to win nineteen out of twenty elections in the space of fifteen years is no small feat. It rests in part on the charismatic personality of the leader, a description that cannot be extended to Thaksin. But it also reflects a capacity to identify a societal cleavage that can be exploited to electoral advantage. This is where the comparison between Chávez and Thaksin is at its strongest. That cleavage was not the urban sophisticated middle class that modernization theory relies on so heavily. It consisted of groups identifying themselves as disadvantaged; low-salaried workers, rural workers, favela dwellers, and generally the economically poorer segments of society that saw little prospect of advancement in unequal oligarchic pre-Chávez Venezuela and that retained its faith in Chávez for as long as he maintained the power of rhetoric and patronage.

Also like Thaksin, Chávez cared little for the rules and disciplines of democracy beyond crude electoral majoritarianism. Civil liberties were eroded, the separation of powers was ignored, the culture of democracy and pluralism that had been building in Venezuela was allowed to whither, and the military became an instrument of government control over domestic policy. Thaksin likewise emasculated the oversight branch of government, infiltrated the nonpartisan Senate, probably bribed or intimidated judges on the highest court, and ignored due process when confronting first narco-gangsters and then local Muslim unrest.

These are all good reasons to oppose both Chávez and Thaksin and to vote for their opponents. But the dilemma confronting opponents of plebiscitary democracy is the doubt they harbor of their ability to win at the polls. The response that both sets of opponents gravitated toward was the most undemocratic of institutions, the coup d'état. Chávez was toppled by a coup in 2002 but regained his office within forty-eight hours. Thaksin was ousted by a coup in 2006, but while he remained in exile his political party, led by his relatives, regained power in 2007, only to be upended by a coup again in 2014. The interesting but difficult question is whether the respective middle classes supported these coups. There is considerable evidence that it did so in Thailand, with the Bangkok elite and middle class pleading for the military to stage a coup for at least a year before it happened. Indeed, the governance formula being touted by Thaksin's opponents was for a nonelected government of technocrats appointed by the king. There is also good evidence that the elites and the middle class in Caracas supported the 2002 coup, which was publicly supported by the Federation of Commerce and preceded by a white-collar strike. Therefore, as in Thailand, the conclusion to be at least suggested, though not conclusively settled, is that the middle class will support anti-democratic methods when it considers its interests at significant risk.

Turkey

Close comparisons between Thailand and Turkey do not spring intu-itively to mind. Yet the closeness of political developments in the two countries is the subject of a political essay by Duncan McCargo and Ayşe Zarakol.[17] Their paths toward democracy shared key similarities. Neither country was colonized, though both suffered the indignities of European intrusive influence. Both entered modernity through local rev-olutionary processes; Kemalism in Turkey, which abolished the Ottoman Empire in 1922, and the People's Party revolt against absolute monarchy in Thailand in 1932. The military remained a key player in politics and development in both countries through to the end of the twentieth century. And, critically, both countries adopted a Western-inspired economic development approach that identified and supported certain industries and companies for state support, placed considerable power in the hands of experts and bureaucrats, and favored "middle-class urbanites who embodied the state's ideal of what it meant to be modern or Thai or Turkish."[18] This excluded from the winners' circle a large class of people who were rural or poor or ethnic or otherwise did not identify with the urban middle class. These people formed the elec-torate that Thaksin accidentally came to champion and that Recep Tayyip Erdoğan far more consciously targeted as his vehicle to power.

The Justice and Development Party (AKP) he helped found from the fragments of other Islamist and reform parties won a sweeping vic-tory in the 2002 elections, and Erdoğan was appointed prime minister the following year. Since that time, Erdoğan can be said to have estab-lished a plebiscitary democracy like those in Thailand and Venezuela.

The AKP either won an outright majority or was the dominant party in each of the next eight elections—three local, two legislative, two referendums, and the 2014 presidential election won by Erdoğan after constitutional changes approved by referendum.

Erdoğan could not at first be said to have attacked the institutions of democracy in the same way as Thaksin and Chávez, though he oversaw a diminution of the enjoyment of civic rights, particularly in relation to the press: Turkey fell to 151st place on the 2016 Press Freedom Index of Reporters Without Borders.[19] According to Nobel laureate for literature Orhan Pamuk, Turkey is "a democracy where the respect of human rights [and] free speech are violated every day."[20] But after the failed coup in 2016, Erdoğan began attacking his enemies pretty much without regard to constitutional or human rights limitations. Erdoğan has also attacked the secular foundation of the modern Kemalist Turkish state to favor Islamist proscriptions against alcohol and sexual choice, and favoring such Islamic symbols as head scarves. His economic policies were clearly successful, growing the economy while reducing inequality and crafting policies favoring his political supporters.

Erdoğan is therefore no darling of the Turkish middle class. But because he was careful to defang the military, the option of a coup was not realistic—as was learned by those who staged the 2016 coup to their cost. There is no evidence that the middle class supported that ill-advised coup attempt, and most commentators swiftly condemned it. What can be said, though, is that the 2013 massive protests against Erdoğan and his government have been led by the middle class. Although ostensibly about the destruction of a small park in Istanbul, the protests were seen as a response to Erdoğan's growing authoritarianism. And it is more than likely that the Istanbul middle class was at least rubbing its hands in glee at the audacious attempt by an erstwhile political supporter of the AKP, the exiled Fethullah Gülen, to infiltrate the police and judiciary and topple Erdoğan through corruption cases. Nevertheless, these instances cannot be said to be evidence for the abandonment of democracy by the Turkish middle class, but as in the former cases, there is at least a suspicion that this would be an acceptable means of ridding themselves of Erdoğan and his AKP.

Egypt

Egypt does not fit nearly as well into this narrative as the first three examples. It is a far poorer country with per capita income of one-third of Turkey's, half of Venezuela's, and two-thirds of Thailand's. Accordingly, the comparative size of the middle class is relatively small. The element that is of interest flows from the fact that the middle class had a distinctive character in the failed Egyptian transition to democracy, as this is where the liberal voice emerged. The small but tight group of civil society activists, many of whose sons and daughters were at Tahrir Square to trigger the fall of President Mubarak, are the product of a sophisticated, partly Western-educated, English- or French-speaking, central-Cairo-dwelling middle class. As can be expected from such a group, during the Mubarak years they campaigned tirelessly for human rights and democracy. Before long, however, they were again in the streets, pleading for the military to rid them of the newly elected Muslim Brotherhood president.

Care is required in framing the Egyptian middle class's support for democracy and ultimately opposition to its crude result. Its support for democracy was never intended to result in an Islamist government, and its opposition to President Morsi can hardly be said to be evidence of its antidemocratic nature given the deep flaws in the Egyptian transition and in Morsi's rule. The liberal voice was not against the Muslim Brotherhood's involvement in public life, but it comforted itself with the vague notion that this role would mainly be directed as a social safety net, assisting Egypt's many poor and disadvantaged people who live on the outskirts of the big cities and in rural communities. It resented the fact that the Brotherhood, invisible during the early Tahrir Square period, suddenly emerged as a dominant player demanding its due. Yet, in the early part of the transition it faced the reality that it had neither the support nor the organization to mount a serious challenge for power and thus was faced with the unenviable choice of continued military domination of the nation or the uncertainties of Brotherhood rule.

Egypt prides itself on its ancient roots. While longevity contributed to the conception of Egypt as an imagined community by its residents, the other requirements for a democracy—accountable and representative institutions governed by the rule of law—never developed. Indeed, Egypt's modern history, beginning with conquest by Napoleon, is one of authoritarianism by colonial, Ottoman, royal, and military rule. This is not a propitious path along which democracy can instantly take hold. Quite the contrary, authoritarian and paternalistic instincts by both the military and the Islamists proved to be the dominant influences.

One lesson that the failed Egypt transition to democracy reinforces is that elections alone cannot establish democracy. Egyptians voted early and often. Between the fall of Mubarak and the coup against Morsi, a period of two and a half years, Egyptians voted five times. They voted for constitutions, legislatures, and presidents, and each contest seemed to complicate the process rather than clarify it. While no one can claim that Egypt is governed by rule of law, its judges nevertheless wielded considerable influence in nullifying elections and constitutions for reasons both significant and trivial. Although the elections were not rigged, the military never let go of the reins of power and ultimately decided the struggle with Morsi by a coup. The Brotherhood at times played on its popularity for electoral purposes and at other times used its muscle on the streets to intimidate opponents.

It is therefore understandable that the liberal voice, the middle-class voice, found it difficult to accept developments as a healthy process of democratization. It is understandable that the liberal segment of society lost patience with Morsi and his incompetent rule. It is also understandable that liberals would time and again return to Tahrir Square as their only means of influence over developments. But to plead for a military coup, as many of them did in the massive demonstrations of mid-2013, is deeply antithetical to democracy. It was clear to one and all that a coup would simply result in a swap of authoritarian rule from obscurantist Islamists to narrow-minded military rule. That is what Egypt now has, and, while certain explanations and justifications are plausible, the fact remains that the middle class supported this result.

Conclusion

This chapter began with a discussion of theories of democratization. Modernization theory is considered to be the leading theory, and it is based on a concept of an educated and assertive middle class reaching a certain critical mass where its demands are influential in shaping society and democratization is one outcome. Beyond the democratization process there is an important argument about the impregnability of democracy, where it is consolidated and where income levels surpass a certain relatively high point. The balance of the chapter looked at the application of modernization theory in certain countries. The concluding part of the chapter will attempt an analysis of the applicability of modernization theory to democratization.

Beginning with the poster children for modernization theory, there is little doubt that the Republic of Korea and Taiwan provide strong evidence for its applicability to democratization. Applying authoritarian discipline favoring industrialization and export policies combined with pronounced cultural traits that favored education, both countries experienced dynamic per capita income growth in the space of a generation.

The educated new generation bridled at the authoritarian aspects of society and called for radical reforms leading to a democratization process that now looks to be consolidated and beyond the impregnability barrier. The next target of both electorates is corruption, which necessarily accompanies authoritarian capitalism, and both polities are taking important strides in taming corruption.

Without disputing this narrative, one also needs to be alive to a companion narrative that may be seen as either competing with or complementary to modernization theory as an explanation for Korea and Taiwan's democratization process. Korea and Taiwan are not "normal" polities; they are each a portion of a larger entity that, though it need not necessarily take Westphalian form, nevertheless qualifies to do so and have adherents wishing it so. And the debate on unification is not only conducted by way of imagination and deliberation but also by way of massive military forces facing each other, separated by a demilitarized zone or a militarized strait. In other words, each polity faces an existential security threat. The guarantor for each polity's existence is the United States, which, especially in the post–Cold War era, respects fellow democracies far more than countries following other systems of government. Thus, an alternative explanation for democratization may be the "pull" factor of the United States. Needing to retain the respect and protection of its security guarantor, both the Republic of Korea and Taiwan undertook their processes of democratization. As noted, this argument can be seen as complementary to modernization theory, but it is nevertheless an alternative argument. Of course, the "pull" factor is a well-accepted argument in the case of the European Union's influence over democratization in candidate countries on its European periphery.

There are also cases where modernization theory has had little role in democratization. India and Indonesia are both poor countries that at the time of their democratization process had relatively small middle classes, though clearly members of the educated elite played leading roles. For all its faults, India's devotion to democracy cannot be doubted. The consistently massive electoral turnout, the meaningfulness of each election in terms of leaders and policies, and the pride taken by the institutions of the separation of powers in their respective roles all point to the consolidation of Indian democracy. With India's recent economic dynamism, the middle class has grown, but the safeguarding of India's democracy is not in its hands alone but in the hands of the entire nation, right down to the millions of homeless people who register to vote. India faces problems of inequality, corruption, inclusion, and service delivery, but in terms of the most widely accepted test of consolidation, no significant political actors are calling for any system other than the democratic system India currently has. It is as if no other system could possibly work in a country as diverse as India. Contraintuitively, there is a type of diversity theory, rather than modernization theory, that best explains India's situation.

While Indonesia cannot yet be equated with India as a consolidated democracy, the pattern of political contestation is encouraging. The 2014 election of Joko Widodo as president marked an important milestone on the process of democratization. Jokowi, as he is known, is the first post-Suharto-era politician to win the highest elected office. The previous occupants were all tied to Suharto in one way or another—as his vice president, ardent opponent, or loyal military officer. Even Jokowi's election opponent, Prabowo Subianto, was a former Suharto-era military officer and, incidentally, a former Suharto son-in-law. A politician of humble origins, who won support because of the effectiveness of his administration as, first, mayor of Surakarta, and then, governor of Jakarta, Jokowi is the first presidential product of Indonesia's new democracy. As in India, the country faces similarly massive challenges; and as in India, an argument can be advanced that a version of diversity theory is at play. Indeed, "Bhinneka Tunggal Ika" is the official national motto of Indonesia: it is an old Javanese phrase for "Unity in Diversity." It might one day be complemented with the concept of democracy through diversity.

Returning to examples in the previous section where the middle class has soured on the results of democracy, a number of patterns emerge. Where the disadvantaged classes cohere around a political champion, the results can be distinctly mixed. Chávez, Erdoğan, and Thaksin portrayed themselves as such champions and succeeded in winning the stubborn loyalty of a majority of the electorate. This opened for each of them the benefits of plebiscitary democracy, where every sin could be washed clean and any policy could be blessed by an election. Chávez, Erdoğan, and Thaksin can hardly be described as committed democrats. They each believed in causes larger than democracy, and each saw the democratic process as a means to reach his own goals. Where the democratic process became inconvenient, they undermined it.

Their supporters benefited—some directly from the personal patronage politics that each had to play, but most, indirectly from policies designed for their short-term benefit. The long-term results are harder to discern. Venezuela may be plunged into recession by its overreliance on a single resource in a coming era of alternative energy and stranded carbon assets. Chávez's legacy may be a dysfunctional economy and an untenable Cuban-style social system. Erdoğan's legacy may be a reemergence of Islamic elements of social life, which may well cost Turkey any slim chance it had of joining Europe. Thaksin's legacy is the reality of political cleavage replacing the official mirage of national unity held together by royalty. The accidental hero, Thaksin, whose main objective was self-enrichment, may nevertheless leave the most enduring legacy.

The theoretical legacy of these three case studies, along with the sobering example from Egypt, is the unreliability of faith in the middle class as the transformative class bent on democratization. The middle classes in these cases understandably opposed the champions of the less-privileged segments of society, but they did so well beyond the bounds of electoral politics. Judging the system to be skewed in favor of their political opponents, they abandoned it and in three of the four cases called for and defended the least democratic method of alternation of power, the coup d'état. In the case of Turkey, the option of a military coup did not seem feasible and failed miserably when attempted. The middle class did not support the coup and had instead turned to mass demonstrations, a legitimate democratic tool. The Gülen oppositionists had previously turned to the use of a type of fifth column within the criminal law enforcement machinery to rid itself of the despised leader, a more doubtful tool.

Turning to the impregnability argument that is also based on modernization theory given its income-level threshold, there is a recent case that is casting doubt on the previously very robust empirical support. Hungary's April 2010 parliamentary balloting, in which Viktor Orbán's Fidesz party won 53 percent of the vote and a seat bonus big enough to give it powers of constitutional amendment, touched off what Orbán himself has called an "electoral revolution." The speed and the scale of the changes have indeed been revolutionary. In the past several years, Hungary has seen the adoption of a new constitution as well as the passage of some 350 bills that have profoundly affected the very foundations of the rule of law and raised doubts about whether the country can still be considered a liberal democracy.

Hungary had been a poster child for postcommunist democratization. Beginning with a slide away from central planning and authoritarianism in the Gorbachev period, followed by a smooth pacted transition toward electoral politics in which pre-Soviet parties miraculously sprang to life, and then a successful negotiation process for accession to the European Union through which it accepted the European *acquis* (a vast body of rights and rules to bring a candidate country up to minimum European standards), Hungary may have been thought to have become a consolidated democracy. Combine this with a per capita income around the $20,000 mark and Hungary falls into the impregnability category. European Union influence may yet put a break on Hungary's backsliding and return it to the democratic fold, but at this stage one can validly sound danger sirens.

The situation in Hungary is a reminder that there may be issues that at times trump the rational choices of voting for economic and political continuity. Hungary has a bad case of social irredentism that feeds a victim's grievance mentality. The Treaty of Versailles stripped it of territory together with five million Hungarian-speaking nationals who continue to live in neighboring countries. The fact that Hungarian is not a Romance, Germanic, or Slavic language like all its neighbors feeds the concept of distinctiveness that fuels its feelings of victimhood. Viktor Orbán's Fidesz party began life in the transition period as a liberal youth party but migrated to the nationalist wing of politics by playing to these Hungarian particularities. Modernization theory has trouble dealing with national particularities.

Modernization theory has many attractions. It is a clear and well-understood path to allow a society to negotiate away from traditionalism. It is a process that relies on a vast number of individuals all proceeding along that path voluntarily. It may be supported by government policies in the industry, trade, and education sectors, but it remains the sum of the many individual parts that are attracted by it. In that sense, modernization theory is an admirable bottom-up process. For all the benefits of modernization, the burden of this chapter is to cast some doubt on its reliance for the purpose of democratization. Economic growth and the commensurate increase in the proportionate size of the middle class may well lead to demands for democratization. But once electoral democratic forms are achieved, its bounty will not invariably benefit the middle class. In some cases, the middle class will turn against the system it fought for.

What are the consequences of this conclusion? The first conclusion to be drawn is not to put all the eggs in one basket. Economic development will resolve many problems and lead to many beneficial outcomes, but it will not resolve everything. If one's ultimate goal is a successful society, then economic development may have to fit in with other processes. Issues of inclusion, participation, quality of life, and equity in opportunity are important companion processes. To describe the sought-after balance between the various processes that will be different in different societies is beyond the scope of this project. But one policy area that will be examined in Chapter 9 is development assistance policies and the impact they are having on development and democracy.

The other conclusion again deals with eggs in baskets. If the middle class is ultimately an unreliable transformative class for democratization, then is there another group that can successfully play this role? The answer to that question is attempted in the next chapter.

Notes

1. E. E. Schattschneider, *Party Government* (New York: Holt, Rinehart and Winston, 1942), p. 1.

2. Adam Carr's Election Archive, http://psephos.adam-carr.net/.

3. Russell J. Dalton and Martin P. Wattenberg (eds.), *Parties Without Partisans: Political Change in Advanced Industrial Democracies* (Oxford: Oxford University Press, 2002).

4. Roland Rich, *Parties and Parliaments in Southeast Asia: Non-Partisan Chambers in Indonesia, the Philippines and Thailand* (London: Routledge, 2013).

5. Office of the High Commissioner for Human Rights, "CCPR General Comment No. 25: Article 25 (Participation in Public Affairs and the Right to Vote)," http://www.refworld.org/docid/453883fc22.html.

6. Same Varayudej, "A Right to Democracy in International Law: Its Implications for Asia," *Annual Survey of International & Comparative Law* 12 (2006): 1–28; Susan Marks, "What Has Become of the Emerging Right to Democratic Governance?" *European Journal of International Law* 22, 2 (2009): 507–524.

7. Alexis de Tocqueville, *Democracy in America* (London: Penguin, 2003). Original 2-volume edition first published in 1835 and 1840.

8. Margaret Keck and Kathryn Sikkink, *Activists Beyond Borders: Advocacy Networks in International Politics* (Ithaca, NY: Cornell University Press, 1998), p. 90.

9. *The Economist,* "Beneath the Glacier," April 12, 2014.

10. UN, "Basic Facts About ECOSOC Status," 2014, http://csonet.org/index.php?menu=100.

11. Robert D. Putnam with Robert Leonardi and Raffaella Y. Nanetti, *Making Democracy Work: Civic Traditions in Modern Italy* (Princeton, NJ: Princeton University Press, 1994).

12. Francis Fukuyama, "Democracy and the End of History Revisited," in Heraldo Muñoz (ed.), *Democracy Rising: Assessing the Global Challenge* (Boulder, CO: Lynne Rienner, 2006), p. 116.

13. Adam Przeworski, Michael E. Alvarez, José Antonio Cheibub, and Fernando Limongi, *Democracy and Development: Political Institutions and Well-being in the World, 1950–1990* (New York: Cambridge University Press, 2000), p. 49.

14. A short history of constitutionalism in Thailand can be found in Rich, *Parties and Parliaments in Southeast Asia,* chapter 5, from which this analysis is drawn.

15. Worawan Chandoevwit, "Thailand's Grass Roots Policies," *TDRI Quarterly Review* 18, 2 (June 2003): 3–8.

16. A concept drawn from Duncan McCargo, "Network Monarchy and Legitimacy Crises in Thailand," *Pacific Review* 18, 4 (December 2005): 499–519.

17. Duncan McCargo and Ayşe Zarakol, "Turkey and Thailand: Unlikely Twins," *Journal of Democracy* 23, 3 (July 2012): 71–79.

18. Ibid., pp. 72–73.

19. Reporters without Borders, *Press Freedom Index, 2016*, https://rsf.org/en/ranking/2016.

20. *Today's Zaman,* February 18, 2015, http://www.todayszaman.com/national_pamuk-authoritarian-military-replaced-with-authoritarian-govt-in-turkey-372624.html.

8

The Bottom Three Billion
Must Be Recruited

I **always considered myself a feminist in a sort of abstract** and theoretical way. After all, I was a flower child in the hippie generation and feminism was one of the self-evident revelations of those times. But it had limited application beyond a vague notion of equality in social relations. Yes, I did a share of the housework and the child rearing, but my feminism was not tested in my own mind until, at a fairly senior level in the Foreign Ministry, I was confronted with the prospect of having a woman as my boss. Let's call her Meredith. Thinking about the situation, I was determined not to use a different standard in my judgment of my new boss. Meredith came with a terrific reputation, and all my dealings with her in the past had been positive, so I had no anxieties. In the event, her reputation preceded her accurately. She was brilliantly analytical, extremely thorough, and driven by a burning ambition. As her deputy, in a unit of about eighty people, I was happy to follow her lead though it was not easy to keep up with her. Meredith was very hard driving and hated any excuse for nondelivery, which she interpreted as weakness. She worked long hours and wasted precious few minutes on extraneous issues such as personal interests or family. Our bosses were delighted with her, and this reflected well on the entire unit. It stopped occurring to me that Meredith was a woman.

Our bosses may have been delighted, but our staff was less so. Meredith was demanding, expecting everybody to live up to her level of competence and drive. She was on top of the issues in everybody's portfolios and was brilliant, to the point of exasperation, in questioning every detail. Meredith was not the easiest person in the world to approach. She played nice but had difficulty hiding an edge of haughtiness in her dealings with members of the team. And she was tough, never budging from a set deadline or requirement. Gradually, I realized that staff were increasingly coming to me whenever they had a problem, personal or professional. Whether it was a difficulty with a child that needed early attention, meaning a missed deadline, or an intractable analytical problem that was resisting imposed order, my office became the place where people would come. In my own mind, I was simply being the loyal deputy, complementing the very busy Meredith and lightening her load. But this aspect of my role seemed to grow, and bit by bit I became an advocate for the staff, an explainer of their problems, a friendly ear to listen to their concerns, and, at times, a flak catcher for them.

It was only after I left that job and had the distance to look back on it that it dawned on me that Meredith and I had unconsciously engaged in a subtle but unmistakable gender role reversal. I am pretty sure that if our positions had been reversed, I would have acted pretty much as Meredith did, though probably less successfully. The work culture required that the head of a large unit be unfailingly focused, unsparingly rigorous, and unapologetically ambitious. Meredith lived up to it and more. But this left a void for the other needs of the unit; caring, mentoring, listening, empathizing. I had no choice but to fill this void. Again, if our roles had been reversed, I am sure Meredith would have tried her best to deal with these issues, though probably less successfully. Surely this is not the best way to divide responsibilities, with the boss taking all the traditional male roles and the deputy all the traditional female roles. Would it not be best if both, indeed all, positions adopted a mix of gender roles? In my next assignment I was determined to be both male and female in my leadership and management role. I think we should think of this as bi-genderness rather than genderlessness.

The Caveman Trope

But before we pursue the issue of bi-gendered roles, we need to deal with the questions raised in the introduction—the caveman trope. Is male dominance a universal phenomenon? Is it innate? Are gender relations among humans as implacably defined as instinctive gender roles in some parts of the animal kingdom? Because if that is the case, then patriarchy should be seen as the natural state of affairs and railing against patriarchy would be to confront basic human instinct. A way to test this key question is to ask whether all human societies are patriarchal. If they are, then perhaps patriarchy is instinctive. But if they are not, then patriarchy must be seen as something learned and thus able to be unlearned.

To answer this question, we need to turn to that most fulfilling of social science disciplines, anthropology. People tend to think of anthropology as the study of distinctiveness among the world's many human societies. This is understandable because the bulk of its product is the description of differences in governance, inheritance, ritual, and the like. But Claude Lévi-Strauss demonstrated that anthropology is also the key to understanding human universalities. And the study of the !Kung people (the exclamation mark is the phonetic symbol for the clicking noise in San languages) debunks the notion that patriarchy is universal. In Patricia Draper's famous 1975 paper on the !Kung, she described both traditionally nomadic and more recent sedentary groups of the San people of Namibia (sometimes called Kalahari Bushmen) and found that while the sedentary groups had adopted the patriarchal practices of their village neighbors, the traditional group had not:

> In the hunting and gathering context, women have a great deal of autonomy and influence. Some of the contexts in which this egalitarianism is expressed will be described in detail, and certain features of the foraging life which promote egalitarianism will be isolated. They are: women's subsistence contribution and the control women retain over the food they have gathered; the requisites of foraging in the Kalahari which entail a similar degree of mobility for both sexes; the lack of rigidity in sex-typing of many adult activities, including domestic chores and aspects of child socialization; the cultural sanction against physical expression of aggression; the small group size; and the nature of the settlement pattern.[1]

Draper's study confirms a long-held view that nomadic societies are fundamentally egalitarian though there may be some gendered divisions of labor. This may simply be a function of the small size of each group and the intimate degree of interdependence. But perhaps a significant contributing factor is the absence of the concept of ownership. Nomadic people carry their meager belongings and manufacture their tools as needs arise. They have no concept of ownership of land, though they might recognize the limits of where it is safe to hunt and forage before running into competitors. Indeed, they share a concept of being a part of the land that sustains them rather than any concept of having dominion over it. That is probably why they did not have a basis for developing the concept of a woman as a chattel. In any case, the !Kung and similar hunter-gatherers disabuse us of the notion of patriarchy as a universal human instinct. It is a learned societal practice dressed up as immutable tradition. And because it is learned, it may also be unlearned if the circumstances allow.

What would a nonpatriarchal society look like? There is no point in trying to dress it up as a form of utopia—humans are flawed creatures and their societies will therefore necessarily be flawed. But what would society look like with the rectification of the major flaw of patriarchy? One clear benefit would be society's capacity to draw from the talent of all its people, not simply that of men. We have already entered the economic era where the major determinant of success is the productivity and ingenuity of human resources. So why play with only half the deck? The corollary is that any limitations placed on human productivity and ingenuity for reasons of gender discrimination will come at a cost to economic success.

The full use of society's talent is an obvious benefit of the end of patriarchy. But surely there are other benefits that are less discernible. Having organized ourselves through centuries of patriarchy, there needs to be a process of feminization of society to find a new balance. The new balance will have an impact on the family, the community, and the governance of society. I will attempt in the following pages an intellectual exploration of what this balance might look like; but, first, we need an unvarnished understanding of from where we are coming.

The Rule of Guns and Beards

Living in cosmopolitan, metrosexual New York, it is hard to conceive of the rule of guns and beards (ROGAB), but go to Afghanistan, as so many Western uniformed people have done over the past fifteen years, and the concept is palpable. Let's start with the beards. No doubt, religious scholars can provide numerous obscurantist reasons why men should grow beards. But if there is one thing anthropology teaches us, it is to look beyond the ostensible reasons given by primitive people to justify custom and to seek understanding in structure and function. Beards may be a fashion statement in some societies, but they are also the simplest and most visible uniform of patriarchy. Men can grow them and women can't. And so it is the easiest mark of distinction in society, the longer the better. Have beard, can rule.

Now let's turn to guns. We need to think of this word as a form of synecdoche to stand for all instruments of violence or intimidation. The gun is probably the single most effective instrument for this purpose, but of course men also use others, such as acid or simply fists. Men justify their monopoly of guns as naturally flowing from the hunter role from which they evolved. But as we have seen, this is a fallacy as hunter-gatherer societies are far more egalitarian. Let's return to that most telling of political explanations—what is convenient. Men claim a monopoly on the use of violence because it allows them to control women. Physical dominion over women is the base from which all other controls over women are constructed. Men claim control over women's bodies, their time, their sexuality, their mobility, and the tasks they can or must perform. Women's protestations will be met with a string of absurd justifications such as the holy book says so, tribal lore says so, tradition says so, and your cowered mother says so, but behind these trails of tendentious teachings stands the ultimate persuader, violence or the threat thereof. Have gun, can intimidate.

Rational choice theory tries to explain a lot about human conduct. Though I harbor doubts about the extent of its applicability, it explains patriarchy pretty well. First, get ahead of half the human race, eliminate half the competition—a coherent rational choice for men. Second, get a lot of unpaid labor to keep your home clean, your hot meals served, and your kids nurtured—again, one can understand *Homo economicus* making that choice. Finally, be dominant in sexual relations without inconvenient consequences such as actually giving birth—most men would make that facile rational choice.

Let's return to Afghanistan for a moment. Why is it that the Taliban has destroyed hundreds of girls' schools in Afghanistan and Pakistan? Why, under Taliban rule in 2002, did only 200,000 of the many millions of girls go to school?[2] There really is no point in trying to understand this phenomenon by reference to obscurantist interpretations of spurious revealed texts. (On this issue, I return to my earlier observation that the content of any religious text is irrelevant. All religious texts can be made to say whatever the speaker wishes them to say. Therefore, to engage in discussion of the holy texts is to fall into a bottomless debating trap. The only relevant issue is what use anybody wishes to make of the texts.) The more useful means of interpretation of these actions is to ask who benefits from them. The Taliban is clearly of the view that educated women are their enemies. They are correct. Educated women will put up a fight against ROGAB. Educated women together with their male allies may even defeat ROGAB. Imagine fighting against millions of Malalas! The Taliban would have to commit autogenocide by putting bullets in all their heads. They are not waging their war against women because of some obscure passage from a so-called revealed text; they are fighting for ROGAB. They are fighting for men's privilege and for men's dominion.

It is easy to lampoon a pariah. It is easy to point to the fanaticism of the Taliban men in Afghanistan who wear the long beards and carry the guns. It is much more painful to identify the little bit of the Taliban in each of us. Again, it is not the absurd beliefs that are relevant, it is the results. How many of us continue to wage our own wars against women? Even in our sophisticated and successful modern societies, we seem to accept the proposition that women should not govern us; we seem to accept that women should be paid less for the same work; we seem to accept that women should carry the bulk of the responsibility for child raising and household maintenance; and women are still fighting a battle to be in charge of their own bodies, this time against a bunch of men preaching obscurantist passages from a different so-called revealed text. We need to fight the Taliban abroad and at home.

Women Need Democracy

The title of this chapter borrows from the title of Paul Collier's famous book about the world's poverty-stricken bottom billion.[3] It is important not to lose track of this vast number of people while the world is congratulating itself on having dragged hundreds of millions of people out of poverty—in fact, the world should be congratulating China, from which most of the success stories come. The Collier number is large, round, and memorable and demonstrates that the global economic development process has not worked for everyone. But if we are to add up all the women of the world who remain in the grip of patriarchy, remain a chattel owned by their husbands or families, and remain economically hobbled by discriminatory inheritance laws, land ownership systems, and employment practices, then we will come to another large, round, and memorable figure—three billion!

The three billion figure includes nearly all the women of the global South and a significant slice of the women of the North as well. The metric for measuring "bottom" in this case is not assets or income but stunted capability. Of course, if we use the Collier measure one would find a disproportionate number of women in the bottom billion. But the stunted capability metric is in many ways more damaging and more galling because aside from the burden of economic hardship, it makes wives, sisters, and female students and workers subordinate to their husbands, brothers, and male colleagues. Three billion people in the world are not being allowed to develop their capabilities fully because of their gender. That is what makes them the bottom three billion.

What is depriving them of the ability to develop their capabilities fully? In the age of Twitter, we seek one-word answers to complex questions. A simple answer therefore is "patriarchy," but it is an unsatisfying answer. While patriarchy is practiced to a lesser or greater extent nearly everywhere in the world, it is not an explicit ideology. Men do not march down the street waving the flag of patriarchy. Political party platforms do not laud its benefits. Poems are not written extolling its virtues. It is in this sense a phantom enemy. A better answer is "tradition." Unlike patriarchy, men venerate tradition, political parties support it, and poems and songs are indeed written about it (perhaps most famously in the opening number of *Fiddler on the Roof,* where the central character, Tevye, explains everybody's place and role in the village in a song appropriately titled "Tradition"). Tradition is invariably deeply patriarchal. It is patriarchy's beard. Its boosters like to make it synonymous with pretty folkloric customs. Its defenders equate it with continuity and harmony. It is often dressed up as religion, which, of course, can and must be sustained by blind belief. In other words, tradition is a formidable adversary.

The bottom three billion must make the painful decision to consider tradition as its adversary. The decision is painful because tradition, unlike patriarchy, is an insidious enemy. There is much in tradition that women and men may wish to retain. Many of those pretty folkloric customs are a comfort and a joy. And for all the ill it brings, its defenders are not wrong when they say that it also instills elements of continuity and harmony. Patriarchy may be the phantom enemy, but tradition is the enemy with which many of its foes will be locked in a love/hate relationship. The proponents of tradition will portray it as an all-or-nothing deal, take it or leave it. This suits their purposes fine, but it is deeply ahistorical. Tradition is portrayed as having been practiced since time immemorial, but it is a living process—and all living things change. The issues are the size and speed of change.

In a previous chapter we learned of the Australian government's inadvertent invention of long-term ethnography when it banished noted anthropologist Bronislaw Malinowski to the Trobriand Islands. The early anthropologists following Malinowski's example did us a great service in recognizing and describing the different means of achieving viable society. They did us a great disservice in describing these primitive (a term used to describe the absence of sophisticated technology) cultures as "timeless." The truth is that the ethnographers simply did not stay

long enough. Each society described was viable in its particular environment. But the environment changes, physically, through contact or
through internal dynamics, and society will change accordingly, dragging tradition along. Tradition is not constant, immutable, or unchang-
ing. It is subject to change; large or small, brutal or subtle. But it won't
change of its own accord. It requires actors to negotiate those changes.

Who will these actors be? The logical answer must be those who
have the most to gain by change. And the largest class of people in this
category is women. Armed with the sure knowledge that tradition is
negotiable, women need to be at the forefront of the battle of tradition.
We have witnessed more than a century of this struggle, from the suffragists to today's oppressed Saudi women seeking the right to drive. The
battlegrounds of women's struggle are in education, employment, inheritance, elections, government, and the home. But perhaps the most basic
battle is the right to be in charge of one's own body—not to have it
mutilated, covered, hidden, beaten, or denied health services. The negotiation over the meaning and path of tradition therefore unfolds in public spaces as well as in the most intimate places. It is fought on the floor
of parliament and over the dinner table at home. The negotiation has an
ebb and flow, and the thought that must sustain women is that history
does indeed curve toward justice.

As every negotiator understands, arguing against something is best
accomplished if there is something positive toward which one is pointing. What should women be struggling for? Again the Twitter world
requires single-concept responses. There is a vast array of motives out
there, and to describe them under a single word is quixotic. But let's tilt
at the windmills and continue this thought experiment. In the previous
paragraph I used the word *justice*. It is a magnificent word for any rab-
ble rouser, and I would never deny its mobilizing value. But its meaning
tends more to philosophy than politics. It is difficult to define and apply.
And, perhaps most disabling, it has an applied meaning that turns it into
the machinery of institutions. The Iranian theocracy's Revolutionary
Guards control the police and the courts, and they would be more than
pleased to have the debate turn on the term *justice*.

A more subtle term is a component of justice—*human rights*. It is one
of modernity's greatest achievements to have cemented the concept of
human rights as an inherent aspect of our humanity. And as Hillary Clinton has been telling us for decades, women's rights are human rights, and
human rights are women's rights. It is therefore an excellent candidate,
and tens of thousands of human-rights defenders have chosen this term as
their positive goal. I applaud them, but I have a nagging doubt about

whether the term can shed its technicalities. Because it encompasses political, civil, economic, social, cultural, and people's rights, the term seems broad enough to cover all of society's ills. But it seems to be locked up in various chambers around the world, where its meaning is dissected and dissimulated. This is the technicality I fear might shackle the use of this term. When Russian athletes are banned for using performance-enhancing drugs, their government, which ran the scam, has the chutzpah to say that these bans are breaches of the athletes' human rights!

A decade ago I would have passionately defended the term *democracy*. But as I have argued in the preceding chapters, democracy has had its soft power dulled. We had no better example of this depressing fact than the term employed by the "square people" of the Arab Spring. It was not justice or human rights or democracy that mobilized them, though they wanted them all, it was the word *dignity*. But as I have previously noted[4] the term *dignity* does not solve the goal problem. It is too amorphous and subjective. It is evidence of the success of a political system, but it is silent about what will get us there.

The antonym of *tradition* is *modernity,* and it is fitting that this should be the goal. Unlike the other candidates, each of which has a saintly feel, *modernity* has a raw quality that gives us pause. But this is in fact its redeeming feature. Just like tradition, modernity must also be negotiated. It is not a take-it-or-leave-it process. If one examines the many different modernities in the world, it becomes clear that there is a threshold and beyond it a menu of options. The threshold is the right to be an individual and to make choices about beliefs and objectives. The threshold may perhaps be drawn from the document that stands as one of the foundational texts of modernity, the American Declaration of Independence, and its radical idea that individuals must be allowed to pursue happiness. This is the point where tradition ends and modernity begins. Beyond this point, let the negotiations begin.

But that cannot be the end of the story. It is well and good to extol the value of negotiations, but as Malala Yousafsai learned, under ROGAB the other side negotiates with bullets. It is at this point that we see the value of democracy. It is the only system that will allow a negotiation to take place. Women cannot rely on the generosity of their husbands, their religious leaders, or their benevolent dictators to negotiate their path from tradition to modernity. They need the weapons that only democracy places in their hands. They need to deliberate, to organize, to convince, and to vote. They need to negotiate their way from tradition to modernity. Only democracy will allow this process to occur. Women need democracy.

Democracy Needs Women

Democracy also needs women for strategic and substantive reasons. Let's first deal with strategy. In the early chapters I traced the roller-coaster ride of democracy promotion in the post–Cold War period. Various strategies employed have shown themselves to be problematic. The cozy idea of nudging authoritarian or illiberal governments toward ever more effective democratic institutions has shown itself to be ineffective. It was simply too easy for autocrats to snow the funding democratic governments by "cooperating" with the democracy promotion organization. On behalf of both the Australian and, separately, the Danish government, I conducted training programs in Vietnam for government institutions such as the National Assembly and the Procuracy (a robust version of a criminal prosecution service), and though there were clearly some younger individuals who were open to new ideas, I have to be honest and admit that on the whole these training programs achieved little discernible change. The uncomfortable aspect of this process was the benefit to the Vietnamese government of being seen to be cooperating and therefore open to democratization. Nothing was further from the truth, however, and the Communist Party is as dominant as ever. There is always some benefit in maintaining lines of communications with such countries, but let's not fool ourselves that these one-party states will allow their authoritarian systems to be undermined by well-prepared syllabi or the critical opinion of peers.

Another big idea was to help strengthen that essential and seemingly irreplaceable building block of democracy, the political party. With the exception of the National Endowment for Democracy (NED), all the largest democracy promoters are offshoots of Western political parties, in particular the US and German party foundations. Let's not forget that democracy promotion was a serendipitous invention of the two major German party foundations assisting their Iberian counterparts in the pivotal period of transition away from authoritarianism. There are some who continue to believe that directing assistance toward political parties remains the key requirement. But my sense is that, in general, the air has gone out of this particular sail. The problem, as Thomas Carothers so vividly described,[5] is the fecklessness, corruption, and incompetence of so many political parties in so many countries around the world. The political party is part of both the public and the private domains. Democracy promotion tends to focus on the public aspects—developing the party platform, crafting campaign tactics, grooming candidates. But the problems are mainly on the private side—the dysfunctional internal dynamics, party leader dominance, and unaccountable money.

This has basically left one major strategy: supporting civil society. This is the strategy followed by the NED, the UN Democracy Fund, and many others. It is the right strategy and it brings dividends. It is also a strategy that necessarily progresses through trial and error, and public money has little tolerance for error, especially if the baleful anecdote is magnified in the media. I understand the taxpayer's intolerance for wasted money, but allow me to inject a little plea in support of failure. It is not a failure if we learn from it. Trial and error is the scientific process, and if scientists were allowed only to be successful it would mean the end of experimentation and instead the continued repetition of projects with sure-fire results we already know. At UNDEF, our external evaluators found about 20 percent of the projects to be failures. I considered this an excellent result—an 80 percent success rate! In hindsight, we learned far more from the failed projects than from the successful ones. We spent more time reading and discussing these reports and trying to determine what they might teach us about project selection and design. Anyway, that's my ode to failure. But the Achilles' heel of civil society projects is not their methodologies but their vulnerability to the actions of hostile governments. This issue was unpacked in a previous chapter.

So here lies the dilemma of democracy promotion: cozy government-to-government projects are ineffective, the beneficiaries of political party strengthening projects are too often dysfunctional, and civil society projects are particularly vulnerable to the predations of their governments. Who can therefore champion democracy successfully? I believe the one-word answer is women. They are the bottom three billion. They need democracy. Democracy provides them with the means to negotiate their way from tradition to modernity, picking and choosing what to leave behind and what to adopt. Strategically, democracy could have no stronger class of advocates than those who have the most to gain by its development. We already know the contours of what this looks like. It involves women leaders, elected women, women academics, business women, women village leaders, and civil society women. It also involves all the men who support them. It takes the form of legislation, government programs, jobs, micro-finance, discussion, and deliberation. The forums range from the UN to the village square to the dining mat in the humblest family home. We have seen this movement building inexorably over recent decades.

Democracy also needs women for a substantive reason: it needs feminized politics. In various ways, overt and insidious, ROGAB has radiated its values into politics everywhere. It is not simply that it has elevated men into the role of "natural" leaders, but it has also privileged the more extreme tendencies on the male spectrum. At this point we can no longer shelter behind any notion of scientific certainty, and we must enter the world of assessment and intuition. But I would list among the male values that dominate in today's politics: fearlessness, self-centeredness, uncompromising confidence, determination to vanquish, and a zero-sum mentality. A politician imbued with these qualities along with a strong speaking voice and good hair will go far. Of course, the more his society has adopted the ways of modernity, the more will the politician have to modify his behavior. But even with modified behavior, we nevertheless see extreme male values inform the political process. Parliament becomes a shouting match complete with finger pointing and fist shaking. Debate turns into hyperbole in supporting one's position and mockery when considering that of the opponent. Cooperation is understood in tribal terms of unquestioning loyalty to one's own and at best shaky short-term truces with those on the other side. It is bad enough when the dividing line between the warring tribes is ideological, but at least then, substance focuses on policy prescriptions. But when politics becomes identity based, as in so many countries of the global South, politics based on extreme male values becomes a game of privileging one's own group over the other, with tragic results we have come to know all too well.

Can there be another form of politics? With apologies to Carl von Clausewitz, is politics the continuation of war by subtler means? In other words, is there no escape from politics based on extreme male values? If the current form of politics is the only possible form of politics, then it makes the case for democracy that much weaker. Why support a system that can only provide this type of aggressive result? Okay, it is nevertheless better than ROGAB in the hands of the autocrat or the theocrat. But is it sufficiently inspiring to fight for? Here we come to one of democracy's great virtues: it allows for peaceful change of government, and it can therefore allow for peaceful change of governance. Politics can change and lead to better results. The key is to feminize our politics.

Returning to the world of assessment and intuition, what are the female qualities we need in order to change our politics and finally to put an end to ROGAB? Some of these flow from biology. Women are child bearers, and this builds in them nurturing and caring values. We need those in politics. I was surprised to read recently about another positive biological feature—menopause. The author said this gave women a deeper perspective because it established a sense of mortality. We need that in politics. Perhaps for reasons of both nature and nurture, women are good at working together, at cooperating, at networking. We need those in politics. Women tend to be more empathetic and forgiving. We need those qualities in politics. And yes, sometimes we need to consult the map or the instructions before we go blundering onward. Others, who understand these things far better, need to take this debate forward, but I remain convinced that a large part of the answer to the problems of society and to the salvation of democracy itself is more feminized politics.

Whenever I discuss this issue with students or colleagues, the same hoary argument invariably is trotted out. It goes something like this: Margaret Thatcher was pretty war-like, or Indira Gandhi suspended democracy, or Dilma Rousseff has been impeached! Pointing to a particular act by a woman politician is an unconvincing piece of inductive reasoning that tells us very little about the general proposition. The problem with this type of argument, however, goes beyond the poor logic. It is the problem of critical mass, an issue identified in a pioneering publication by the International Institute for Democracy and Electoral Assistance.[6] In short, when women are in token numbers in a particular institution, they tend to adopt the culture of that institution and behave like their colleagues, the men. It is only when women form a critical mass in an institution that they can develop and display their feminine qualities. What is that critical mass? The publication hazards the figure of 30 percent, and in our need for quantitative measures this figure has been adopted as an international benchmark. The parliaments of the world are now subject to the same numerical scrutiny as the racing guide at Belmont Park Race Course, leading to about the same degree of understanding.

I visited Dhaka a few years ago to meet with several UNDEF project deliverers. One project focused on women's issues and led to a useful publication.[7] To welcome me, this group held a dinner and invited the women members of the national parliament. It was one of my more disappointing events. Having looked forward to discussing women's issues with women's champions, I instead had paraded before me the worst of Bangladesh's politics; blind partisanship, nepotism, privilege, and disregard for others. Yet this is a country where politics is dominated by two women—the daughter and widow of former leaders. I doubt the men could be as violent or ruthless as the women leaders of the country. Critical mass may be an important element, but it is an insufficient ingredient if the numbers comprise the wives of oligarchs who are no different from their husbands.

Feminized politics has to be about quality as well as quantity. It has to be about men as well as women. It needs to be about the best qualities of both men and women. Because today's politics flows from ROGAB and its more polished successors, it needs to be feminized so that the correct balance can be found. This is not a prescription for utopia, a concept democracy rejects. Women are just as human as men and are therefore just as flawed. They can make mistakes too. But feminized politics holds out the promise of avoiding the obvious mistakes that flow from male-centered politics. It may not promise peace, but it suggests a more peaceful world. It may not promise harmony, but it suggests more cooperation. It may not promise the end of identity politics, but it suggests far more empathy in the conduct of politics.

This should not become a battle between men and women. Each individual is a complex sum of his or her parts and can draw on both masculine and feminine qualities. As has so tellingly been demonstrated, there is not one single masculinity.[8] Men can find their feminine qualities, and women can draw on their male qualities as well. In this regard, we all need to be bi-gendered.

Notes

1. Patricia Draper, "!Kung Women: Contrasts in Sexual Egalitarianism in Foraging and Sedentary Contexts," *Anthropology Faculty Publications Paper* 45 (1975): 78, http://digitalcommons.unl.edu/anthropologyfacpub/45.

2. World Bank, "Bringing 6 Million Children Back to School in Afghanistan," April 17, 2013, http://www.worldbank.org/en/results/2013/04/17/bringing-6-million -children-back-to-school-afghanistan.

3. Paul Collier, *The Bottom Billion: Why the Poorest Countries Are Failing and What Can Be Done About It* (Oxford: Oxford University Press, 2007).

4. Roland Rich, *Dignity Through Democracy and Human Rights* (New Delhi: Institute of Social Sciences, 2012).

5. Thomas Carothers, *Confronting the Weakest Link: Aiding Political Parties in New Democracies* (Washington, DC: Carnegie Endowment for International Peace, 2006).

6. Azza M. Karam, Frene Ginwala, and Gehan Abu-Zayd, *Women in Parliament: Beyond Numbers* (Stockholm: International IDEA, 2002; since revised several times).

7. Rokeya Kabir (ed.), *Policies Budget and PRSP: Are They Promoting Women's Rights in Bangladesh?* (Dhaka: University Press Limited, 2011).

8. R. W. Connell, *Masculinities* (Berkeley: University of California Press, 2005).

9

Democratizing
Development Assistance

To recall the adaptation of the showbiz joke about death and comedy from the introduction—analysis is easy, action is hard. We can fill libraries with analyses, the inescapable starting point, but when it comes to policies we quickly learn how few action options are at our disposal. This is true of issues as intractable as homelessness and recidivism, and it is certainly true of democratization. A previous chapter analyzed theories of democratization. None of those theories suggested that it could be triggered by military action, yet we have recently seen the military ostensibly used as a powerful tool to bring about democratization. Some fifteen years later in Afghanistan that policy option has failed, and many Iraqis think the same can be said for the military intervention in their country. Investment and globalization are also available policy tools, especially if one adheres to modernization theory, but they follow a long-term market logic that is not at the beck and call of governments. Governments have certain limited means of influencing the direction of trade and investment, such as tax policies, investment treaties, and reductions of official barriers to trade and investment. Though these are useful tools, they do not fundamentally influence the rational economic decisions based on comparative advantage that direct the flow of trade and investment. Soft power is a mighty tool, but it is necessarily a long-term strategy and cannot be readily wielded by governments. It is slow moving and has become subject to millions of authors in the world of social media. In the world of policy prescriptions, soft power is a fairly inaccessible tool. In relation to strengthening democracy at home, the final chapter will suggest a few action options. In relation to democratization in the global South, the tool of direct foreign funding of champions of democracy is being compromised by the Putin model. This leaves one rather weak tool available to policy wielders: official development assistance.

Official development assistance is a twentieth-century invention born during the decolonization period. The amount spent for ODA by OECD countries in 2014 reached $135 billion.[1] While there are many admirable aspects of the phenomenon—including its capacity for self-criticism, its relative openness, and its engagement with the scholarly literature[2]—ODA remains anchored securely to the twentieth century. To be a more effective tool for democratization, ODA needs to break free from its old paradigms by democratizing itself, in both delivery and implementation.

Twentieth-Century Aid and Its Two Paradigms

There is no doubting the impressive achievements of ODA over the past half century, especially in disease control, humanitarian emergencies, and human development, but it is also clear that ODA has failed in its stated purpose of fostering economic development. ODA was built on a precedent it did not follow, the Marshall Plan, and based on a theory that its author quickly disavowed—Domar's theory of filling the savings gap.[3] During the Cold War years, it morphed into a support mechanism for the governments of developing countries underpinned by two key paradigms.

The first and most obvious paradigm underpinning ODA is the Westphalian concept of sovereignty. ODA began as and largely remains a government-to-government enterprise. The early days saw massive infrastructure projects, many of which brought few dividends because of their inappropriate designs, the lack of sustained maintenance, and limited buy-in from locals. In my travels I have seen far too many examples of useless infrastructure spending: highways to nowhere, abandoned factories, and water projects that exacerbate desertification. Disappointment with the results of high spending on building up developing countries' physical assets led to the next phase, trying to build their governments' human assets. These civil-service capacity-building and institution-building programs continue to be in fashion and remain firmly in the clutches of the Westphalian paradigm.

The Westphalian paradigm is convenient to both sides of the ODA divide. It allows the aid agency to deal with a single interlocutor. This often translates into a search for a "champion," a common description of which is an enthusiastic government minister who speaks the language of the donor and employs the jargon of ODA. And on the receiving side, for all the complaints about the plethora of uncoordinated donors, the advantage of having government donors is their general predictability, being rules-based institutions driven by declared public policy. Governments on both sides of the ODA divide have an interest in maintaining the Westphalian basis of ODA.

The second paradigm imposing itself on ODA is less obvious. It is the Soviet five-year plan (S5YP), which was born and died in the twentieth century along with the polity it so ill-served. I am not the first to make the link between Soviet planning and ODA. William Easterly argues that the apparent initial success of the USSR in a system of planning and forced savings had a big influence on development economists.[4] Of course, the S5YP is a different concept from ODA, and the modern aid agencies are very different creatures from the Gosplan, the Soviet agency in charge of planning. The Gosplan directed the entire planned economy whereas the aid agencies direct less than 1 percent of their nations' gross national income. It is not the command economy aspect of the S5YP that ODA embraced but the conceit of omniscience, the top-down design, the power of bureaucracy, the "experts know best" posture, the dirigisme and control, the insufficiency of listening to affected voices, and the authoritarian developmentalism implicit in its delivery. I am not a Thatcherite. Planning has a role in government. We need environmental planning, health and education planning, and social safety net planning. But planning cannot take the place of the basic role of the market. This is in effect what has happened in the ODA experience.

The S5YP model also has an understandable attraction to officials on both sides. For the aid-giving administration, large programs delivered over several years and encompassing broad goals allow a big slice of the aid pie to be served with one set of documents. These programs give the impression that size leads to impact. They can be sold to an at-times skeptical domestic audience with simple sound bites ("abolish poverty"; "health for all"). From the perspective of the aid-receiving government, large projects basically allow for impressive ribbon-cutting ceremonies and give the impression of government activism. They also allow for large tenders to be called, opening the possibility of rent-seeking behavior.

ODA is not as powerful an economic weapon as those flowing from finance and trade, but because of its altruistic rhetoric, its charitable status, and its dealings with a wide range of receiving state actors beyond trade or finance ministries, ODA developed an agenda-setting capacity that even the Bretton Woods and GATT stakeholder communities had to take into account. Since the 1940s, ODA has migrated from infrastructure and capital, to basic human needs, to structural adjustment, to the environment, to governance and human development results until coming the currently fashionable term, the all-encompassing and therefore rather meaningless *partnership*. The adoption of "governance" around the turn of the millennium was particularly influential from the perspective of democracy.[5]

ODA's process of self-awareness began with a realization that it was all well and good to strive for infrastructure construction or meeting basic human needs or saving the environment but that none of these would bring results if the delivery mechanism for these programs did not work. The delivery mechanism was aid-receiving ministries and other government instrumentalities. To cure this problem, the early steps included civil service training projects, efficiency studies, and an attempt to improve management processes. Before too long it became clear that the focus on the bottom of the governance pyramid—the field workers, managers, and bureaucrats—was at best insufficient and at worst ill-directed. The issue of poor project delivery flowed from problems at the top of the governance pyramid; incompetence, fecklessness, clientelism, and the issue that could finally dare speak its name, corruption. These were problems involving heads of governments and ministries that did not lend themselves to the normal ODA panacea—training. These were problems that required the introduction of difficult practices such as accountability, meritocracy, and contestability. And from the perspective of the ODA donors, the only system that could foster such practices was democracy.

The effect of twentieth-century aid was to try to help nations build themselves from the top down. The simplest idea was to replicate the governing structures of the donors as closely as resources and circumstances would allow. This tended to focus much aid spending on the receiving nation's governing structures on the theory that those structures would then service the needs of the people. But this clearly entailed a shortcut not taken by the donor countries themselves, whose own government structures were built up over centuries of contestation and deliberation. As has become all too clear, five decades of projects, technical assistance, and training in which some $5 trillion in ODA has been spent[6] has not led to the sought-after result. The majority of people in the majority of aid-receiving countries remain as poor as they were at the beginning of the process.

The "Ownership" Fallacy

Accepting its lack of effectiveness and therefore recognizing the need for change and reform, the ODA community turned to the notion of receiving country ownership as the way forward. The theory is that ownership of projects by the receiving countries will cause them to value those projects, integrate them into their planning cycles, and contribute their own resources in support. It was an attempt to move aid out of the donor-driven paradigm that had led to inappropriate aid, tied aid, and donor competition to be involved in the most salient sectors.

The problem with the ownership concept is that while it may have reformed some donor practices, it does not deal with the two outdated twentieth-century paradigms. The Westphalian hold is unrelenting. Aid remains the subject of government-to-government decisionmaking. On the practical side, this creates the funnel effect whereby the $5 trillion is moved through decisionmaking taken in the two government bottlenecks meeting at the spouts. The perennial complaint is that aid-receiving governments must place their spouts against those of each of the donors, thus exhausting their capacities and redirecting their energies from domestic governance issues to engagement with donors.

Beyond the practical problem, however, there is a much sterner problem of principle with the receiving government ownership concept. Once ownership changes hands, where are the oversight mechanisms? Donor countries with their well-established systems of vertical and horizontal accountability no longer "own" the aid or the issues it generates. Receiving countries, with feeble oversight processes and often little or no accountability to the people the aid is intended to benefit, now own these issues. From an accountability perspective, a backward step has been taken.

The proposed cure for this problem is to convert receiving-country ownership to democratic ownership whereby the beneficiaries and the public at large have a say in aid design and delivery processes. Admirable as this idea may be, it cannot be satisfactorily engineered. Nondemocratic states will simply set up fake consultation processes with civil society representatives friendly to the government. Other civil society organizations will then complain to the donor community, sidetracking the process. Even in developing countries practicing democratic processes, the consultation mechanisms remain problematic. Civil society is unlikely to speak with one voice, and the issues involved are unlikely to be the subject of political party planks in an election campaign. The problem is not a deficiency in the concept of democracy; it is caused by having aid issues locked up within the duopolies of West-phalian polities engaging with each other at the government level.

The other twentieth-century paradigm also rears its ugly head in the "ownership" model because it privileges S5YP behavior. One of the few governance propositions in which we can have confidence is that economic development is not the product of S5YPs but of market-based initiatives. Even though this proposition is broadly accepted by donor countries whose own wealth has been generated by their respective private sectors, it is remarkable that in a half century of ODA, the donor community has not invested in the private sectors of developing countries. If anything, ODA has had a distorting effect on the private sector: undermining agricultural production by dumping food aid, confusing the labor market with expatriat salaries, and encouraging a large public sector role in the economy.

Why can't ODA assist the private sectors of poor countries? The main problem is the logic that clings to taxpayers' money from which ODA is drawn. Public money should not be used to allow an individual or private company to be enriched; it should be used for the benefit of the broader public. Existing ODA projects in favor of the private sector are therefore usually designed to improve the enabling environment for the private sector, often in the form of helping to develop government rules and services. While these rules and services, such as developing bankruptcy courts and intellectual property rules, are not in themselves controversial, being imposed on a rudimentary private sector, they all too often lead mainly to opportunities for rent-seeking by government gatekeepers.

Twenty-First-Century Aid

Twenty-first-century aid needs to break free from its Westphalian and S5YP paradigms. Twenty-first-century aid needs to move away from the government-to-government bottlenecks. Twenty-first-century aid needs to help build societies organically from the bottom up instead of from the top down. Twenty-first-century aid needs to be democratized to allow a flow of ODA to the private sector and to civil society in addition to an appropriate and modest proportion for receiving government projects or budgets.

Tentative steps in that direction have already been taken, largely through donor experimentation fueled by the frustrations of not seeing the expected returns on ODA investment. Accordingly, the ODA community has worked to take decisions about educational scholarships out of the hands of local officials; they are now decided by open competitive processes. ODA has already recognized that investment in civil society brings significant dividends, including in democratization processes. And ODA has dipped its toe in the enormous lake that is direct support for the private sector.

Twenty-first-century aid needs to find ways of strengthening all these processes. In doing so it needs to be influenced not by Westphalia or the S5YP but by people's participation and market mechanisms. It will be people—in the form of entrepreneurs, innovators, designers, risk-takers, civil society activists, consumer activists, environmental activists, public intellectuals, and voters—who will bring about economic and social development, not governments. It will be the basic building blocks of the market—competition, private property, meritocracy, freedom of information, risk, reward, free decisionmaking—that will provide the mechanism for economic development, not the S5YP. The question that needs to be addressed is how to change the small tentative steps in this direction into a completely new paradigm of democratizing ODA.

The Receiving Bottleneck

The key is to avoid the government spout-to-spout bottlenecks. On the receiving side, the problem has already been solved, though only in pilot form, through various schemes that require open competitions for grants: establish a fund, draft rules and guidelines for its operation, allow open applications, assess applications through disinterested consultants, establish an independent executive board to make final decisions, establish a secretariat to manage the system, and commission independent evaluations of results. The flexibility of such a system is that it can allow for donor funds, public and private, to be blended seamlessly; different funds can be directed at different issues; the mechanism can support different types of projects from civil society voice projects to social safety net delivery projects to innovative problem-solving projects. Having established the funds and their governance and management mechanisms, governments on both sides of the ODA divide can get on with their other pressing problems, returning periodically to review issues of effectiveness and impact.

ODA has also taken tentative steps in establishing investment funds for private-sector entities decided by open competition. It is perhaps to be expected that the ideas behind these funds came from the private sector and from groups such as the Gates and Rockefeller Foundations. The Africa Enterprise Challenge Fund provides grants and interest-free loans to businesses that wish to implement innovative, commercially viable, high-impact projects in Africa.[7] The African Agricultural Capital Fund will deliver much-needed growth capital to boost the productivity and profitability of Africa's undercapitalized agriculture sector.[8] The new African Cocoa Initiative is a public-private partnership to invest in sustainable cocoa farms in West Africa.[9] Such investment funds have the same advantages and flexibility as the existing civil society funds and can be readily scaled up. Once again, these structures allow public and private donor funds to be blended. The logic of public money is filtered away by the arm's-length involvement of public officials and by the meritocracy inherent in the decisions taken. Governments, angel investors, and the public can all contribute.

At the grassroots level, the microfinance revolution has demonstrated that poor people—especially women—when given access to modest loans can lift themselves out of poverty through engaging in the market. ODA had a significant role to play in the early days of microfinance by guaranteeing the loans made by local lenders to microfinance borrowers, and ODA may have a continuing role to play in scaling up microfinance in parts of the world where it is not well-established. Once again, however, ODA for this purpose need be directed not at governments but rather at capitalizing or guaranteeing private microfinance banks.

A criticism that will be made by governments is that such funds are not "coordinated" and do not necessarily align with government plans (thus clinging to the S5YP mentality). The response is that civil society and private-sector activities in donor countries are also not "coordinated" by governments and are not subservient to government plans. Governments have a critical role in security, regulation, and taxation, and all actors need to conform to the rules adopted by democratically elected governments. Government actions in rich countries are directed toward regulating, monitoring, and measuring the economy as well as public investments in certain areas of infrastructure and social safety nets. This leaves most of the economy open to companies and individuals exercising the freedom to take risks and accept rewards, which then generate economic growth. Why should this concept not work just as well in poor countries?

In delivering the limited macro role in regulating, monitoring, and measuring the economy as well as public investments in certain infrastructure and social safety net areas, governments may seek assistance from donors—and there is no reason why this should not be part of the future ODA mix. But just as the government role in society, however important, should be limited, so should the share of ODA directed toward a government be commensurately limited. Receiving governments will need to be very strategic in determining their priorities for the limited slice of ODA that will come their way. Developing-country ministers will no longer have cause to complain about the amount of time they are being asked to devote to donor requirements as they will be dealing with a much smaller and more focused slice of the ODA pie than is currently the case.

The obvious criticism of this plan for ending the receiving government bottleneck is that the receiving governments will kick up a hue and cry. The new idea is disruptive. Government ministers and their domains will be disrupted. The role of patronage will be greatly diminished, and this will disrupt the political clientelism so prevalent in aid-receiving countries. What will become of those ribbon-cutting ceremonies? And what about all those trips to London and Stockholm for "consultations"? Yes, government officials would lose some of their privileges. This problem needs to be managed because we cannot rely on decisionmaking from receiving governments to be taken solely in the interests of their people. There needs to be a trade-off. Once again, ODA has already invented it.

For decades, ODA focused on projects. I know them well. The Mandalay Dairy Development project intended to produce milk for people who did not drink it, which was finally privatized through its sale to Nestlé, which then mothballed the plant to ensure it did not compete with a Nestlé plant in neighboring Thailand.[10] Or a market-opening road in Northern Samar, the Philippines, that was mainly used by the military in search of insurgents. But ideally, project aid is worthwhile and contributes to economic development. The latest ODA innovation, however, is budget support.[11] If a country is performing well in a certain sector with a functioning bureaucracy and workable delivery mechanisms, why should aid be project based? Why not simply give the money to that ministry and let it get on with its work? The trade-off would be that in return for the democratization of ODA at the receiving end, that slice of the ODA pie going to governments would be steadily transformed from project aid to budget support. This would be an attractive offer. Those being disrupted according to this plan would be the aid bureaucrats in the donor countries who would no longer have projects to plan and manage. The aid-receiving bureaucrats would now truly "own" the ODA coming their way, though they would need to account for it in a way that is sufficiently transparent to meet the needs of their people and of the donors. ODA remains, after all, public money.

The Donor Bottleneck

These processes will clear the bottleneck on the receiving end, but dealing with the bottleneck at the donor end will require some innovative thinking. As things stand, ODA comes from taxpayers' money; it is collected by the tax office, passed to the aid agency through the annual parliamentary budget process, subjected to aid agency planning, and then disbursed and monitored as ODA. Parallel governmental processes occur at the receiving end. Each of these processes has staffing and transaction costs paid for ultimately by reducing the amount of ODA available for delivery to recipients. This design is due to the Westphalian and S5YP assumptions underpinning ODA. A far more efficient way of dealing with ODA is only to collect as tax that smaller amount of ODA that will be used as budget support for receiving governments. The balance of ODA should never enter into any public account, either at the donor or receiving end.

This may sound like a radical approach, but once again the tools for achieving this result have already been invented and are already in use; it is simply a matter of scaling them up. The existing tools are civil society activism, corporate social responsibility, and, critically, tax deductibility.

Civil society organizations have had a prominent place in ODA processes, particularly since the end of the Cold War. Turning to CSOs for aid delivery coincided with a growing disillusionment on the part of donors in the capacities of receiving governments.[12] Beginning as vehicles for service delivery, CSOs quickly demonstrated that they were also the vehicles for advocacy, reflecting the policy positions of social movements and groups.[13] The question arises, however, whether it is necessary for funds directed to CSOs to go through the donor-government funnel.

The main advantage in channeling funds to CSOs through government ODA agencies is strong accountability. But there are also disadvantages. There may be a propensity for internal political reasons to deliver ODA through CSOs based in the donor country rather than in the receiving country, thus increasing the costs and probably decreasing the effectiveness of the grant.[14] There will also be a tendency for supposed reasons of efficiency to channel the funds in large amounts, thus favoring large CSOs that have the management and accounting capacity to handle relatively large funds for large projects, another throwback to the S5YP. And in the increasingly harsh partisanship of politics in donor countries, there may well be a tendency to favor "our" CSOs over "theirs."

Would it not be better to allow market forces to operate in this field? Rather than coming from taxpayers, money for civil society work should come from individual and corporate voluntary contributions, thus bypassing governments on both sides of the ODA process. There should be no doubt about the generosity of the nongovernment sector. In 2009, according to the OECD, $17 billion of ODA was channeled by donor governments through CSOs while in the same year CSOs themselves raised $22 billion.[15] The market is already showing the way.

But what about the supposed efficiencies of ODA agencies to direct funding to the most effective CSOs? In some cases, such as delivery of emergency humanitarian assistance, ODA agencies may well have useful background on which to draw in the selection process. But any efficiencies that may accrue are outbalanced by inefficiencies flowing from the inevitable influence of politics on government decisionmaking. As noted, governments like to give grants to CSOs in their own countries as this is clearly good politics. When governments give grants to CSOs in the receiving country they are usually careful not to "upset" their official interlocutors in those countries, thus selecting politically acceptable CSOs—believing this to be good diplomacy. Market-based mechanisms would avoid this sort of politicization.

How can one tackle the issue of weak knowledge about the situation in receiving countries on the part of the general public in donor countries as against the supposed expert knowledge of ODA officials? The market will respond to this pressure in a number of ways. The power of franchise is one way already at work. When a CSO develops a powerful brand, it then franchises groups in other countries to use that brand, taking care to protect the brand by only franchising reputable applicants. This is what Transparency International does in the anticorruption field. In the field of development, it is what ActionAid does. Another way is for groups to develop a reputation for expertise in certain regions and thus attract funds for disbursement to their selected CSOs in those regions. These groups will be subject to competition from other groups, thus keeping transaction costs lower than in ODA agencies that are beyond competition. Whereas these "bundlers" of funds may initially come from donor countries, eventually they will be based in receiving countries because their costs will be lower and their expertise greater. In other words, the market will develop means whereby the public can be relatively confident in its investments even though the individual members of the public have limited expertise.

The ideal role of donor governments in this regard is also a well-known current practice—to allow tax deductibility for private contributions to development aid. As will be elaborated in the next section, the tax system is the best way for governments to provide incentives for development assistance.

The Private Sector

The key issue that ODA has failed to address is how to grow the private sector in developing countries. This is a devastating indictment because it is the private sector that fuels economic growth, and without the ability to grow the business sector, ODA has in effect given up on its objective of *economic* development and has settled for more indirect interventions by focusing on human development and emergency assistance. As noted, the constricting logic of public money militates against the sort of risk and innovation needed to grow the business sector. To achieve that indispensable outcome, it is necessary to turn to funds that have not been collected by governments.

Yet again, the basic means of doing so have already been invented. The digital revolution has facilitated the possibility of individuals from wealthy countries investing directly with entrepreneurs from poor countries. Since Kiva was founded in 2005, 1.6 million Kiva lenders have invested almost $1 billion in loans to 2.3 million borrowers.[16] This is less than 1 percent of total ODA, but the Kiva experiment should be seen as a pilot for what can be achieved on a far larger scale. Transfers in the form of grants rather than loans should be tax deductible where those grants are to local companies in poor countries. Such transfers in the form of venture investment should get a lesser tax break.

The corporate world knows a lot more about business and economic growth than do governments. If the objective is to grow the business sector in poor countries, it stands to reason that corporate actors are more likely to be successful at this venture than are donor governments. Is the corporate world willing to take on this role? In the past couple of decades, the corporation has adopted a more sophisticated path to success than focusing solely on short-term maximization of profits. Corporations both large and small have understood that the key to success is to invest in the brand. This means going beyond the immediate requirements of shareholders to respond to the wishes of consumers, critics, and other stakeholders. An important way to invest in the brand is through corporate social responsibility (CSR). CSR is itself developing its concepts, and today we speak less of CSR and more of socially responsible corporations (SRCs) that view their responsibilities beyond simply putting a slice of profits aside for CSR and require responsible decisionmaking as befits a corporate citizen of the world.

The question that governments should be asking is how to involve the private sectors of wealthy countries in helping to grow the private sectors of poor countries. CSR and SRCs make corporations in general more willing to do so, but incentives are also required. The best answer is to provide those incentives through the tax system. Donor governments need to design a system whereby corporations from which they collect taxes are encouraged to get involved in the developing world by investing in small local companies, training entrepreneurs and specialists, and sharing their innovations and expertise.[17] Current market forces tend to direct most investment funds to those countries providing the likeliest means of a strong return, and therefore these funds are not directed toward the poorest countries. That is why incentives are needed in the form of tax concessions. This concept offers far brighter prospects for economic development than the present system, which has failed to deliver on economic development for half a century despite a $5 trillion investment.

The Role of Donor Governments

Delivering most development support through private means does not eliminate the role of donor governments. There remains a modest role in delivering aid to receiving governments, probably in the form of budget support and emergency assistance. But there is also a regulatory role. A system of encouraging private involvement in development assistance through individuals, civil society, and corporations by way of the tax system needs careful design and oversight. Regulations need to define the parameters within which such tax deductions will be allowed. As with any tax system, oversight is necessary. These are traditional government roles, unlike the Sisyphean task of economic development of the poorest countries in which government aid agencies have inappropriately been engaged.

How can we measure ODA under the proposed system of democratizing it? After all, there are internationally encouraged goals for the quantum of ODA that form an important part of the workings of the international system. The answer is quite simple: count as ODA the *tax foregone* due to the deductions allowed for private and corporate transfers to people and businesses in aid-eligible countries. It is the tax foregone by governments by allowing these deductions that makes it *official* development assistance. Donor governments must again shed their Westphalian assumptions by allowing transfers to people, civil society, and businesses in poor countries as deductible, regardless of whether the receiver is registered as a "charity" in the donor country. A people-to-people ODA system would reflect the interests and passions of democratic societies: entrepreneurship, charity, education, and no doubt sports and the arts.

The crafting of rules in this regard should not be beyond competent government agencies. There will be rules required to determine what is and is not tax deductible. Religious proselytization, for example, should clearly be excluded from tax deductibility benefits. And there may well be other groups—such as the anti-tax, anti-vax, antigovernment, and pro-gun fanatics—that should also be excluded. Why should there be any eligibility restrictions? Because it remains ODA, which is subject to agreement on both sides. Receiving governments should have an important input in the discussions. The Development Assistance Committee would be an excellent forum in which to iron out the details. It already has strong definitions of what is development assistance and what is not, and this would be the template for any new system of democratized ODA. Receiving countries would also have considerable say in the oversight of the system. Again, pilot steps have been taken where reputable umbrella groups in civil society or the business communities of developing countries act as certifying authorities in a form of self-regulation.[18]

Would this new method of delivering aid directly from people to people, civil society to civil society, and companies to companies lead to a reduction in ODA? If governments were simply to commit to maintaining ODA at current levels but counting most of it as tax foregone, the amount of funds actually transferred will be considerably greater than at present. Assuming for the sake of simplicity an effective tax rate of one-third of income, it would take three times the amount of financial flows claimed as tax deductions to generate the amount of tax foregone. Assuming that ODA by the United States is $10 billion, and assuming generously that half of it will be channeled in government-to-government and other donor government flows, the remaining $5 billion in ODA as tax foregone will be generated by $15 billion in tax-deductible aid flows. US ODA would remain at $10 billion, but the aid flow from the United States will be $20 billion, a doubling of the current flow and far better directed at the bottom of the pyramid.

Conclusion

There is a delicious irony in this proposal. It turns out Evsey Domar may have been right all along. Domar's theory that poor countries cannot generate the savings required for the necessary investment in capital provided the intellectual justification for the ODA phenomenon. Domar quickly disavowed the theory because of its unrealistic simplicity. But, in fact, the problem with the theory as applied was its unarticulated

Westphalian and S5YP assumptions—which had aid flowing to governments to deliver large development projects. Financial flows directly to local companies, civil society organizations, and entrepreneurs may well fill the savings gap that Domar identified by allowing these flows to be used in a more organic and appropriate way in each locality.

Some may worry that the democracy and human rights projects currently being funded by donor governments will disappear in a new ODA system of budget support plus people-to-people funding. This is a risk. Instead of the planning model we are currently employing, the system would move to a market model. But the market is not simply a market for goods and services. It is also a market for ideas. If local groups put together coalitions in support of democratization or human rights or women's empowerment and seek funding from the wealthy people in donor countries, why would they not receive those funds? The market will accommodate issues that are popular with donors. Whereas the business-to-business transfers will probably concentrate more on production of goods and services, the people-to-people transfers will no doubt focus on the big ideas that motivate people in the developed world—environment protection, human rights, and, hopefully, democracy. What will probably dry up are the big civil service training projects. They will now have to compete for funding with other receiving-government priorities decided by receiving governments with control over their budgets. Yes, there is a risk. But the reward is a better form of international solidarity.

It is time to democratize ODA. It is in keeping with the times to let people and companies from different countries deal with each other directly rather than through their governments. It is facilitated by the information and communication revolution. It is about helping nations to build up from the bottom rather than from the top down. It is time to finally let go of the conceit of the S5YP and to recognize the nonlinear, surprising, and human ways of development. It is time to give serendipity a chance.

Democratizing ODA will have a direct impact on democratization more generally. It will facilitate a more organic bottom-up means of development rather than the current concepts, which infantilize the population by simply treating them as the passive recipients of others' plans. It will require local people, not simply their governments, to take responsibility for development. This will be an important form of economic empowerment. Economic empowerment will be accompanied by demands for political empowerment. And that must mean demand for democracy.

Notes

1. Development Co-operation Directorate (of OECD), "Development Aid Stable in 2014 but Flows to Poorest Countries Still Falling," 2015, http://www.oecd.org/dac /stats/development-aid-stable-in-2014-but-flows-to-poorest-countries-still-falling.htm.

2. For example, William Easterly, *The Elusive Quest for Growth: Economists' Adventures and Misadventures in the Tropics* (Cambridge, MA: MIT Press, 2001); William Easterly, *The White Man's Burden: Why the West's Efforts to Aid the Rest Have Done So Much Ill and So Little Good* (New York: Penguin, 2006); R. Glenn Hubbard and William Duggan, *The Aid Trap* (New York: Columbia Business School, 2009); D. Moyo, *Dead Aid: Why Aid Is Not Working and How There Is a Better Way for Africa* (New York: Farrar, Straus and Giroux, 2009); Jeffrey Sachs, *The End of Poverty: Economic Possibilities for Our Time* (London: Penguin, 2006).

3. Roland Rich, "Applying Conditionality to Development Assistance," *Agenda—A Journal of Policy Analysis and Reform* 11, 4 (2004): 321–334, http:// epress.anu.edu.au/agenda/011/04/11-4-A-3.pdf.

4. Easterly, *The Elusive Quest for Growth*, pp. 30–31.

5. Homi Kharas, "Development Assistance," in Bruce Currie-Alder, Ravi Kanbur, David M. Malone, and Rohinton Medhora (eds.), *International Development: Ideas, Experience, and Prospects* (Oxford: Oxford University Press, 2014), p. 9, http:// hdl.handle.net/10625/51592.

6. William Easterly and Claudia R. Williamson, *Rhetoric Versus Reality: The Best and Worst of Aid Agency Practices*, p. 4 (figure updated to reflect post-publication flows), http://williameasterly.files.wordpress.com/2010/08/61_easterly_williamson_rhetoric vsreality_prp.pdf.

7. Africa Enterprise Challenge Fund, "About Us," http://www.aecfafrica.org /about-us.

8. The African Agricultural Capital Fund, "Feed the Future," https://www .feedthefuture.gov/model/african-agricultural-capital-fund.

9. World Cacao Foundation, "African Cocoa Initiative," http://www .worldcocoafoundation.org/wcf-african-cocoa-initiative.

10. An account of this story can be found in Roland Rich, *Pacific Asia in Quest of Democracy* (Boulder, CO: Lynne Rienner, 2007), pp. 227–229.

11. See Netherlands Ministry of Foreign Affairs, *Budget Support: Conditional Results—Review of an Instrument (2000–2011)*, 2011, https://www.oecd.org/derec /netherlands/IOB_BS.pdf.

12. M. Edwards and D. Hulme (eds.), *Making a Difference: NGOs and Development in a Changing World* (London: Earthscan, 1992), p. 20.

13. Norman Uphoff, *Nongovernmental Organizations and Accountability: Beyond the Magic Bullet* (London: Earthscan, 1995), p. 123.

14. "In 2009 members provided around five times more aid to NGOs based in their countries (national NGOs) than to international NGOs and local NGOs in developing countries." OECD, *How DAC Members Work with Civil Society Organizations: An Overview* (Paris: OECD, 2011), p. 19.

15. Ibid., p. 10.

16. Kiva, "About Us," http://www.kiva.org.

17. I first proposed this idea in 2007; Roland Rich, "Hercules or Sisyphus? Building Capacity in the Asia-Pacific," *Australian Strategic Policy Institute Insight No. 33*, 2007, Canberra, http://www.aspi.org.au/publications/publications_all.aspx.

18. See, for example, the Philippine model in Fely I. Soledad, "The Philippine Council for NGO Certification," *International Journal of Not-for-Profit Law* 3, 2 (December 2001).

10

We Need Resilience
and Resurgence

Democracies are in crisis everywhere, placing democracy itself in crisis. What can we do about it? Flowing from the range of problems outlined in previous chapters, there may well be a feeling of helplessness creeping in. The problems seem too numerous and deep, the solutions too difficult and contested. Where to start? There are three kinds of responses available to us. The first two can be described as the "invest in" and "stand up to" schools. The third school of action might be called the "resilience and resurgence" school. We need all three, but in particular the last.

Invest In

The "invest in" school of thought is to keep doing what we are doing to invest in the forces in favor of global democratization but to do it smarter. This deceptively simple formulation needs a little unpacking. Whether they realize it or not, the investors first need a theory of democratization. Only then can they determine how to direct their investment.

If the underlying theory of democratization is modernization theory, then ODA needs to be directed to grow the economy and grow the middle class, and globalization needs to be encouraged to provide opportunities all around the world. The best-documented empirical cases of modernization leading to democratization in South Korea and Taiwan were middle-class led, though governments and business elites also played a significant role. These success stories occurred in the early days of globalization. But here's the rub: although modernization theory remains the leading theory of democratization, the globalization policies that are the surest bet to grow the global economy are under threat in a Brexit-and-Trump world. There is no other candidate to stimulate growth. Globalization is the only game in town for modernization. So a necessary step is to rehabilitate globalization.

There is nothing wrong with the concept of comparative advantage applied on a global scale. The problem is the lack of fairness in the way countries seek to gain that advantage. Low wages are clearly a valid comparative advantage but only when the workers have the right to organize and bargain collectively. The toleration of certain extractive and energy industries is a comparative advantage, but not if the advantage is derived from polluting the spaceship, our world. Globalization needs certain disciplines to make it a fairer process. The policy of making globalization more fair was one the Obama administration pursued in a groundbreaking document—the Trans Pacific Partnership (TPP). I asked my students to write an essay about it. They were all Bernie Sanders people and relished the thought of trashing the treaty. But then they did something that hardly any of its critics had done: they read it. Their essays all pointed to the ways in which TPP would make globalization fairer and, incidentally, would retain America's global leadership. Automation is costing lots more jobs than globalization. So are we all to become Luddites? Should we bring back the blacksmiths? One thing the world needs is leadership to rescue globalization—from itself by making it work better, and from the ignorance that currently surrounds it.

If not modernization through globalization, are other theories the locus of our investment? A trickle of funds goes toward political parties, and there are some solidarity networks among like-minded political parties. But the amounts are small, and the networks tend mainly to be used as good reasons for conferences in nice places. Political parties are not inspiring a great deal of confidence. The most dynamic among them tend to be populist parties nursing grievances but without any solutions as to how to rectify the problems. It is difficult to support parties such as in Schattschneider's theory. And in any case, those sort of parties tend to be anti-foreigner and would not welcome international support except from like-minded bigots. In fact, the problem of political parties goes deeper that those radical parties at the edges of the spectrum. They are no longer performing the key roles required in a democracy. They decreasingly represent political cleavages in society and increasingly represent identity cleavages. They focus less on issues and more on facile slogans. They are less effective at aggregating various coalitions of opinion than they used to be. They still form governments, but even this role is being usurped by charismatic outsiders. Finally, there is a subtle change occurring from parties to movements, from formal structures to informal ones, from long-term horizons to ever shorter attention spans.

More money is spent in support of human rights, another presumed path toward democratization, but, again, the figure is tiny. The international community has a courageous group under the leadership of the UN High Commissioner for Human Rights, but it rarely has the support of the Security Council. There are powerful international CSOs that promote and protect human rights, but they are little more than irritants to increasingly confident autocrats. The invention of human rights is one of modernity's greatest achievements. The concept of human rights continues to have the power to inspire. The dividends will be greater human dignity, less impunity, and perhaps even more democracy. And let's not forget that human rights are women's rights. It would be wrong to give up on the human rights discourse. It is one of the fields we need to invest in.

Alongside human rights, there seems to be a growing acceptance of the central place of civil society as the key element in democratization, and in recent years there has been more investment in that direction. In a longer-term perspective, it doesn't matter whether the civil society group is engaged in poverty alleviation, education, health, human rights, or democracy promotion. Any contribution to the growth and self-confidence of the civil society sector is positive. Societies need to build social capital, and investing in civil society is the surest means of doing so. Ideally, that investment should cover advocacy CSOs as well as delivery CSOs. There can be no illusions about the difficulty of this path now that authoritarian governments have found ways to asphyxiate civil society by cutting off foreign funding. We need to find a range of responses to this challenge.

When I visited Najaf in southern Iraq in 2016, I dropped in on a CSO receiving funding from the UN Democracy Fund. It was run by a group of idealistic and savvy young folk. They understood that their sustainability could not be based on lurching from one foreign grant to another. So, alongside their advocacy work, they ran small businesses— secretarial training, English-language teaching, translation, and other office services. This struck me as a sensible strategy. In the three ring Venn diagram, this work would be in the overlap between the business sector and the civil society sector.

But when we speak about investing in human rights or civil society, we are relying mainly on that rather modest instrument known as ODA. Current levels of ODA are running at about 0.3 percent of the gross national income of the twenty-eight OECD countries. That still adds up to about $130 billion or so annually, but that sum needs to cover many issues, including refugees and emergency situations. The strategy discussed in the previous chapter outlines a means to increase this flow and democratize it. What we would be losing out on are the many programs targeting officials of countries that are trying to transition away from whatever sort of authoritarianism they experienced to some sort of more democratic and open society. They might be senior figures in the executive, such as elected officials, civil servants, and members of independent oversight bodies, or even judges and lawyers. They are an obvious target for government-to-government aid in what the international community has come to call "strengthening" projects. That term is not accidental; it flows from an unarticulated analogy that is subconsciously widely held to apply. Just like we strengthen our bodies by spending time at the gym, so must these officials strengthen their performance by spending time in the training room. Training is the panacea. Through ODA, the established democracies provide some of the gym equipment and send over personal trainers. The obedient trainees duly fill out the feedback forms, saying how much the training has assisted them. Taxpayers in ODA donor countries are expected to believe that having attended a training session, these officials will no longer be corrupt, no longer favor their families or clans in exercising their discretion, and no longer be slack and lazy in the workplace. What planet are we on?

ODA can be transformed into a better tool by democratizing it and narrowing down the role of governments at both ends of the process. All the OECD countries that constitute the club of donors are democracies. Let their taxpayers get involved in people-to-people ODA, and the values of democratic societies will be reflected in the ODA product in a way in which it is not today. One of the incidental benefits of this change in ODA practice will be a shift in recipients. Civil society will become the major recipient of the foreign flow of development funds into the country. Let us recall that a vibrant civil society is an end in itself and perhaps the trigger and guarantor of democratization. Theory and practice will be coming closer together. I suspect that another category of significant beneficiaries overlapping civil society will be women. Women are the better networkers and perhaps have more patience to stick to a task. Women understand the notion of solidarity with other women in a way that does not occur to men in their relationships with other men. Women would thus be empowered as agents for modernity and democracy.

But is the world moving in this direction? Only at the edges, not in the mainstream. The mainstream is represented by the magic letters SDG, the sustainable development goal. This is not the place for an examination of these goals, but what we can conclude is that the dysfunctional current system of ODA remains with us and is ratified by the SDGs, which continue the process of putting governments at the center of the development process to the practical exclusion of both civil society and the private sector. And whereas the MDGs—millennium development goals—for the fifteen years that preceded the 2016 SDGs at least had the advantage of parsimony with, in effect, only seven goals to choose from, thus achieving better donor alignment, the SDGs' seventeen goals will work more like a menu than a coordination mechanism. And it goes without saying that democracy is not explicitly one of the seventeen goals nor one of the 169 targets.

We can expect governments at both ends of the ODA process to fight to keep the system as it is; after all, they are the primary beneficiaries of the process. It gives them influence, diplomatic clout, patronage power, and primacy in the development process. The shiny new SDGs are simply a means of packaging the continuation of the system. So "investing in" remains a good strategy, but in its current form it is unlikely to be the means of consolidating democracy around the world.

Stand Up To

Every election season some candidate or another criticizes whatever administration is in power for being spineless. The answer, they tell us in three simple words, is to "stand up to" whatever tyrant, evil empire, or vicious ideology is currently the bogeyperson. Any solution to a complex problem that comes in three words should be examined with suspicion. A more sophisticated version of the "stand up to" injunction is to accuse those in power of appeasement. The appeasement canard dates back to pre–World War II, when Neville Chamberlain, then prime minister of Great Britain, returning from Munich, did not stand up to Hitler, who was claiming territory outside Germany. Because of the obvious failure of Chamberlain's policies in avoiding the need to eventually confront Nazi Germany, the term *appeasement* has a powerful impact.

As with most simple injunctions, there may be a kernel of truth in the proposition in some circumstances. Clearly, Europe needed to stand up to Hitler, though the time to start doing so would have been prior to Munich when he boldly remilitarized the Ruhr contrary to the conditions imposed on Germany. In the far simpler situation of the "civil war" in the Solomon Islands at the turn of the millennium, standing up to the rascals was clearly the right course of action. Ambitious wannabe politicians stoked the embers of interisland rivalry and obtained dominance by getting their hands on high-powered weapons. This "political" violence quickly degenerated into brazen criminality, which the local constabulary was unable to counter. Here was a situation that called for an outside force to "stand up to" the criminals, which Australia and its Pacific allies did, allowing the Solomon Islands to begin the process of returning to normality.

Popular perceptions of recent history have Ronald Reagan winning the Cold War by standing up to the evil empire. This argument implies that his predecessors from Eisenhower to Carter did not stand up to the Soviet Union. What malarkey! Yes, it is true that Reagan challenged the USSR to a game of military spending that the latter was in no position to undertake. But responsibility for the end of the Cold War must be primarily attributed where it belongs, to Mikhail Gorbachev. As I noted in a previous publication, "unlike his predecessors who were prepared to use force to punish deviation, Gorbachev understood the futility of maintaining an untenable system and holding together an impossible empire by force."[1] Gorbachev let go of the Cold War and inadvertently also let go of the Soviet Union.

There is a formidable list of tyrants, autocrats, and vicious ideologues out there. Do we "stand up to" all of them? Most of the blowhard candidates who employ the "stand up to" language think it is sufficient to sound tough and issue severe threats. But this is a lesson that any major power learns at its cost: threats are meaningless unless that power is prepared to carry them out. Another lesson that is still in the process of being digested is that resorting to the use of force necessarily cannot be cost-free. Disputes cannot be resolved through drones and precision bombs. Imposing a foreign nation's will on any local situation will take boots on the ground and cost blood and treasure, as well as running the risk of triggering unintended consequences. Yes, the Bush administration stood up to Saddam, with the unintended effect of strengthening both Iran and jihadism.

So we need to accept that though the "stand up to" formulation remains a policy option, it is a blunt tool with limited capacity and requires the appetite for war. It needs to be sparingly used. It needs to be strategically calculated. And in those rare circumstances when it is the best option, it needs to be decisively deployed. I don't believe we can improve much on the work of the International Commission on Intervention and State Sovereignty (ICISS), from which the "responsibility to protect" doctrine emerged. The responsibility to protect is a doctrine of high principle and good intentions, but it is also a doctrine of realpolitik. Among its important wisdoms is that embarking on a path of use of force to end or avert a genocide or massive abuses of human rights should only be exercised in accordance with "the principles of right intention, last resort, proportional means and reasonable prospects."[2] It is the "reasonable prospects" admonition that makes it such a useful doctrine.

Resilience and Resurgence

"Investing in" is a difficult long-term undertaking, and "standing up to" is a limited strategy requiring a particular set of circumstances, and though we have to continue to do both in the right way at the right time, there is another line of action on which we can work continuously and profitably. We need to fix our own democracies. We need to demonstrate political resilience. We need to revert to the concept of the "surge" but this time deploy it domestically and politically. We need to rebuild democracy's soft power.

Democracy is a never-ending journey. Democracy is an aspiration toward which we must work. We cannot be content to think of having happily arrived at our destination. We must continue to strive for democracy to become "more perfect." In doing so, we will assert considerable power—soft power. How will this power work in favor of democratization around the world? The bottom line is that we need once again to make democracy admirable. The greatest power is to have others wish to emulate one's success. The established democracies thus carry the great responsibility of being seen to strive to make democracy work. Admittedly, some ideas and policies will be rejected or even if adopted will fail to have the intended impact. No matter! It is the process of trying to make democracy ever better that is the lesson that needs to be absorbed. And the posture that needs to be avoided is that of "end of history" self-satisfaction mixed with paternalistic condescension of others.

Where to begin? Clearly, as this is a journey, we should pay heed to its previous milestones, from Runnymede to Philadelphia. We never start with a blank page. We must always build on our foundations. In all democracies there is much to preserve and indeed cherish. But the hubris of self-satisfaction lurks. The United States is the world leader and therefore has the responsibility to demonstrate leadership by example. It has always been the mission of the United States to develop democracy. It should continue to be its mission to make its democracy emulatable.

There are large problems and small; some are intractable and some simply need a little common sense to resolve. Issues such as the growing inequality in economic results, plutocratic money politics, and the continuing grip of racial disadvantage are in the large and intractable camp. They are not beyond solution, but each would take a book-length treatment to tackle, and I am not sure I have anything particularly original to add. My suggestion is to pluck a few relatively low-hanging fruit while not losing sight of the big-picture problems. Solving a few manageable problems could embolden Americans to take on the bigger ones. I would like to make some suggestions of how to tackle a few problems and thus make American democracy more resilient and resurgent. In doing so, I make a plea to the American body politic to put aside short-term political calculation and keep an eye on the big picture. It is in everybody's interests for American democracy to be developed and improved.

Declare Election Day an Official Holiday

Americans know when Election Day occurs in November—the Tuesday after the first Monday. Every four years they troop off to elect a president and a bunch of other representatives, and in the two years in between they vote in smaller numbers just for those other representatives. That's how it is. But wait a minute; Tuesday is a weekday, when people troop off to work, not to vote. And the way the economy is developing, the unskilled and even the slightly skilled don't just troop off to work in the singular, they often have to hold down more than one job. And, by the way, don't forget that in many places, perhaps intentionally to dissuade people from voting, one has to stand in line a long time in the cold to vote.

Why are commentators surprised that for most of the past fifty years voter turnout hovered around 50 percent in presidential elections and dipped to closer to 40 percent in mid-term congressional elections?[3] Voter turnout rose to 62.3 percent in 2008 and around 57.5 percent in 2012 in the excitement of the Obama years.[4] In 2016 it stayed around that number.[5] European voter turnout is closer to 80 percent.[6] Clearly, we have a problem.

Analysts look for sophisticated reasons for the low turnout rate in the United States, ranging from disaffection with politics to concerns about the voting system, but surely the reason is much simpler. Voting in the United States is not easy. In fact, it's downright difficult. Voter registration is a discreet step and can be complicated and convoluted. Then one has to find the time to vote on Election Day, and that may not be straightforward if one votes at peak periods and must stand interminably in line. None of this makes American democracy particularly admirable.

The obvious thing to do is to make voting much easier. It's actually quite a simple thing to do. First, make voter registration part of the process of obtaining a driver's license, as required under the Motor Voter Act of 1993. Very few states comply fully, Oregon being a felicitous exception. Exactly the same information is being collected for each process. For libertarians among us who do not wish to compel anything, there could be a box to be ticked to opt out of voting. Very few would tick that box. Eighty-seven percent of Americans have driver's licenses,[7] so very quickly the problem of registration will shrink dramatically.

Second, make Election Day an official holiday. Nearly every other country in the world that holds meaningful elections holds them on a weekend or on an official holiday. One day off every two years! That will not break the bank or reduce American productivity.

Why haven't these simple steps already been taken? While there will be no articulation of the reasons and while I am not suggesting that there is a vast conspiracy at the heart of this issue, the political economy answer is simple: the elites of America do not encourage the working people to vote. Without wishing to turn this into a partisan issue, it is also pretty clear that conservatives have adopted a secret policy (under the disguise of fighting nonexistent electoral fraud) of depressing the vote in the hope of partisan advantage by dissuading younger voters and minorities from voting.

As an outsider observing America with foreign eyes, I find it amazing that so few people even raise these simple design issues.[8] Because the solution seems so obvious: simplify registration and accommodate voting, and voter turnout will increase. The country will get a better idea of what its citizens want, and more people will have skin in the game. That is good for democracy.

End the Electoral College Farce

The Electoral College is a good system . . . for the eighteenth century. Back then, communications were difficult and information flowed ever so slowly. How could someone in far-off Ohio decide between candidates in distant Washington? It made sense to elect someone good and true to travel to Washington and decide on a candidate on behalf of his or, very occasionally, her community. Hence the quaint institution of the Electoral College. But, lo and behold, we are in the twenty-first century and the quaint institution is still with us. The justification has, however, changed. It has been bent to the will of politics to achieve a completely different objective than that for which it was designed. State assemblies one after the other decided on the winner-take-all rule whereby all the Electoral College votes for that state go to the candidate who wins the majority or even plurality of votes in the state. This had nothing to do with communications and information and everything to do with maintaining the duopoly of Democrats and Republicans, thus freezing out even the most remote possibility of allowing a third party to crash the party.

The Electoral College has achieved its objective of cementing the duopoly, as Ross Perot learned in 1992 when he gained almost 20 percent of the national vote but earned not a single elector. Indeed, today it is a better tactic for party outsiders such as Donald Trump and Bernie Sanders to try to capture one of the two duopolistic parties rather than form their own. The Electoral College also has other negative impacts.

The most obvious is that the will of the majority may not prevail. This has happened several times in American history, most recently in 2000 and again in 2016, when the candidate with the most votes did not win the presidency. This can also happen in parliamentary elections, where it might be reflective of broader geographic rather than narrow numerical popularity. But it should not happen in a nationwide presidential election where it is so easy to simply count the popular vote. In fact, a mathematician with clearly too much time on his hands worked out that a candidate in a two-horse race could win the Electoral College while winning only about 22 percent of the nationwide popular vote.[9] This is demonstrated through a neat *reducto ad absurdum* process of having one candidate win no votes in some states while winning by only one vote in other states and thus racking up the requisite number of electors even though the opponent obtained 78 percent of the vote.

The result in 2016 is particularly disturbing. It is not like the few thousand votes by which Al Gore won the popular vote in 2000. Hillary Clinton won almost three million more votes than her opponent.[10] She won by more than two percentage points. If there are doubts about the legitimacy of Donald Trump's victory, it has less to do with Putin's meddling and more to do with the clarity of the will of the American people.

Aside from the inherent unfairness of not following the will of the majority, the Electoral College distorts the electoral process and effectively disenfranchises the majority of voters. With the red/blue divide in the country expressing itself dominantly in about forty states, the election is decided in those ten or so states where swings are possible. The result is that presidential elections are fought in swing states such as Arizona, Colorado, Florida, Michigan, North Carolina, Ohio, Virginia, and Wisconsin. Voters in the two most populous states can live through the entire campaign without seeing a political advertisement. But the hapless Floridian or Ohioan is inundated with political messaging for the best part of a presidential election year. One desperate voter from Miami went so far as to ask for those treacly Cialis ads to return to his screen.

A handful of states are therefore singled out for special attention. Their issues receive special attention. And even in the first term, any president has to avoid policies that may be particularly unpopular in those states. The absurd veto that the small Cuban American community based in the swing state of Florida held for decades over US policy toward Cuba could only finally be over-ridden in President Obama's second term.

The Electoral College is, of course, not the only poor piece of institutional design in American politics. The two-year term for members of the House of Representatives is another holdover from the eighteenth century, but it would take a constitutional amendment to establish more sensible four-year terms. The decision to hold primaries first in the small and unrepresentative state of Iowa means that the country has to continue its counter-productive corn ethanol subsidy. To set a fairer tone for the primary campaign, the first should be held in a relatively large and diverse state. But the Electoral College strikes me as the most egregious piece of poor design, and clearly many Americans agree because there has been a concerted campaign to get rid of it, as shown by the National Popular Vote Interstate Compact. On April 15, 2014, Governor Andrew Cuomo signed the National Popular Vote bill, making New York the eleventh jurisdiction to enact the law. Once there are enough jurisdictions to cover half the Electoral College votes (270, therefore standing about 100 votes short in 2016), the compact will come into effect. At that time, those states will direct all their Electoral College votes to the candidate who wins a majority or plurality in the election. The effect, once the compact comes into force, will be to achieve the popular vote result, though by indirect means, and kill off the worst impacts of the Electoral College.

A Federal Election Management Body
Should Run Nationwide Elections

Let me remind you of two words that cast an ugly stain on America's reputation as an admirable democracy—*hanging chads*. The level of incompetence that leads to hanging chads flows from simple mathematics—the United States has some nine thousand electoral management bodies![11] Nearly every American voter with whom I speak has a story along the lines of going home to Georgia (or wherever) to vote and being confronted by elderly ladies with blue hair and old men with dysfunctional hearing aids who have no idea how to run an election. After the 2000 election fiasco, Congress showed a hint of spine and common sense and passed a law requiring greater uniformity and higher standards in the conduct of elections. The carrot was federal funding. There was no stick. The situation improved but cannot yet be described as satisfactory, let alone excellent. But there is no excuse for anything short of excellence in the conduct of elections in a high-quality democracy.

For those who think this is only a problem in the Ozarks, allow me to quote from a *New York Times* editorial of July 29, 2016:

> In New York, there is no early voting in person. Absentee ballots are a pain. The boards that run elections have barely acknowledged the arrival of the computer, let alone the Internet. Anyone who votes in New York City, for example, must first sign a large paper ledger that looks like something from the Smithsonian archives.

Americans will argue that their country is exceptional. They might argue that the highly decentralized nature of electoral management in their country flows from its federal nature and is a bulwark against tyranny. But there are lots of federations around the world, and, aside from the United States, all but one have a federal election management body that runs nationwide elections. Americans need only look at neighbors to the north and south to see two examples of competent federal election management bodies. The world leader in conducting elections is probably India, with its 800 million voters, all, including the homeless, duly registered, all on digital and searchable electoral rolls, leading to results immediately accepted by voters. There are no hanging chads in India. Incidentally, the federal state with elections run by its constituent units is Switzerland. As this is the country that comes closest to the concept of direct democracy with many questions, national and cantonal, going to the electorate, it is understandable that cantons should run elections. And somehow, I would place more confidence in the twenty-six cantonal electoral administrations in efficient Switzerland than in the nine thousand county electoral administrations in the United States.

It is not as if the federal parts of the system have taken no interest in the running of elections. The United States has a body called a Federal Election Commission (FEC) and one called the Electoral Assistance Commission (EAC). The former deals with campaign finance. But the *Citizens United* case made most campaign money unaccountable, which combined with the fact that presidential candidates no longer accept federal campaign money (which would preclude them from raising their own) gives the FEC hardly anything worthwhile to do. The EAC hands out the carrots to those electoral managers who meet the federal standards. But this is simply tinkering with the edges of the problem. Please bite the bullet and follow international best practice by establishing a federal electoral management body to actually run nationwide elections. Oddly, the 2016 elections threw up an argument in favor of decentralized election administration. In one of his many evidence-free and fact-free accusations, Trump, who was convinced he would lose the election, accused the electoral system of being rigged. Otherwise sensible people rallied to its defense with the argument that it would be a practical impossibility to rig an election in the United States because it is conducted by nine thousand different bodies. Really? Is this the best argument we can muster for inertia? There is no point retaining a broken system because it responds to spurious allegations.

And if I may be permitted a final peavey word on this issue: drop the failed practice of partisan appointment to the federal electoral management body. Surely the United States can find a way to appoint an independent body that wins the respect of the electorate. Elections are too important to be part of the spoils system. The calls made by electoral commissioners often have significant political impact. Can't the United States find a way to appoint people who will make these calls fairly and dispassionately? When there was a need to have a body to undertake this task in relation to interest rates, the nation created the Federal Reserve Board, whose members are not partisan creatures but are, according to the 1935 Banking Act, a "fair representation of the financial, agricultural, industrial, and commercial interests and geographical divisions of the country." Surely the United States can get its act together and do the same for national elections.

Conclusion

I need to conclude on a somber note. Those halcyon post–Cold War days when every problem seemed soluble are gone. The problems faced by the international community are getting much harder. We are faced by an existential climate crisis that requires some very tough decisions to mitigate its worst impacts. This will entail changing deeply ingrained production and consumption patterns. That is a lot more than the tinkering we are currently playing with. It will require the world to strand vast hydrocarbon deposits. Industries will be dislocated, and some will go the way of the blacksmith. Our consumption patterns need to change, including in the way we consume food. It simply makes no ecological sense to graze vast herds of beef for our cheap hamburgers. We need to negotiate our way through this crisis, and it is difficult to see today's democracies having the competence and conscientiousness to do so. We have just had two presidential terms of an incumbent who understood the climate change challenge but was unable to do much about it.

We are faced with the gathering realization that our global economic system is not producing the results we seek in view of the unacceptable inequality it has triggered. Inequality is growing in nearly every country in the world. It is not the fact of inequality that is the problem. Every society has always accepted some inequality. But the trend of concentrating ever more wealth into ever fewer hands has clear zero-sum implications. It is almost quaint to realize that in 1984, management guru Peter Drucker advocated that a CEO should be paid no more than twenty times what his average worker earned.[12] Today the ratio is around three hundred.[13] In previous centuries, the solutions to growing inequality were war, plague, or state collapse. These are not the solutions we are seeking. Are our democracies sufficiently farsighted and innovative to find sustainable solutions to the problem of growing economic inequality?

We are confronted with the return of the ugliest face of tradition. This is taking the form of racism and misogyny, and it threatens to take the form of religious intolerance, which some wish to provoke into a war of religions. We have seen massive refugee movements and stingy responses in too many instances. Will our democracies practice inclusiveness and accommodation, or will they be swayed by demagogues preaching majoritarianism and intolerance?

And even as we deal with these fresh problems, we have one of the oldest international relations problems to manage—the rising power problem. To date, it has been handled rather well. There has been no policy to contain China. The rich countries instead opened their borders to its products and allowed China to develop a huge middle class. But now we need modernization theory to work and for China to democratize. We are not seeing that happen. And alongside, we must also deal with another difficult international relations problem, that of the waning power. Russia is no longer a superpower but wishes to continue to act that way. The only theory that may lead to democratization in Russia is civil society theory, and Putin is doing all in his power to ensure Russian civil society is stillborn. There is yet another traditional international relations quandary that continues to bedevil us: how should we deal with authoritarian states? Should we be amoral realists and give them their space, or should we be idealist internationalists and struggle for a better world? Is our democratic debate sufficiently informed and knowledgeable to tackle this question? Again, the signs are not positive.

In other words, our global energy, security, and economic systems are out of whack. They can be fixed or at least ameliorated to an acceptable level. But to do so requires our political systems to intervene quickly and wisely. We are in need of high-quality democracy producing sharp leadership to tackle this contentious array of problems.

The alarm I am raising in this extended essay is that our political systems are not up to the task. In theory, the world has at its disposal a political system that is able to make high-quality decisions—democracy. Informed voters electing wise representatives to serve in well-functioning governments is the way to deal with difficult problems faced by society. With the end of the Cold War we thought the world would move in that direction. It has not. Democracy is in trouble at home and abroad. If we can't fix it, we won't be able to fix any of our other problems.

Notes

1. Roland Rich, *Pacific Asia in Quest of Democracy* (Boulder, CO: Lynne Rienner, 2007), p. 7.

2. Report of the International Commission on Intervention and State Sovereignty, December 2001, p. IX, http://responsibilitytoprotect.org/ICISS%20Report.pdf.

3. Thomas E. Patterson, *The Vanishing Voter: Public Involvement in an Age of Uncertainty* (New York: Vintage, 2003).

4. Bipartisan Policy Center, *Voter Turnout in 2012*, 2012, http://bipartisanpolicy.org/library/2012-voter-turnout/.

5. Gregory Wallace, "Voter turnout at 20-year low in 2016," November 30, 2016, http://www.cnn.com/2016/11/11/politics/popular-vote-turnout-2016/.

6. International Institute for Democracy and Electoral Assistance, *Voter Turnout: A Global Survey—Regional Differences*, http://www.idea.int/vt/survey/voter_turnout3.cfm.

7. Department of Transport, *Our Nation's Highways: 2011*, https://www.fhwa.dot.gov/policyinformation/pubs/hf/pl11028/chapter4.cfm.

8. Fareed Zakaria advocated this holiday recently; http://globalpublicsquare.blogs.cnn.com/2012/10/12/do-americans-need-more-holidays/.

9. C. G. P. Grey, "The Trouble with the Electoral College," https://web.archive.org/web/20120121133239/http://blog.cgpgrey.com/the-electoral-college/.

10. Clinton 65,844,610 to Trump 62,979,636; http://cookpolitical.com/story/10174.

11. Robert Pastor, "The US Administration of Elections: Decentralized to the Point of Being Dysfunctional," in International Institute for Democracy and Electoral Administration, *Electoral Management Design: The International IDEA Handbook* (Stockholm: IDEA, 2006), p. 273.

12. John Hunter, "Peter Drucker Advocated a Ratio of 20 to 1 for CEO to Average Worker Pay," *The W. Edwards Deming Institute Blog*, 2015, https://blog.deming.org/2015/02/peter-drucker-advocated-a-ratio-of-20-to-1-for-ceo-to-average-worker-pay/.

13. Ira Kay and Blaine Martin, "CEO Pay Ratio and Income Inequality: Perspectives for Compensation Committees," *Harvard Law School Program on Corporate Governance*, 2016, https://corpgov.law.harvard.edu/2016/10/25/ceo-pay-ratio-and-income-inequality-perspectives-for-compensation-committees/.

Postscript:
Has Democracy Been Trumped?

Like for everybody else, Donald Trump included, the results of the 2016 presidential election came as a shock. I was pretty sure the polls had been wrong. The death of the landline spelled the end of traditional polls, as it is no longer possible to be confident of finding a geographically and socioeconomically representative sample. Also, so many people refuse to cooperate with unsolicited phone callers, again making the representativeness of any sample quite murky. But I was also pretty sure that the polls were overrepresenting Trump's support, with many people expressing their unhappiness before coming to their senses on Election Day. How wrong I was! I placed far too much faith in the American people.

The semester was not yet finished and the syllabus is unrelenting, but my students' suffering could not be ignored. And so in each class I went around the room to allow them to express themselves. Always heedful of the need for structured discussion, I suggested that each student explain where they were in relation to Elisabeth Kübler-Ross's five stages of grief.[1] But there is no point in hiding the obvious, I was as needful of therapy as my students. It was vicarious healing.

Denial

I plunged into that Egyptian river early and deep. For two days I refused to read or watch any news. Escapism works if there is an attractive and distant destination. Frank Tallis's *A Death in Vienna* took me away to Hapsburg-era Vienna, where a Sigmund Freud acolyte helped the police solve a murder mystery in a room locked from the inside. In between chapters I binged on HBO's *Westworld,* leaping into a gaudy future. But escapism doesn't work for long. I soon emerged from both the future and the past to rejoin the present ugly new world.

Anger

They have put the fox in charge of the hen house. They have let loose a raging bull in their very own china shop. They have allowed the snake to slither into the crib. As you can tell, I was running out of well-worn anthropomorphic metaphors for the Trump victory. The anger seethed nevertheless. How can so many voters act against their own interests? How can people be so gullible as to accept Trump's substance-free one-liners? How can they ignore the vile things the candidate did and said? Anger has a soothing, cleansing quality, especially if it is caused by something other than one's own folly. So let's wallow a little longer.

There have been policy-free candidacies in the past but surely never one so brazen as Trump's. It reminded me of nothing more than George Orwell's "four legs good, two legs bad." Here were his policies: "repeal and replace"; "lock her up"; "kick them out." What can it mean to elect a candidate with no platform? Either that candidate has no mandate or he has a mandate to do whatever he damn well pleases. That is all well and good for Marshal Jean-Bédel Bokassa of the short-lived Central African Empire, but what can it mean to have a president of the United States with no sensible policy ideas? Bokassa and Trump share one important quality: an unshakable psychotic egomania. Trump was happy to exhibit it without shame or hesitation. The campaign to retake Mosul—timed to assist his opponent. The nine thousand electoral management bodies of the United States—plotting to steal the election from him. Media criticism—revenge by Mexican billionaire Carlos Slim. Whatever the issue, it is always about Trump. So the new president has no policies but comes armed with a psychiatric disorder.

And what about the people around him? Nobody respectable! What more does one need to know than that his three most virulent defenders were Chris Christie, Rudy Giuliani, and Newt Gingrich. Yuck! Sleazy failed politicians who saw in Trump their one tiny glimmer of hope for political redemption. At least Christie had a small redeeming quality: his wife, Mary-Pat, could not hide her spontaneous disgust on camera when Trump made one of his many misogynistic comments. Even Trump understood how a candidate might have to scrape the muck in the bottom of the barrel, but a president should try not to taint himself with it.

In 2015, if a screenwriter had written a treatment for a movie remake called *The Siberian Candidate* in which Putin manipulates the American election by hacking and attacking his preferred candidate's opponent and has that candidate extol Putin's virtues and then appoint as Secretary of State someone who has been decorated by Putin, no sane producer would have touched it. The writer would have been counseled to be more subtle, to hint at the relationship rather than spell it out so blatantly, and to make the candidate smarter and Putin not so smart. Well, what does Hollywood know, anyway!

But what truly made me fume above all else was not about Trump at all. It was the meaninglessness of all the supposed knowledge acquired in my discipline of political science. Every theory, precedent, and instinct explains why a divided party cannot win. Common sense explains that a party that tries to suppress the vote instead of winning it is doomed. A party cannot prosper when its candidate spends half his time attacking its establishment, mocking his party colleagues, and demeaning the party elders. And, of course, a Republican nominee attacking Wall Street is like the Pope attacking the Vatican. Every law of political science broken. Result? Control over the three branches of government, including both houses of Congress. Add to that the 60 percent of governorships and state legislatures in Republican Party hands and you have a picture of a party that wrote its own obituary in 2012 and then refused to follow any of its own prescriptions, only to reap the wages of sin with . . . unadulterated victory.

Bargaining

How long can one wallow in anger? It stops feeling good after a while. It goes from righteous to ruinous in so a short time. One has to move on, but to where? The bargaining stage shows the true genius of Dr. Kübler-Ross. Whereas the other stages are rather generic, the bargaining stage is individualistic. This struck me with the variety of bargains my students were making. They ranged from the personal to the political, from spatial to temporal, from material to spiritual. Bargaining is an astute human quality allowing us to rationalize and contextualize. For the next few weeks I engaged in more bargaining ratiocination than would go on in an Arabian bazaar at the height of the oil glut.

First, I replayed the entire Brexit debate . . . my way. The Brexit vote had importance beyond Europe because it validated the subsequent Trump vote in both subtle and direct ways. I have been to England many times. I've participated in conferences at Chatham House, Ditchley House, and Marlborough House; I've given papers at Cambridge and Oxford; I've engaged in a *tour d'horizon* with colleagues at the Foreign and Commonwealth Office at Whitehall; and I've chaired meetings of the International Maritime Organization on the Albert Embankment of the River Thames. In other words, I know nothing about England. The closest I came to filling this regretful lacunae was at Upton Park, home of West Ham United. My late cousin Walter had indulged my lifelong obsession with Aston Villa by getting tickets to their game at Upton Park. As a schoolboy in Australia we all had to pick an English football club. Most of my friends went for Liverpool for the sensible reason that it kept winning. But I never liked going with the pack so I took recourse to the unimpeachable logic of a twelve-year-old. My hero, James Bond, drove an Aston Martin so of course he must live in Aston Villa. Now the tickets Walter procured were "away" tickets. Because fans of the visiting team behave like uncivilized wild animals, they have to be segregated, monitored, and roundly insulted. I was thus among future Brexiteers and privy to their vulgarity, belligerence, and occasional flashes of wit. From this one afternoon I can claim some understanding of the scepter'd isle.

The Brexit campaign was all bombast and insult, selling a product that sounded like a breakfast cereal and laxative all rolled into one, what fun! The Remain campaign sounded somnolent and pettifogging, selling a boring old-fashioned gizmo. So let's dress it up. It should have been called Connect or some other modern action word. And instead of the paternal, finger-wagging "this will cost ya" warning, the campaign should have sounded a dire threat: Brexit will mean the end of the English Premier League! How's that? The end of football as we know it? Yes, if our opponents wish to fight in a postfactual world, we should follow their lead. All one needs is the merest plausibility. Leaving the EU will end the applicability of the European Court of Justice's Bosman rule[2] whereby European players come to play for English soccer teams. No more Zlatans or Edens or Cescs in English football. Back to ugly kick-and-chase route-one football. That's what you'll get if you vote Brexit! Ah, if only they had followed this course . . . David Cameron would still be prime minister . . . the UK would remain in the EU . . . Trump would have no chance. . . .

But what's done is done. Bargaining also deals with the future. January 20 is around the corner. I then conjured up a sentence that I thought could not possibly be formulated in my brain. "Ted Cruz is right!" How could that hypocrite, whose only promise is a never-ending battle of the culture wars, be right about anything? He told the gullible Republican primary voters not to trust Trump, whose upbringing had given him "New York values." Trump has New York values. Well, New York values mean not poking your nose in other people's business or bedroom. New York values are immigrant values because New York is an immigrant town. New York values are live and let live. Maybe, imbued with those values, a Trump presidency will not be that bad.

When all is said and done, how much damage can a Trump presidency do? Titles such as "leader of the free world" disguise the fact that an American president has limited powers and must share these with Congress and the states. Yes, he can make the tax system more unfair by making it less progressive under some discredited trickle-down theory. Yes, he can squander yet more soft power both for the nation and for democracy. And yes, this administration will probably end up giving Russia and China a free ride by simply accepting their systems as amorally equivalent. But he can't bring back the coal industry any more than he can bring back the blacksmiths; the market will decide that. He can't repeat the Spanish Inquisition and expel ten million people, because that would require money and competence—Congress won't grant him the former and he clearly lacks the latter. And of course he won't build a superfluous wall while the nation's infrastructure crumbles all around him.

I was toying with this sort of wishful thinking when my psychologist niece explained to me that the five stages of grief are not necessarily linear or sequential. OK, back to anger.

Depression

Before I knew it the Christmas season was upon us. It is not my favorite time of the year—a celebration of consumer capitalism and a time to suffer fools and jingles gladly. My children and grandchildren were thousands of miles away. Depression hit. Hard.

Politics has been turned upside down, inside out, and back to front! There are no verities left on which to cling. There were never any political certainties, but we have now been robbed of predictable likelihoods. Nothing is clear, no possibility is excluded. For some two hundred years we have employed the left-right dichotomy to make sense of politics. It was bequeathed to us by the French revolution, where those who wished to execute the king sat on the left and those who did not sat on the right.[3] It was then hijacked by Marxism, where the spectrum ran from state control of the economy to laissez-faire savagery. Eventually it narrowed down to questions of how large should the welfare state grow and how progressive should taxation become. Post-Trump, the spectrum has lost economic sense, and the dichotomy now is between rational and irrational, competent and incompetent. That sort of spectrum has no place for cleavage expression or party politics. Nor is it clear that democracy can tolerate a political system shorn of policy content attempting to respond to group interests. If what we expect from leaders is titillation, shock, and entertainment, then democracy has morphed into a giant version of *American Idol*.

Depression calls for comfort food and its intellectual equivalent. I returned to an old favorite, Umberto Eco. Eco lived under Mussolini's fascism as a child, and in his essay "Ur-Fascism"[4] he searches for the font of fascism, the basic meaning of fascism, and the common indicators of fascism. Let's play a mind game and try to measure the future Trump administration on that basis. On the first two criteria, the Trump phenomenon does not seem to fit. Ur-fascism harks back to traditionalism and rejects modernism. Trump, in contrast, would happily tear down the old to build the gaudy new. But in a more nuanced way it may yet fit. Trump must play to his gallery, and this includes the evangelicals, the Tea Party, and the alt-right, all of whom take comfort in traditionalism. Trump likes modern buildings, but he may have to follow his supporters and reject modernist notions such as empirical evidence, deliberation, and consensus.

As to the next half-dozen criteria, Trump is the square peg in the square hole. Rationalism is rejected because it is hard work and requires knowledge and scholarship. Debate and disagreement are rejected as effete games played by the establishment whereas the people understand full well what is black and what is white. Politics becomes an appeal to those people frustrated by the current system and thus simply requires leaders to play to those frustrations—Trump scores a direct hit on that one. The "people" become a mythic single body losing individual disaggregation. This loss of political individuality is particularly convenient because it means there can be no disagreement with those speaking in the name of the self-same "people." Trump is therefore by definition always right, regardless of contradiction or confusion. Which leads neatly to the next feature of Ur-fascism, the imagined common identity of the "people" based on race or nation. In the Trump case it is the latter with broad hints at the former.

Ur-fascism must deal with its opponents. Here again Trump is comfortably in line. Opponents are always enemies, and they are forever mounting conspiracies against the courageous leader. The vast conspiracy against Trump includes such useful enemies as the media, Democrats, Wall Street, Hollywood, judges, NGOs, and pretty much all foreigners (unless they are in business with Trump). And another feature of Ur-fascism that Trump has taken to his ample bosom is a hatred of elites. They are the true enemy, so we must drain the swamp and reject all expert advice. Parliamentary government with its interminable debates beyond the ken of the ordinary "people" is a form of elitism and thus must also be shunned. The leader knows what the "people" want, and they must trust him to deliver it.

But there are two other criteria where it is difficult to fit in Trump. Ur-fascism sees life as permanent warfare. Ur-fascism worships heroism. Permanent warfare and heroism require a little bit of effort and sacrifice. This seems well beyond what Trump and most of his followers are prepared to tolerate. Trump is, after all, intellectually lazy, and his attention span can't reach far beyond 140 keystrokes. It is difficult to see Trump in uniform, posing for a Jacques-Louis David painting. Where these two terrifying aspects of ur-fascism may have salience is if one slice of the Trump base were to take charge of his presidency under his inadvertence. That slice is represented by the gun lobby and the alt-right, who may well see themselves heroically fighting a permanent war against . . . pick one or more of the following: liberals, globalizers, atheists, gays, blacks, feminists, and (of course) foreigners.

The final feature of ur-fascism is its most insidious. Ur-fascism develops its own "*new*speak" as in Orwell's *1984*. In Trump's case the newspeak is not particularly eloquent or deep. It uses little Anglo-Saxon words and avoids the big Normand interlopers. Here is what will happen. All criticism of Trump will be deemed to be in oldspeak and therefore illegitimate. Concepts such as social safety net, equality before the law, and loyalty to allies are all in oldspeak and can therefore be dismissed as nothing more than the bleating of the old, displaced elites. Newspeak will use simple words such as *great, white,* and *win.* Only newspeak will be responded to.

Where does this leave democracy? In a bad place. Fascism and democracy cannot live side by side. Mussolini said that "the struggle between the two worlds, Fascism and Democracy, can permit no compromises. It's either their ideas or ours, either our State or theirs!"[5] So democracy is an inefficient and outdated system to be replaced by the gleaming new engine of fascism running on time and in accordance with the people's will—as discerned by the great leader. Today's authoritarian leaders are not so brazen. They will claim to worship at the altar of democracy while manipulating its rules to their benefit, excoriating opponents, and hobbling civil society. Mussolini has become Putin.

The only defense is activism on the part of politicians, civil society leaders, and engaged citizens. Democracies have at times succumbed to fascism, but they have also faced it down. The danger is that activism in defense of democracy will be portrayed by those in power as a conspiracy by the enemies of the "ordinary people." The activists will use old-speak, which will be met by derision from the leader and the minority that elected him. Complaints about policies will be described on a spectrum ranging from sour grapes to sedition.

Oh yes, depression hit hard. But no, I am not accusing Trump of being Mussolini. It is too soon for that. But is it not disturbing to be able to play this mind game and make Trump's fit with ur-fascism so snug?

Acceptance

Inauguration Day is looming and life must go on. There is a new normal, and we must accommodate ourselves to it as best we can. Though I cycle back and forth through the first four stages, I eventually come to the fifth with a heavy heart and a deep sigh.

The dominant school in American political science is based on rational choice theories. In some ways, rational choice theory is to capitalism what class struggle is to communism. According to this school, the best way to explain social behavior is through a calculation of what action by any given individual will improve his or her material well-being. We have thus become *Homo economicus,* forever scanning for ways to marginally improve our lot. Because wealth and material well-being is measurable, rational choice theories lend themselves to mathematical calculation, and much of political science can now be expressed numerically. Though I am uncomfortable with this school of thought, I have to concede that it has brought us considerable and useful scholarship. After all, we do spend a great deal of time worrying about getting by in this material world. Aggregating calculations for this mass of individuals as they strive for wealth or even subsistence will provide broad answers about public wants and acts. My concern with rational choice theory is that it cannot tell when *Homo economicus* morphs into *Homo philanthropicus*. We often don't know ourselves. So while it explains a lot, it cannot explain all, and ultimately we can never be sure that it explains any particular conduct.

It came to me as a shock to realize that while I was critical of rational choice ideas, I was in fact applying similar principles to electoral and political behavior. I was seeing humans as *Homo politicus.* *Homo politicus* spends every moment researching politics and assessing policy ideas. *Homo politicus* has a political philosophy and applies it rationally when casting votes or expressing opinions. *Homo politicus* understands the consequences of her political actions and is therefore careful in taking it. But people are not like that all the time, or perhaps not even often. Most people are *Homo apatheticus* and they can easily become *Homo perversicus*. They don't place that much importance on politics and they don't spend too much time thinking about it. They may or may not vote. They may or may not care. While it is not a great thing to be *Homo apatheticus* it is certainly an option.

In 2016 *Homo apatheticus* stirred and decided to become *Homo perversicus* and flip the system the bird, give the finger to the establishment, and be an irrational choice proponent. Democracy needs to accept and accommodate *Homo perversicus*. Electorates have been known to make bad choices in the past, and they surely will make them again in the future. Progress is never a straight line. It has peaks and troughs. We simply took a stomach-churning drop on the political roller coaster. Democracy has to demonstrate it is tough enough to survive a Trump.

What does democracy being Trumped entail? Trumpism would mean the end of rational politics, where policy ideas contest to determine which best fits the electorate's needs. It would mean the beginning of purely transactional politics where those who can win today's argument by whatever means prevail regardless of tomorrow's consequences. And it would mean the end of civility (disparagingly called *political correctness*) in politics, which rescues democracy from brute majoritarianism. Finally, it would cause the death of democracy's soft power. So, has democracy been Trumped? Not yet. Democracy is in crisis, but the crisis is not yet life-threatening. Voters can make mistakes. Voters can fall for the dubious charms of the charlatan. Voters are even entitled to vote against their interests. But voters have to learn from their mistakes. That is the strength of democracy. It has in its methods a mechanism for self-correction. Mistakes can be rectified, charlatans unmasked (over and over again), and interests reclaimed. History may one day look back on 2016 and say that America suffered a fit of temporary insanity but then came to its senses. The test will be 2020.

I am not even sure Trump will run again. The job of president is grueling. Trump doesn't do grueling. But that sounds a bit like wishful thinking. He will simply change the job. He will delegate widely and then describe every result as a great victory and every criticism as a lie. The United States will live through Potemkin politics in which everything is great again. His ego will win the day; of course he will run in 2020 (unless all those hamburgers finally get him). So in 2020, the wisdom of the American voter will again be tested. Will my faith again be misplaced?

I have a painful memory. It is all the more painful because it is quite recent. As an international lawyer, I have a belief in a rules-based world where the Charter of the UN acts as a basic constitution of humankind and the international community moves, however falteringly, toward a time of very few wars and only very occasional famines. We were moving pretty much in that direction since the end of World War II, as argued so convincingly in Steven Pinker's 2011 book *The Better Angels of Our Nature: Why Violence Has Declined*. But George W. Bush dealt a grievous blow to that world when he rode roughshod over international law, ignored the warnings of the international community and didn't give a damn about the opinion of the people of the rest of the world, and invaded Iraq. At a conference of international lawyers held at my university in Canberra in 2003, I said that it is not too late to mitigate the damage, to undo much of the harm and get us back on track: the American people simply have to reject a Bush second term. We all know what happened—Karl Rove.

Which brings me to another author and another theory that may have some bearing on the question of whether democracy has been Trumped. In 2004 Dick Stoken published *The Great Game of Politics: Why We Elect, Whom We Elect*. It contains a useful little theory about the vicissitudes of American politics, which Stokes sees as an endless arm wrestle between different visions of America. The originality is in the arm wrestle rather than the visions. Stoken sees the decisive changes in American politics following a simple quantitative test: a two-term president, followed by a supporter of that president. Presidents Bush, Clinton, and Obama all failed the decisiveness test. Indeed, the last decisive presidency was Reagan's, and before him Roosevelt's. Were there to be a two-term Trump followed by a pensive supporter, then, yes, democracy in America will be Trumped.

Notes

1. Elisabeth Kübler-Ross, *On Grief and Grieving: Finding the Meaning of Grief Through the Five Stages of Loss* (New York: Scribner, 2005).

2. *Union royale belge des sociétés de football association ASBL v. Jean-Marc Bosman* (Judgment of the European Court of Justice, 1995), http://eur-lex.europa.eu /legal-content/EN/ALL/?uri=CELEX:61993CJ0415.

3. Sudhir Hazareesingh, *How the French Think* (London: Penguin, 2016), p. 140.

4. Umberto Eco, "Ur-Fascism," *New York Review of Books*, June 22, 1995.

5. AZQuotes, "Benito Mussolini," http://www.azquotes.com/quote/1085806.

Bibliography

Africa Research Institute. *Between Extremes: China and Africa,* Briefing Note 1202. October 2012. http://www.africaresearchinstitute.org/files/briefing-notes /docs/Between-extremes-China-and-Africa-P2E56236DQ.pdf.

African Union. African Charter on Democracy, Elections, and Governance. http://www.ipu.org/idd-E/afr_charter.pdf.

Baregu, Mwesiga. "From Liberation Movement to Ruling Parties in Southern Africa." Pp. 92–103 in Chris Landsberg and Shaun McKay, eds., *Southern Africa Post-Apartheid? The Search for Democratic Governance.* Capetown: IDASA, 2004.

Bell, Daniel. *China's New Confucianism: Politics and Everyday Life in a Changing Society.* Princeton, NJ: Princeton University Press, 2008.

Bipartisan Policy Center. *Voter Turnout in 2012.* http://bipartisanpolicy.org/library /2012-voter-turnout/.

Borooah, Vani, and Martin Paldam. "Why Is the World Short of Democracy? A Cross-Country Analysis of Barriers to Representative Government." Paper presented at the European Public Choice Society Annual Conference, Durham University, England, March 31–April 3, 2005.

Carothers, Thomas. *Confronting the Weakest Link: Aiding Political Parties in New Democracies.* Washington, DC: Carnegie Endowment for International Peace, 2006.

———. "The End of the Transition Paradigm." *Journal of Democracy* 13, 1 (January 2002): 5–21.

Carr, Adam. *Election Archive.* http://psephos.adam-carr.net/.

Chandoevwit, Worawan. "Thailand's Grass Roots Policies." *TDRI Quarterly Review* 18, 2 (June 2003).

China Daily. *China in Brief.* 2000. http://app1.chinadaily.com.cn/highlights/ChinaInBrief /economic_d.html.

Cockett, Richard. *Blood, Dreams, and Gold: The Changing Face of Burma.* New Haven, CT: Yale University Press, 2015.

Collier, Paul. *The Bottom Billion: Why the Poorest Countries Are Failing and What Can Be Done About It.* Oxford: Oxford University Press, 2007.

215

Connell, R. W. *Masculinities*. Berkeley: University of California Press, 2005.

Cordesman, Anthony. *Russia and the "Color Revolution."* Center for Strategic and International Studies. May 28, 2014. http://csis.org/publication/russia-and-color -revolution.

Dalton, Russell J., and Martin P. Wattenberg, eds. *Parties Without Partisans: Political Change in Advanced Industrial Democracies*. New York: Oxford University Press, 2002.

De Beer, Patrice. "Europe: Flailing or Divided?" *World Policy Journal*, Winter 2014– 2015. http://www.worldpolicy.org/journal/winter2014/europe-flailing-or-divided.

Dershowitz, Alan. *Supreme Injustice: How the High Court Hijacked Election 2000*. New York: Oxford University Press, 2001.

De Tocqueville, Alexis. *Democracy in America*. London: Penguin, 2003. Original 2-vol. edition first published in 1835 and 1840.

D'Hooghe, Ingrid. *China's Public Diplomacy*. The Hague: Netherlands Institute of International Relations Clingendael, 2015.

Diamond, Larry. *Squandered Victory: The American Occupation and the Bungled Effort to Bring Democracy to Iraq*. New York: Henry Holt, 2005.

Dollar, David. *China's Engagement with Africa—From Natural Resources to Human Resources*. Washington, DC: Brookings Institution, 2016.

Dorsey, James M. "Creating Frankenstein: The Saudi Export of Wahhabism." 2016. http://mideastsoccer.blogspot.sg/2016/03/creating-frankenstein-saudi-export-of.html.

Draper, Patricia. "!Kung Women: Contrasts in Sexual Egalitarianism in Foraging and Sedentary Contexts." *Anthropology Faculty Publications Paper 45*, 77–109. http://digitalcommons.unl.edu/anthropologyfacpub/45.

Duverger, Maurice. *Political Parties: Their Organization and Activity in the Modern State*. London: Methuen, 1954.

Easterly, William. *The Elusive Quest for Growth: Economists' Adventures and Misadventures in the Tropics*. Cambridge, MA: MIT Press, 2001.

———. *The White Man's Burden: Why the West's Efforts to Aid the Rest Have Done So Much Ill and So Little Good*. New York: Penguin, 2006.

Easterly, William, and Claudia R. Williamson. *Rhetoric Versus Reality: The Best and Worst of Aid Agency Practices*, p. 4. http://williameasterly.files.wordpress.com /2010/08/61_easterly_williamson_rhetoricvsreality_prp.pdf.

Eco, Umberto. "Ur-Fascism." *New York Review of Books*, June 22, 1995.

Edwards, M., and D. Hulme, eds. *Making a Difference: NGOs and Development in a Changing World*. London: Earthscan, 1992.

Evans, Grant. *Asia's Cultural Mosaic—An Anthropological Introduction*. Singapore: Prentice Hall, 1993.

Foster, Steven. *The Judiciary, Civil Liberties, and Human Rights*. Edinburgh: Edinburgh University Press, 2006.

Freedom House. *Freedom in the World*. 2014. http://freedomhouse.org/report-types /freedom-world#.U_Nz5PldVlo.

Frum, David. *How We Got Here: The '70s*. New York: Basic, 2000.

Fukuyama, Francis. "Democracy and the End of History Revisited." Pp. 115–120 in Heraldo Muñoz, ed., *Democracy Rising: Assessing the Global Challenge*. Boulder, CO: Lynne Rienner, 2006.

Grey, C. G. P. "The Trouble with the Electoral College." https://web.archive.org /web/20120121133239/http://blog.cgpgrey.com/the-electoral-college/.

Halperin, Morton, Joe Siegle, and Michael Weinstein. *The Democracy Advantage: How Democracies Promote Prosperity and Peace*. New York: Routledge, 2005.

Hazareesingh, Sudhir. *How the French Think*. London: Penguin, 2016.

He, Baogang. *Rural Democracy in China: The Role of Village Elections.* London: Palgrave, 2007.

Hong, Zhou. "China's Evolving Aid Landscape: Crossing the River and Feeling the Stones." Pp. 134–168 in Sachin Chatuvedi, Thomas Fues, and Elizabeth Sidiropoulos, eds., *Development Cooperation and Emerging Powers: New Partners or Old Patterns?* London: Zed, 2012.

Hubbard, R. Glenn, and William Duggan. *The Aid Trap.* New York: Columbia Business School, 2009.

Hunter, John. "Peter Drucker Advocated a Ratio of 20 to 1 for CEO to Average Worker Pay." *The W. Edwards Deming Institute Blog.* https://blog.deming.org/2015/02 /peter-drucker-advocated-a-ratio-of-20-to-1-for-ceo-to-average-worker-pay/.

Huntington, Samuel. *The Third Wave: Democratization in the Late Twentieth Century.* Norman: University of Oklahoma Press, 1991.

ICNL and WMD. *Defending Civil Society Report.* 2012. http://www.movedemocracy .org/defending-civil-society-project.

International Commission on Intervention and State Sovereignty. December 2001, p. IX. http://responsibilitytoprotect.org/ICISS%20Report.pdf.

International Institute for Democracy and Electoral Assistance. *Voter Turnout, A Global Survey—Regional Differences.* http://www.idea.int/vt/survey/voter _turnout3.cfm.

Kabir, Rokeya, ed. *Policies Budget and PRSP—Are They Promoting Women's Rights in Bangladesh?* Dhaka: University Press Limited, 2011.

Kanninen, Tapio, and Katerina Sehm Patomaki, eds. *Building Democracy from Manila to Doha: The Evolution of the Movement of New and Restored Democracies.* Helsinki: Helsinki Process Publication Series, 2005.

Karam, Azza M., Frene Ginwala, and Gehan Abu-Zayd. *Women in Parliament: Beyond Numbers.* Stockholm: International IDEA, 2002.

Kay, V., and Blaine Martin. "CEO Pay Ratio and Income Inequality: Perspectives for Compensation Committees." *Harvard Law School Program on Corporate Governance.* 2016. https://corpgov.law.harvard.edu/2016/10/25/ceo-pay-ratio -and-income-inequality-perspectives-for-compensation-committees/.

Keane, John. *The Life and Death of Democracy.* New York: W. W. Norton, 2009.

Keck, Margaret, and Kathryn Sikkink. *Activists Beyond Borders: Advocacy Networks in International Politics.* Ithaca, NY: Cornell University Press, 1998.

Kharas, Homi. "Development Assistance." In Bruce Currie-Alder, Ravi Kanbur, David M. Malone, and Rohinton Medhora, eds., *International Development: Ideas, Experience, and Prospects.* Oxford: Oxford University Press, 2014. http://hdl.handle.net/10625/51592.

Kitano, Naohiro, and Yukinori Harada. "Estimating China's Foreign Aid 2001–2013." *JICA Research Paper 78.* June 2014. http://jica-ri.jica.go.jp/publication /assets/JICA-RI_WP_No.78_2014.pdf.

Klitgaard, Robert. *Controlling Corruption.* Berkeley: University of California Press, 1988.

Kübler-Ross, Elisabeth. *On Grief and Grieving: Finding the Meaning of Grief Through the Five Stages of Loss.* New York: Scribner, 2005.

Kumar, Krishna, ed. *Postconflict Elections, Democratization, and International Assistance.* Boulder, CO: Lynne Rienner, 1998.

Lahoud, Nelly. *The Jihadis' Path to Self-Destruction.* London: Hurst, 2010.

Li, Tianchen. "New Trends in the Studies on Confucius and Confucianism." *Culture Mandala: The Bulletin of the Centre for East-West Cultural and Economic Studies* 3, 2 (1999): article 6.

Linz, Juan J., and Alfred Stepan. "Toward Consolidated Democracies." *Journal of Democracy* 7, 2 (1996): 14–33.

Little, Reg. "Confucius in Beijing: The Conference of the International Confucian Foundation." *Culture Mandala: The Bulletin of the Centre for East-West Cultural and Economic Studies* 1, 2 (1995): article 4.

Luttwak, Edward N. *The Rise of China vs. the Logic of Strategy.* Cambridge, MA: Belknap, 2012.

Marks, Susan. "What Has Become of the Emerging Right to Democratic Governance?" *European Journal of International Law* 22, 2 (2009): 507–524.

McCargo, Duncan. "Network Monarchy and Legitimacy Crises in Thailand." *Pacific Review* 18, 4 (December 2005): 499–519.

McCargo, Duncan, and Ayşe Zarakol. "Turkey and Thailand: Unlikely Twins." *Journal of Democracy* 23, 3 (July 2012): 71–79.

McCregor, Richard. "Zhou's Cryptic Caution Lost in Translation." *Financial Times,* June 10, 2011.

Moore, Barrington. *Social Origins of Dictatorship and Democracy.* Boston: Beacon, 1966.

Moyo, D. *Dead Aid: Why Aid Is Not Working and How There Is a Better Way for Africa.* New York: Farrar, Straus and Giroux, 2009.

Netherlands Ministry of Foreign Affairs. *Budget Support: Conditional Results—Review of an Instrument (2000–2011).* https://www.oecd.org/derec/netherlands/IOB_BS.pdf.

O'Donnell, Guillermo A. "Delegative Democracy." *Journal of Democracy* 5, 1 (1994): 55–69.

OECD. *Aid at a Glance: Flows of Official Development Assistance to and Through Civil Society Organizations in 2011.* October 2013. http://www.oecd.org/dac/peer-reviews/Aid%20for%20CSOs%20Final%20for%20WEB.pdf.

———. *Education Indicators in Focus.* 2012. https://www.oecd.org/edu/50495363.pdf.

———. *How DAC Members Work with Civil Society Organizations: An Overview.* Paris: OECD, 2011.

OECD Development Co-operation Directorate. *Development Aid Stable in 2014 but Flows to Poorest Countries Still Falling.* 2015. http://www.oecd.org/dac/stats/development-aid-stable-in-2014-but-flows-to-poorest-countries-still-falling.htm.

Orwell, George. *1984.* New York: Signet Classics, 1949.

Pastor, Robert. "The US Administration of Elections: Decentralized to the Point of Being Dysfunctional." Pp. 273–276 in International Institute for Democracy and Electoral Administration, *Electoral Management Design: The International IDEA Handbook.* Stockholm: IDEA, 2006.

Patterson, Thomas E. *The Vanishing Voter: Public Involvement in an Age of Uncertainty.* New York: Vintage, 2003.

Pei, Minxin. "Is CCP Rule Fragile or Resilient?" *Journal of Democracy* 23, 1 (2012): 27–41.

Piccone, Ted. *Five Rising Democracies: And the Fate of the International Liberal Order.* Washington, DC: Brookings Institution, 2016.

Pinker, Steven. *The Better Angels of Our Nature: Why Violence Has Declined.* New York: Viking, 2011.

Przeworski, Adam, Michael E. Alvarez, José Antonio Cheibub, and Fernando Limongi. *Democracy and Development: Political Institutions and Well-being in the World, 1950–1990.* New York: Cambridge University Press, 2000.

Putin, Vladimir. Annual Address to the Federal Assembly of the Russian Federation. April 25, 2005. http://archive.kremlin.ru/eng/speeches/2005/04/25/2031_type70029type82912_87086.shtml.

Putnam, Robert D., with Robert Leonardi and Raffaella Y. Nanetti. *Making Democracy Work: Civic Traditions in Modern Italy.* Princeton, NJ: Princeton University Press, 1994.

Rich, Roland. "Applying Conditionality to Development Assistance." *Agenda—A Journal of Policy Analysis and Reform* 11, 4 (2004): 321–334. http://epress.anu .edu.au/agenda/011/04/11-4-A-3.pdf.

———. "Crafting Security Council Mandates." Pp. 62–85 in Edward Newman and Roland Rich, eds., *The UN Role in Promoting Democracy—Between Ideals and Reality.* Tokyo: United Nations University Press, 2004.

———. *Dignity Through Democracy and Human Rights.* New Delhi: Institute of Social Science, 2012.

———. "Hercules or Sisyphus? Building Capacity in the Asia-Pacific." *Australian Strategic Policy Institute Insight* 33 (2007). http://www.aspi.org.au/publications /publications_all.aspx.

———. *Pacific Asia in Quest of Democracy.* Boulder, CO: Lynne Rienner, 2007.

———. *Parties and Parliaments in Southeast Asia: Non-partisan Chambers in Indonesia, the Philippines, and Thailand.* London: Routledge, 2013.

———. "Recognition of States: The Collapse of Yugoslavia and the Soviet Union." *European Journal of International Law* 4, 1 (March 1993): 36–65. http://ejil .oxfordjournals.org/content/4/1/36.full.pdf.html.

Ricklefs, Merle. *Mystic Synthesis in Java: A History of Islamization from the Fourteenth to the Early Nineteenth Centuries.* Norwalk, CT: EastBridge, 2006.

Sachs, Jeffrey. *The End of Poverty: Economic Possibilities for Our Time.* London: Penguin, 2006.

Schattschneider, E. E. *Party Government.* New York: Holt, Rinehart, and Winston, 1942.

Sen, Amartya. "Democracy as a Universal Value." *Journal of Democracy* 10, 3 (1999): 3–17.

Shambaugh, David. *Wall Street Journal.* March 6, 2015.

Simon, Zoltan. "Orban Says He Seeks to End Liberal Democracy in Hungary." *Bloomberg News.* July 28, 2014.

Soledad, Fely I. "The Philippine Council for NGO Certification." *International Journal of Not-for-Profit Law* 3, 2 (December 2001).

Stoken, Dick. *The Great Game of Politics: Why We Elect, Whom We Elect.* New York: Forge, 2004.

Strange, Austin, Bradley Parks, Michael J. Tierney, Andreas Fuchs, Axel Dreher, and Vijaya Ramachandran. *China's Development Finance to Africa: A Media-Based Approach to Data Collection.* Working Paper 323. Washington, DC: Center for Global Development, 2013. http://www.cgdev.org/sites/default/files/chinese -development-finance-africa_0.pdf.

Sun, Yun. *Africa in China's New Foreign Aid.* White paper. Washington, DC: Brookings Institution, July 16, 2014. http://www.brookings.edu/blogs/africa-in -focus/posts/2014/07/16-africa-china-foreign-aid-sun.

Traub, James. *The Freedom Agenda: Why America Must Spread Democracy (Just Not the Way George Bush Did).* New York: Farrar, Straus and Giroux, 2008.

UN. "Basic Facts About ECOSOC Status." 2014. http://csonet.org/index.php?menu=100.

United Nations Office for the High Commissioner for Human Rights. *Report of the Commission of Inquiry on Human Rights in the Democratic People's Republic of Korea.* 2014. http://www.ohchr.org/EN/HRBodies/HRC/CoIDPRK/Pages /ReportoftheCommissionofInquiryDPRK.aspx.

Uphoff, Norman. *Nongovernmental Organizations and Accountability: Beyond the Magic Bullet.* London: Earthscan, 1995.

Varayudej, Same. "A Right to Democracy in International Law: Its Implications for Asia." *Annual Survey of International and Comparative Law* 12 (2006): 1–28.

Warren, Mark E., and Hilary Pearse, eds. *Designing Deliberative Democracy: The British Columbia Citizens' Assembly.* Cambridge: Cambridge University Press, 2008.

Whitehead, Laurence. "State Sovereignty and Democracy." Pp. 23–41 in Peter Burnell and Richard Youngs, eds., *New Challenges to Democratization.* Oxford: Routledge, 2010.

Williamson, John. *The Washington Consensus as Policy Prescription for Development.* 2004. http://www.iie.com/publications/papers/williamson0204.pdf.

World Bank. "Bringing 6 Million Children Back to School in Afghanistan." April 17, 2013. http://www.worldbank.org/en/results/2013/04/17/bringing-6-million -children-back-to-school-afghanistan.

———. *China: Overview.* 2016. http://www.worldbank.org/en/country/china/overview.

Zakaria, Fareed. *The Future of Freedom: Illiberal Democracy at Home and Abroad.* New York: W. W. Norton, 2003.

Zhao, Ziyang. Translated and edited by Bao Pu, Renee Chiang, and Adi Ignatius. *Prisoner of the State: The Secret Journal of Premier Zhao Ziyang.* New York: Simon and Schuster, 2009.

Index

About the Book

Democracy is in crisis. After the hope engendered by the Third Wave, democracies around the world are beleaguered with threats from multiple sources. What are these threats? Where did they come from? And how can the challenges to democratic governance best be overcome?

Grappling with these questions, Roland Rich interprets the danger signs that abound in the United States and Europe, in Asia and the Arab World, in Africa and Latin America, and offers innovative strategies for turning the tide.

Roland Rich is on the faculty of the Department of Political Science at Rutgers University and is an honorary professor at the Australian National University. Previously, he served as executive head of the UN Democracy Fund (2007–2014), director of the Centre for Democratic Institutions at the Australian National University (1998–2005), and in the Australian Foreign Service including as ambassador to Laos (1994–1997). His publications include *The UN Role in Promoting Democracy* and *Pacific Asia in Quest of Democracy*.